THANK YOU, ANARCHY

Ed,

For rich comments
& generous
support!

The publisher gratefully acknowledges the generous support of the General Endowment Fund of the University of California Press Foundation.

THANK YOU, ANARCHY

NOTES FROM THE OCCUPY APOCALYPSE

NATHAN SCHNEIDER

Foreword by Rebecca Solnit

UNIVERSITY OF CALIFORNIA PRESS

BERKELEY LOS ANGELES LONDON

University of California Press, one of the most distinguished university presses in the United States, enriches lives around the world by advancing scholarship in the humanities, social sciences, and natural sciences. Its activities are supported by the UC Press Foundation and by philanthropic contributions from individuals and institutions. For more information, visit www.ucpress.edu.

University of California Press
Berkeley and Los Angeles, California

University of California Press, Ltd.
London, England

Library of Congress Cataloging-in-Publication Data

Schneider, Nathan, 1984–.
    Thank you, anarchy : notes from the occupy apocalypse / Nathan Schneider; foreword by Rebecca Solnit.
        pages   cm.
    Includes bibliographical references.
    ISBN 978-0-520-27679-6 (cloth : alk. paper)
    ISBN 978-0-520-27680-2 (pbk. : alk. paper)
    1. Occupy Wall Street (Movement).   2. Occupy movement—New York (State)—New York.   3. Occupy movement.   4. Protest movements—United States—History—21st century.   5. Equality—United States.   6. Income distribution—United States.   I. Title.
    HC110.I5S36   2013
    339.20973—dc23
                                                                    2013007879

Manufactured in the United States of America

22 21 20 19 18 17 16 15 14 13
10 9 8 7 6 5 4 3 2 1

In keeping with a commitment to support environmentally responsible and sustainable printing practices, UC Press has printed this book on Rolland Enviro100, a 100% post-consumer fiber paper that is FSC certified, deinked, processed chlorine-free, and manufactured with renewable biogas energy. It is acid-free and EcoLogo certified.

Once to every man and nation comes the moment to decide,
In the strife of Truth with Falsehood, for the good or evil side;
Some great cause, God's new Messiah, offering each the bloom or blight,
Parts the goats upon the left hand, and the sheep upon the right,
And the choice goes by forever 'twixt that darkness and that light.

JAMES RUSSELL LOWELL, "THE PRESENT CRISIS" (1844)

I think you have to engage in almost revolutionary
strategies to achieve reform.

FRANCES FOX PIVEN, LECTURE AT NEW YORK UNIVERSITY (FEBRUARY 16, 2012)

CONTENTS

FOREWORD | MIRACLES AND OBSTACLES

REBECCA SOLNIT

I would have liked to know what the drummer hoped and expected. We'll never know why she decided to take a drum to the central markets of Paris on October 5, 1789, and why that day the tinder was so ready to catch fire and a drumbeat was one of the sparks. The working women of the marketplace marched all the way to Versailles, occupied the seat of royal power, forced the king back to Paris, and got the French Revolution rolling. It was then the revolution was really launched, more than the storming of the Bastille—though both were mysterious moments when citizens felt impelled to act and acted together, becoming in the process that mystical body *civil society,* the colossus who writes history with her feet and crumples governments with her bare hands.

She strode out of the 1985 earthquake in Mexico City: parts of the central city collapsed in that disaster, but so did the credibility and the power of the PRI, the Institutional Revolutionary Party that ruled Mexico for seventy years. These transformative moments happen in many times and places, as celebratory revolution, as terrible calamity, and they are sometimes reenacted as festivals and carnival. In these moments the old order is shattered, governments and elites tremble, and in the rupture civil society is reborn. The old rules no longer apply in that open space of rupture. New rules may be written, or a counterrevolution may be launched to take back the city or the society, but the moment that counts is the one in which civil society is its own rule, taking care of the needy, discussing what is necessary and desirable, improvising the terms of an ideal society for a day, a month, a season, the duration of the Paris Commune or the Oakland Commune (as Occupy Oakland was sometimes called), or the suspension of everyday life during disaster.

Those who doubt that the significance of these moments matter should note how terrified the authorities and elites are when such moments erupt. Those who dismiss them because of their flaws need to look harder at what joy and what hope shine out of them and ask not what these moments produce in the long run but what they are in their heyday (though they often produce profound change in the long run—and when it comes to long runs, there's always that official of the Chinese government who some decades back was asked what he thought of the French Revolution: "Too soon to tell," he said).

In these moments of rupture, people find themselves members of a "we" that did not exist, at least not as an entity with agency and identity and potency, until that moment; new things seem possible, or the old dream of a just society reemerges, and for a little while it shines not just as a possibility but as how people live with one another. Utopia is sometimes the goal, it's often the moment, and it's a hard moment to explain, since it usually involves hardscrabble ways of living, squabbles, and eventually disillusion and factionalism—but also more ethereal things: the discovery of personal and collective power, the realization of dreams, the birth of bigger dreams, a sense of connection that is as emotional as it is political, and lives that change and do not change back to what they were before, even when the glory subsides.

Sometimes the earth closes over these moments, and they have no obvious consequences—sometimes they're the Velvet Revolution and the fall of the Berlin Wall and all those glorious insurrections in the East Bloc in 1989, and empires crumble and ideologies fall away like shackles. Occupy was such a moment, and one so new that it's hard to measure its consequences. I have often heard that Freedom Summer in Mississippi registered some voters and built some alliances, but more than that, the young participants were galvanized into a feeling of power, of commitment, of mission, perhaps, that stayed with them as they went on to do a thousand different things that mattered and joined or helped build the slow anti-authoritarian revolution that has been unfolding for the last half century or so. It's too soon to tell.

Aftermaths are hard to measure and preludes are often even more elusive. And one of the great strengths of this book is its recounting of the many people who laid the fire that burst into flame on September 17, 2011, giving light and heat to many of us yet. The drummer girl of that moment in Paris walked into a group where many people were ready to ignite, to march, to see the world change—injustice and difficulty as well as hope and devotion make these conflagrations. We need, with every insurrection, revolution, and social rupture to remember that we will never know the whole story of how it happened and that what we can't measure still matters.

Early in this superb book, Nathan Schneider cites Mike Andrews talking about how the general assemblies of the group by that name, the General Assembly of New York City, with their emphasis on egalitarian participation, respect, and consensus decision making, retooled him: "It pushes you toward being more respectful of the people there. Even after General Assembly ends I find myself being very attentive in situations where I'm not normally so attentive. So if I go get some food after General Assembly, I find myself being very polite to the person I'm ordering from, and listening if they talk back to me." This is the kind of tiny personal change that can be multiplied by the hundreds of thousands, given the number of Occupy participants globally. But there have been quantifiable consequences too.

Everyone admitted almost immediately after Occupy Wall Street (OWS) appeared in the fall of 2011 that the conversation had changed—the brutality and obscenity of Wall Street was addressed, the hideous suffering of ordinary people crushed by medical, housing, and college debt came out of the shadows, and Occupy became a point at which people could testify about this destruction of their hopes and lives. California passed a homeowners' bill of rights to curtail the viciousness of the banks, and Strike Debt emerged as an Occupy offshoot in late 2012 to address indebtedness in creative and insurrectionary ways. Student debt came up for discussion, and student loan reform began in various small ways. Invisible suffering had been made visible.

Occupy Wall Street also built alliances around racist persecution, from the Trayvon Martin case in Florida to stop and frisk in New York to racist bank policies and foreclosures in San Francisco, where a broad-based housing rights movement came out of the Occupy movement. It was a beautiful movement, because the definition of "we" as the 99 percent was so much more inclusive than almost anything before, be it movements focused on race or gender, or on class when class was imagined as the working class against a middle class that also works for a living (rather than against the elites that were christened the 1 percent in one of Occupy's most contagious memes). Though the movement abounded in young white people, many kinds of people were involved, from kids to World War II veterans and ex–Black Panthers, from libertarians to liberals to insurrectionists, from tenured to homeless to famous.

And there was so much brutality, from the young women pepper-sprayed early on at an OWS demonstration and the students famously pepper-sprayed while sitting down peacefully at UC Davis to the poet laureate Robert Hass, clubbed in the ribs at UC Berkeley's branch of Occupy, to eighty-four-year-old Dorli Rainey, assaulted by police at Occupy Seattle, and the Iraq War veteran Scott Olsen, whose skull was shattered by a projectile fired by Oakland police. The massive institutional violence made it clear Occupy was a serious threat. At the G-20 economic summit in 2011, President Dmitry Medvedev of Russia warned, "The reward system of shareholders and managers of financial institutions should be changed step by step. Otherwise the 'Occupy Wall Street' slogan will become fashionable in all developed countries." That was the voice of fear, because the 99 percent's realized dreams were the 1 percent's nightmares.

We'll never know what the drummer girl in Paris in 1789 was thinking, but thanks to this meticulous and elegant book, we know what one witness-participant was thinking all through the first year of Occupy, and what many of the sparks and some of the tinder were thinking, and what it was like to be warmed by that beautiful conflagration that spread across the world, to be part of that huge body that wasn't exactly civil society but was something akin and sometimes even larger, as Occupy encampments and general assemblies spread from Auckland, New Zealand, to Hong Kong, from Oakland to London, and to many small towns and counties in 2011. Some Occupy encampments lasted well into 2012, and others spawned things that are still with us: coalitions and alliances and senses of possibility and frameworks for understanding what's wrong and what could be right. It was a sea change, a watershed, a dream realized imperfectly (because only unrealized dreams are perfect), a groundswell that is still ground on which to build.

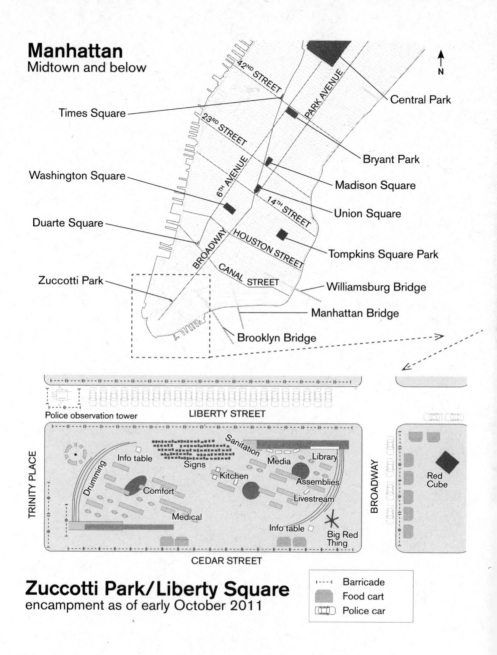

Manhattan
Midtown and below

N

42ND STREET

PARK AVENUE

Central Park

Times Square

23RD STREET

6TH AVENUE

Bryant Park

Madison Square

14TH STREET

Washington Square

Union Square

Duarte Square

BROADWAY

HOUSTON STREET

Tompkins Square Park

Zuccotti Park

CANAL STREET

Williamsburg Bridge

Manhattan Bridge

Brooklyn Bridge

Police observation tower

LIBERTY STREET

Sanitation

TRINITY PLACE

Drumming

Info table

Signs

Media

Library

Kitchen

Comfort

Assemblies

Livestream

BROADWAY

Red
Cube

Medical

Info table

Big Red
Thing

CEDAR STREET

Zuccotti Park/Liberty Square
encampment as of early October 2011

⊢--⊣	Barricade
	Food cart
⊂⊐	Police car

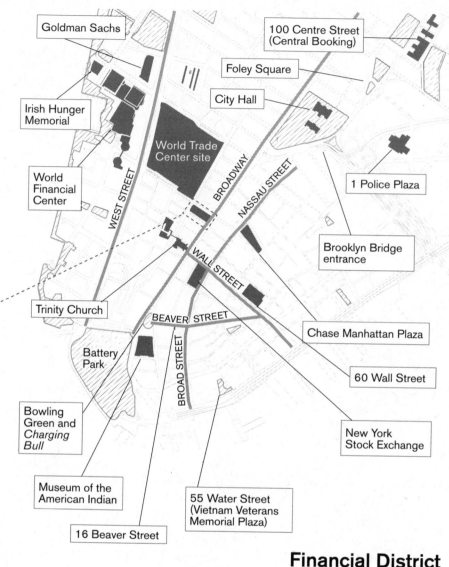

Goldman Sachs

100 Centre Street
(Central Booking)

Foley Square

City Hall

Irish Hunger
Memorial

World Trade
Center site

1 Police Plaza

World
Financial
Center

WEST STREET

BROADWAY

NASSAU STREET

Brooklyn Bridge
entrance

WALL STREET

Trinity Church

BEAVER STREET

Chase Manhattan Plaza

Battery
Park

BROAD STREET

60 Wall Street

Bowling
Green and
*Charging
Bull*

New York
Stock Exchange

Museum of the
American Indian

55 Water Street
(Vietnam Veterans
Memorial Plaza)

16 Beaver Street

Financial District

Map design: Ingrid Burrington

PART ONE

SUMMER TO FALL

ONE | SOME GREAT CAUSE

#A99 #Bloombergville #Jan25 #SolidarityWI #NYCGA
#OCCUPYWALLSTREET #October2011 #OpESR #OpWallStreet
#S17 #SeizeDC #StopTheMach #USDOR

Under the tree where the International Society for Krishna Consciousness was founded in 1966, on the south side of Tompkins Square Park in the East Village, sixty or so people are gathered in a circle around a yellow banner that reads, in blue spray paint, "GENERAL ASSEMBLY OF NYC." It is Saturday, August 13, 2011, the third of the General Assembly's evening meetings.

"No cops or reporters," someone decrees at the start of the meeting. Others demand a ban on photographs.

From where I'm sitting in the back, my hand inches up, and I stand and explain that I am a writer who covers resistance movements. I promise not to take pictures.

Just then, a heavyset man in a tight T-shirt, with patchy dark hair and a beard, starts snapping photos. He is Bob Arihood, a fixture of the neighborhood known for documenting it with his camera and his blog. People shout at him to stop; he shouts back something about the nature of public space. Soon, a few from the group break off to talk things through with him, and the discussion turns back to me.

The interrogation and harrowing debate that follow are less about me, really, than about them. Are they holding a public meeting or a private one? Is a journalist to be regarded as an agent of the state or a potential ally? Can they expect to maintain their anonymity?

After half an hour, at last, I witness an act of consensus: hands rise above heads, fingers wiggle. I can stay. A little later, I see that Arihood and the people who'd gone to confront him are laughing together.

Those present were mainly, but not exclusively, young, and when they spoke, they introduced themselves as students, artists, organizers, teachers. There were a lot of beards and hand-rolled cigarettes, though neither seemed obligatory. On the side of the circle nearest the tree were the facilitators—David Graeber, a noted anthropologist, and Marisa Holmes, a brown-haired, brown-eyed filmmaker in her midtwenties who had spent the summer interviewing revolutionaries in Egypt. Elders, such as a Vietnam vet from Staten Island, were listened to with particular care. It was a common rhetorical tic to address the group as "You beautiful people," which happened to be not just encouraging but also empirically true.

Several had accents from revolutionary places—Spain, Greece, Latin America—or had been working to create ties among pro-democracy movements in other countries. Vlad Teichberg, leaning against the Hare Krishna Tree and pecking at the keys of a pink laptop, was one of the architects of the Internet video channel Global Revolution. With his Spanish wife, Nikky Schiller, he had been in Madrid during the May 15 movement's occupation at Puerta del Sol. Alexa O'Brien, a slender woman with blond hair and black-rimmed glasses, covered the Arab Spring for the website WikiLeaks Central and had been collaborating with organizers of the subsequent uprisings in Europe; now she was trying to foment a movement called US Day of Rage, named after the big days of protest in the Middle East.

That meeting would last five hours, followed by working groups convening in huddles and in nearby bars. I'd never heard young people talking politics quite like this, with so much seriousness and revelry and determination. But their unease was also visible when a police car passed and conversation slowed; a member of the Tactics Committee had pointed out that, since any group of twenty or more in a New York City park needs a permit, we were already breaking the law.

Fault lines were forming, too. Some liked the idea of coming up with one demand, and others didn't. Some wanted regulation, others revolution. I heard the slogan "We are the 99 percent" for the first time when Chris, a member of the Food Committee, proposed it as a tagline. There were murmurs of approval but also calls for something more militant: "We are your crisis." When the idea came up of having a meeting on the picket line with striking Verizon workers, O'Brien blocked consensus. She didn't want the assembly to lose its independence by siding with a union.

"We need to appeal to the right as well as the left," she said.

"To the right?" a graduate student behind me muttered. "Wow."

Just about the only thing everyone could agree on was the fantasy of crowds filling the area around Wall Street and staying until they overthrew the corporate oligarchy, or until they were driven out. As the evening grew darker, a pack of intern-aged boys walked by, looking as if they had just left a bar, and noticed the meeting's slow progress. One of them, wearing a polo shirt, held up a broken beer mug and shouted, at an inebriated pace, "If you always act later, you might forget the now!"

Bob Arihood died of a heart attack at the end of September, after he exhausted himself photographing a march from the Financial District to Union Square. By then, the idea that the General Assembly had been planning for was a reality, spreading fast. One of his photos of the meeting survives on his blog, the only picture of its kind I've found. In that cluster of people around the banner, almost everyone is looking toward the camera; a guy I now know as Richie, dressed in white, is pointing right into the lens. Some look curious, some suspicious, some scared, some indifferent. I'm barely visible in a far corner of the group.

I recognize most of the others now in a way I couldn't then. Some have had their names and faces broadcast on the news all over the world. There's the woman from LaRouchePAC with such a good singing voice, and the group who went to high school together in North Dakota. When I showed Arihood's picture to a friend, he recognized his former roommate from art school. I try to guess what the ones I know best were thinking, what it was exactly that they imagined they were doing there—so expectant, so at odds with one another, so anxious about being watched.

The saying "You had to be there" typically comes at the end of a joke that didn't get the right reaction, that set up high hopes but by the time of the punch line fell flat. If you were there, after all, you'd know that something happened that really was significant or funny or worth repeating. I keep wanting to say those words again and again about Occupy Wall Street—"you had to be there," *"you had to be there!"*—but I stop myself, because doing so would also be an admission of defeat. Those words are a conversation stopper. If I say them I'm giving up on even trying to convey why Occupy Wall Street was such a momentous thing and such a rare moment of political hope for us who were born during the past thirty years in the United States of America.

For nearly two months in the fall of 2011, a square block of granite and honey locust trees in New York's Financial District, right between Wall Street and the World Trade Center, became a canvas for the image of another world. In occupied Zuccotti Park, thousands of people ate, slept, met, talked, argued, read, planned, and were dragged away to jail. Many came to protest the most abstract of wrongs—the deregulation of high finance, the funding of electoral campaigns, the erosion of the social safety net, the logic of mass incarceration, the failure to address climate change—but what they found was something more tangible. There was a community in formation, which they would have a hand in forming; there was work to be done, which they would do with people and ideas that the world outside had insulated them from ever considering.

Before the occupation itself, there was a process by which a few hundred people, inspired by what they saw happening overseas, found the wherewithal to imagine, plan, and resist. After the encampment ended, the many thousands who had experienced it faced a crisis of what to do next.

Over the course of a year of being immersed in Occupy Wall Street, I saw a veil being lifted. Etymologically, the lifting of a veil is what the word *apocalypse* refers to; after that, one can't go back unchanged. The preceding world has passed, and a new revelation is at hand. Nobody who worked to make Occupy Wall Street happen imagined anything much like what actually did: it altered them and transformed them and messed with them. The movement's most unsettling features were often the same ones that made it work—in addition to being at fault for the extent to which the Occupy joke ended up falling flat.

But disappointment is part of any apocalypse. The fact that the most radical aspirations of Occupy Wall Street remain unrealized is also a symptom of success; images that it promulgated of shutting down Wall Street and mounting a general strike became implanted in people's minds, if even just to provide a measure of how those images failed to become manifest.

This was movement time, the nonlinear and momentous kind of temporality that the Greeks called *kairos*. The dumb piece of red sculpture that towers over Zuccotti Park—the "Big Red Thing"—now has in my nervous system the chill-inducing and undeserved status of Beacon of the Real, as the first thing I'd see when approaching the occupation from the subway. Under that distracting piece of corporate abstraction, a living work of art brought every aspect of life into a sharper kind of focus. It was a utopian act, but in the form of realism. With artists mainly in charge, Occupy Wall Street was art before it was anything properly organized, before it was even politics. It was there to change us first and make demands later.

And so it did. Like probably thousands of other underemployed Brooklynites who otherwise had no business being in the Financial District, I came to know that area's twisty streets like the neighborhood I grew up in.

And, now, fearing that my generation might slip back into irony and apathy and unreality, I feel an urgent, evangelistic duty to record as best I can the sliver of this reality that I experienced.

What first brought me to Occupy Wall Street, in some respects, dates back to 2001. I was in high school and had an internship at Pacifica Radio in Washington DC. My first and only reporting job there was to cover a protest against the invasion of Afghanistan, just a few days before the invasion began. I followed the course of the march, and interviewed people, and wasn't sure whether I should be marching too or standing at a professional distance. It was a moderately impressive display, and yet of course the war went on.

Then, in early 2003, the same thing happened, only more so. The world-wide protests against the invasion of Iraq were the largest mobilization in history, and the war happened anyway. The newspapers hardly even noticed the opposition. A lot of us who were young enough to believe that we could turn back the bombers if our slogans were loud enough retreated into disappointment and the complacent cynicism of *The Daily Show with Jon Stewart*. But those protests lodged a question in my head: What would it have taken to make a difference? What would it have taken to capture people's imaginations and keep them from letting the politicians lead us into disaster again?

For the most part, though, I turned my attention to other things. I converted to Catholicism and studied religion. I went to graduate school and started writing for magazines. By the time the middle of 2011 came around, I was putting off finishing a quixotic book I'd been writing for years about how and why people concoct proofs about the existence of God. This put me in a fidgety mood, primed for apocalyptic distractions.

I had been watching revolutions from a distance since the beginning of the year, when people rose up and expelled dictators in Tunisia and Egypt, stirring up Libya, Bahrain, Syria, Jordan, and more. Continually refreshing my social media feeds, with Al Jazeera on in the background, I tried my best to blog each day about whatever was happening in the Middle East. I wanted to understand where these movements came from, who organized them, and how. Experts in the United States were satisfied with attributing the uprisings to global food prices and Twitter, but the revolutionaries themselves didn't use the language of economic or technological determinism. In interviews, they seemed instead to talk about having rediscovered their agency, their collective power, their ability to act.

Over the summer, I attended a seminar in Boston with civil resisters from around the world. Some were still glowing from recent success, like the

Egyptians who'd helped overthrow Hosni Mubarak, while others, like the Tibetan and the two from Burma, remained so far from what they longed for. They shared their goals and their strategies, as well as their sacrifices—for many of them, imprisonment and torture. They had arguments and epiphanies. They learned from what one another was doing and thinking, and grew stronger as a result.

During a break in the discussion, I noticed a photocopied essay by one of those at the seminar, a memoir of her time in the civil rights movement. The essay opened with a passage from a nineteenth-century poem born of the struggle over slavery. It described a moment arising, or a movement, in which a whole society is forced to choose where it stands: "Some great cause, God's new Messiah." When might such a moment, or a movement, come to us in the United States again? Those words became my mission.

I left that meeting with something lit up inside me. I now knew the kinds of stories I needed to learn how to tell—the stories of how people go from wanting to resist to actually doing so, of how by reasoning and creativity they learn to build power. I wasn't interested so much in reporting on more protests, coming and going with the spectacle; I wanted to experience the planning and organizing by which the spectacle, and whatever comes of it, came about. So when I returned home to New York, I started looking for the planning process of some great cause to follow and to learn from. It turned out that this would be easier than I expected—and that the spectacle would be the process itself.

Revolution didn't seem like such a crazy idea in 2011. Just a few weeks into the year, two dictators had already bowed to the power of the people. By late February, the victorious Egyptians were phoning in pizza-delivery orders to the occupied Wisconsin state capitol, in Madison. Unrest followed the summer's heat to Greece, Spain, and England. Europe's summer was Chile's winter, but students and unions rose up there too. Tel Aviv grew a tent city.

While Tahrir Square in Cairo was still full, the boutique-y activist art magazine *Adbusters* published a blog post imagining "A Million Man March on Wall Street." But the United States appeared to go quiet after Madison, its politics again domesticated by talk of the "debt ceiling" and the Iowa straw poll; when tens of thousands actually did march on Wall Street on May 12, few noticed and fewer remembered.

While following the march that day on Twitter from Florida, however, a thirty-two-year-old drifter using the pseudonym Gary Roland read about another action planned near Wall Street for the next month: Operation Empire State Rebellion, or OpESR. That tweet led him to a dot-commer-turned-activist-journalist named David DeGraw. DeGraw was working through the Internet entity known as Anonymous, which over the past year or two had been emerging from various cesspools online into a swarm of vigilantes for justice. With Anonymous, DeGraw had helped build safe networks for the dissidents of the Arab Spring. Since early 2010 he had also been writing about his vision of a movement closer to home, a movement in which the lower 99 percent of the United States would rebel against the rapacity and corruption of the top 1 percent. An Anonymous unit formed to organize OpESR, calling itself A99.

Through DeGraw's website, Roland helped make plans. Having recently lost his job as a construction manager for a New York real estate firm, he was familiar with the city's public spaces and the laws applying to them. He proposed that OpESR try to occupy Zuccotti Park, a publicly accessible place privately owned by Brookfield Office Properties. On June 14—Flag Day—Zuccotti Park would be its target.

Anonymous-branded videos announcing the action had begun to appear in March and got hundreds of thousands of views. Momentum seemed to be building. When the day came, though, only sixteen people arrived at Chase Manhattan Plaza, where the march to Zuccotti was to commence, and of the sixteen only four intended to occupy.

Undeterred, Roland decided to join another occupation that was beginning the same day near City Hall, a few blocks north. Organized by a coalition called New Yorkers against Budget Cuts, the so-called Bloombergville occupation would turn into a three-week stand against the city's austerity budget. It didn't seem to amount to much on its own, but it eventually proved to be another step building toward something that would.

"The attention we were able to get online," David DeGraw wrote after the flop on June 14, "obviously doesn't translate into action." Consoling himself with the thought that the attempt was at least spreading awareness, he started talking about trying again on September 10, a date chosen in deference to the Anonymous convention of operating in three-month cycles.

More simultaneity, more synchronicity: September 10 was also the day on which a completely separate mass action was slated to happen in Washington. Seize DC, as it was called, came from a small organization called Citizens for

Legitimate Government (CLG), which had experienced a period of some prominence during the Bush years.

"We're thinking of this as a guerrilla protest," CLG's Michael Rectenwald told me on a bench in Washington Square Park. (In addition to being the group's founder, chair, and "chief editorialist," he is a professor at New York University who writes about nineteenth-century working-class intellectuals.) The goal was to mount a protest against wars abroad and corporate control at home, beginning on the eve of the tenth anniversary of the September 11 attacks but possibly continuing much longer. "We're trying to get the maximum impact for the numbers we have," Rectenwald said. The details would be worked out more or less on the fly.

Numbers, however, were again the problem. CLG had called for Seize DC on its seventy-five-thousand-member e-mail list, but by late August it was clear that a turnout of even a thousand wasn't likely. This, too, had to be put on hold.

The call that came on July 13 from *Adbusters* was just one more among the others. Like OpESR and Seize DC, its prospects were entrusted to the Internet. The name was in the idiom of a Twitter hashtag: #OCCUPYWALL-STREET. Accompanying that was an image of a ballerina posed atop the Financial District's *Charging Bull* statue, with police in riot gear partly obscured by tear gas in the background. Red letters at the top asked, "WHAT IS OUR ONE DEMAND?" At the bottom, in white, it said "SEPTEMBER 17TH"—the birthday of *Adbusters* founder Kalle Lasn's mother—and "BRING TENT." The image appeared as a centerfold in an issue titled "Post Anarchism," which also included an article by David Graeber. With that, more or less, the magazine's logistical guidance ended.

"What we want to play is a more philosophical role," *Adbusters'* twenty-nine-year-old senior editor, Micah White, told me in August. Not dirtying its hands with organizing became just part of the aesthetic, part of the mystique.

Almost at once, Twitter accounts, Facebook pages, and Internet Relay Chat channels started appearing and connecting. "#OCCUPYWALLSTREET goes viral," *Adbusters* announced in a "Tactical Briefing" e-mail on July 26. The following day, Alexa O'Brien's US Day of Rage declared its support for the occupation. O'Brien and the colleagues she'd found online were organizing actions on September 17 in Los Angeles, Portland, Austin, Seattle, and San Francisco, in addition to Wall Street. Her press releases and tweets became so ubiquitous that people started referring to #OCCUPYWALLSTREET and US Day of Rage interchangeably.

I first heard about the idea of occupying Wall Street while attending the planning meetings of yet another group that, since April, had been planning another indefinitely long occupation of a symbolic public space. In late July I attended one of its meetings, around a conference table in an office above Broadway shared by a handful of New York activist organizations. Those present, both in person and over video-chat, included some of the hardiest survivors of Bush-era dissent. They were mostly middle-aged, frustrated, and ready for a breakthrough. This October 2011 Coalition intended to set up camp at Freedom Plaza in Washington DC starting on October 6, in time for the tenth anniversary of the war in Afghanistan. "Stop the machine!" went their slogan, "Create a new world!"

In early August, Al Gore told TV commentator Keith Olbermann, "We need to have an American Spring." But people all over the country were already fumbling toward an American Autumn.

What, if anything, the hubbub online actually amounted to remained opaque. "We are not a political party," Alexa O'Brien told me when I asked her about the nature of US Day of Rage in mid-August. "We are an idea." Here's how she described its genesis, out of the inspiration of the Arab Spring:

> I felt that something needed to be done to help people have a space where they could discuss these issues and their self-interest without ideological talking points. I asked them to list their grievances on a hashtag—US Day of Rage asked people to list their grievances. Originally we were going to put them into columns. But what ended up happening is we realized that most of the grievances, whether on the left or the right, could be linked to corrupt elections. So we decided to keep it really simple. We need to reform our elections.

The idea that emerged out of these discussions on social media was an especially drastic kind of campaign finance reform: "One citizen. One dollar. One vote."

She went on:

> I wouldn't even call myself an activist. I'm a normal nobody. I'm a nobody. I always say that. For me, this is an avocation. It's an idea of service to my country, to my community, and to other people. In the beginning it was me, but I have to say "we," because there was the hashtag as well. And it's not me. In the

beginning we had the hashtag, and we had a Facebook page. And what we did was we built a platform.

The platform also had a theme song, which appeared on the website in the form of an embedded YouTube video: the theme from the 1970s show *Free to Be . . . You and Me.*

On August 23, an *Adbusters* e-mail featured a video of Anonymous's headless-man logo and a computerized voice declaring support for #OCCUPYWALLSTREET. Soon there were rumors that the Department of Homeland Security had issued a warning about September 17 and Anonymous; Anonymous bombarded mainstream news outlets with tweets demanding that they cover the story.

Micah White:

> I see stuff on Twitter from people saying that we had interaction and then we cut off communication, but we never had any. I never communicated with Anonymous.

Alexa O'Brien:

> They [Homeland Security] believe that we are high-level Anonymous members, which is really a joke. . . . We have had no contact with Anonymous. And that's the honest truth.

An occupation, by definition, has to start with people physically present. Social media, even with whatever aid and cachet Anonymous might lend, isn't enough—witness the failure of OpESR. Until August 2, when the NYC General Assembly began to meet near the *Charging Bull* statue at Bowling Green, #OCCUPYWALLSTREET was still just a hashtag.

That first meeting was hosted by the coalition behind Bloombergville, New Yorkers against Budget Cuts, which had exchanged e-mails with *Adbusters*. Others learned about the assembly at a report-back from anti-austerity movements around the world at the nearby 16 Beaver Street art space on July 31. What was advertised as an open assembly began like a rally, with Workers World Party members and those of other groups making speeches over a portable PA system to the hundred or so people there. But the anarchists started to heckle the socialists, and the socialists heckled back. The meeting melted down. Here's how one participant, Jeremy Bold, described what took place in an e-mail the next day:

[A] few participants were adamantly opposed to the initial speak-out sessions being voiced through the loudspeaker, proclaiming that it was "not a general assembly" and demanding that a more open GA be created. Though organizers quickly shifted to the general assembly structure for the meeting, maintaining use of the loudspeaker caused the opposed participants to organize their own assembly, causing a brief bifurcation in the group: one group utilizing the GA structure of an open floor but maintaining the loudspeaker to contend with the traffic noise, the other group seating themselves in a circle closer to Bowling Green park. The breakaway faction had objected to the format because it appeared to function more like a rally than a GA and expressed concerns about being forced to speak under a particular political party or viewpoint [, and the breakaway faction] voiced this criticism; as they broke off to begin the GA, participants were stuck between the two groups. As the power began to die from the loudspeaker, the group voted by simple majority to move to the traditional GA and joined the circle, in which the GA was already under way.

Those who stuck around got what the anarchists wanted, and perhaps more: a leaderless assembly, microphone-free and in a circle, that dragged the 4:30 P.M. event on until 8:30, with some people staying around to talk until eleven o'clock. They started using the language of the 1 percent versus the other 99—independently, it seems, of David DeGraw and A99. Working groups formed to do outreach, to produce media, to provide food.

Despite the presence of people from various contingents of the sectarian left who made their affiliations known with T-shirts and specialized rhetoric, none of these groups could dominate the NYC General Assembly. New York's activists at that point were splintered and frustrated, and no one group could do much of anything on its own. One of them with a considerable role, the invitation-only Organization for a Free Society, was not the kind to announce its presence, and its members seemed to operate as individuals, not as representatives of a bloc. Even the anarchists, who set the format of the GA and furnished some of its more influential interventions, were in no position to run the show entirely. David Graeber told me,

The anarchist scene in New York had been very fragmented. The insurrectionists versus the SDS people—there'd been all these splits. It had become a little dysfunctional. The New York scene was fucked up, to be perfectly honest.

Describing the makeup of the GA, Graeber continued:

> There was one fairly small crew—capital-*A* insurrectionary anarchists, they were there. But there was mainly what I like to call the small-*a* anarchists, people like myself.
>
> I couldn't tell you what kind of anarchist I am. I don't feel any need to work in groups that are made up exclusively or mainly of anarchists, as long as they operate on anarchist principles. I see anarchism more as a way of doing things, a broad series of ethical commitments and principles, rather than an ideology. So people like that, there were a lot of them.

In lieu of anything else, small-*a* anarchy was an acceptable enough common denominator for the anarchists and everyone else. On that basis, the General Assembly would continue to meet about once a week.

The second meeting I attended was on August 20, the fourth in all. It was relatively productive at first, even if short on consensus. The group didn't, for instance, make any outright commitment to nonviolence, largely because its members couldn't agree on what it would mean to do so. No text for the Outreach Committee's fliers could be passed. But people wiggled their fingers in the air when they liked what was being said and wiggled them down at the ground when they didn't, so through these discussions everyone got to know one another a little better.

Soon, even that modicum of process started to fail. Georgia Sagri, a performance artist from Greece, paced around the periphery of the circle with a large cup of coffee in her hand, making interjections whether or not she was "on stack" to speak. She seemed less interested in planning an occupation than in the planning meeting itself. "We are not just here for one action," she declared. "*This* is an action. We are producing a new reality!" The pitch of her voice rose and then fell with every slogan. "We are not an organization; we are an environment!"

Georgia's powers of persuasion and disruption were especially on display when the discussion turned to the Internet Committee. Drew Hornbein, a red-haired, wispy-bearded web designer, had started putting together a site for the General Assembly. Georgia thought he was doing it all wrong. She didn't trust the security of the server he was using—not that she knew much about servers—and wanted to stop depending on Google for the e-mail group. Her concern was principle, while his was expediency.

As Georgia and her allies denounced Drew publicly, he apologized as much as he could, but then he eventually got up and left the circle with others who'd also had enough. "I'm talking about freedom and respect!" Georgia cried. "This is not bullshit!"

She continued to hold the floor, proposing every detail of what the website would say and how it would look, reading one item at a time from her phone and insisting that the General Assembly approve it. The facilitators seemed exasperated. A passerby began playing Duck, Duck, Goose on the shoulders of those sitting under the Hare Krishna Tree.

The thrill I'd felt the previous Saturday turned to pretty thoroughgoing disappointment. I abandoned my reportorial post: I left early, after three and a half hours.

On the way out, I ran into a couple I knew from the October 2011 Coalition, Ellen Davidson and Tarak Kauff, who were just arriving from another gathering in Harlem. They had met each other at protests over the past few years, in jail after an action at the Supreme Court in DC, and in Cairo during a mobilization against Israel's blockade of the Gaza Strip. I updated Tarak—who had served in the army in the early 1960s and could still do a hundred push-ups—on what had been going on. None of it appeared to surprise or trouble him.

"It's really, really hard," he said in his Queens accent, as the Internet Committee proposals ground through consensus a few steps away. "They're doing fine."

Micah White of *Adbusters* said, when I called him on August 12:

> The worst outcome would be to get there and they just fumble it by doing this whole lefty game we always play, which is self-defeatist. We go there, make some unreasonable demand, like, we want to abolish capitalism and we won't leave until we do. And well, that's like the war on terrorism; that's an impossible dream. Or they just squander it by being some hipster, anarchist insurrection like, we're gonna smash some stores and make a spectacle. And everyone's like, "Why?"
>
> Because we have something beautiful going here. So we're trying to rise above the sectarian clashings of whether or not US Day of Rage is tweeting too much or whether or not the libertarians are—you know? And reach out to the Tea Party too. This is a moment for all of America.
>
> I don't see why this has to be a lefty moment or a righty moment, because this is a moment for us to reinvent democracy in America, because it's getting to be too late. If we don't do it now, we are reaching the end.

In the NYC General Assembly, as well as on the Internet, the idea of "one demand" that *Adbusters* had promulgated was a topic of perpetual discussion. Some of the proposals that were being suggested:

- Impose a Tobin tax (or a "Robin Hood tax") on financial transactions, a popular proposition among some economists for simultaneously bringing the most speculative markets a bit more under control while generating revenue for social programs. This idea was described in one of the planning GAs on a photocopied sheet of paper signed under the activist pen name "Luther Blissett."

- Restore the Glass-Steagall Act of 1933, which was repealed by Bill Clinton in 1999. It prevented investment banks from gambling with money deposited in their commercial affiliates, putting a further brake on speculation and lessening the public's exposure to the banks' risk.

- Overturn the Supreme Court's *Citizens United* decision, which massively deregulated the campaign finance system.

- Demand universal employment in New York, with the accompanying socialist mantra "A job is a right!"

- "End the Fed." The various libertarian contingents (and fans of the online documentary sensation *Zeitgeist*) were especially insistent on this proposal for the abolition of the Federal Reserve.

- "End the wars, tax the rich." This slogan of the antiwar movement tended to come from older voices, and it figured prominently in the October 2011 Coalition.

None of these was to win out. "One demand is dangerous," I remember someone saying in Tompkins Square Park. "This is for the long haul." Another added, "Personally, I'm not asking anything of Wall Street." And another: "Once you get pigeonholed into one demand, it becomes easy to be just about winning or losing."

At first the "one demand" was simply hard to agree on. But gradually its absence seemed to make more and more sense.

The August 27 GA meeting didn't happen because there was a hurricane that weekend—weird for New York City, just like the earthquake a few days earlier. I missed the following weekend's meeting because I went to the October 2011 Coalition's retreat at Ellen and Tarak's house up in Woodstock, where a dozen organizers holed up for two nights and a long day of planning the DC occupation. They were eating well, singing protest songs, and debating the theories of Gene Sharp, the scholar who from his home office in Boston helped inspire revolutions as far away as Serbia and Egypt. Everyone in the group came with some deep well of experience—a Ralph Nader presidential campaign manager, leaders of major antiwar groups, and the gruff Veterans for Peace, whose youthfulness returned to them with any talk of tactics. After decades of trying leaderless activism, they affirmed to one another that identifying leaders is really okay. It was conspicuous that only the very youngest—a sober-minded, thirty-eight-year-old Israeli who managed their website—had any real Internet expertise.

The goal of the occupation was to create a space for people to come into their own, explained Margaret Flowers, a pediatrician and a mother of three teenagers, who became radicalized while fighting for single-payer health care. She was among those who first conceived of the plan for October 6, but Margaret and the other organizers realized that the moment they succeeded—if they did, by some definition of the word—would be the moment they'd have to let go and let this take a life of its own.

"I just think of how I raised my children," she said.

The organizers gathered in the living room the first night, after dinner on the screened-in porch out back, for a meeting over Skype with a guru-type old man in Santa Cruz. His expertise was in a technique for "grounding" oneself with chi—or energy, or qigong, or the earth, or plain love—pointing one's attention to the ground underneath and feeling oneself as connected to it. For too long, they put up with him explaining all this—as strange women strolled by in the background, occasionally pausing to look at the camera or to stand in as demonstration subjects when he attempted to explain just what he was talking about and what it had to do with revolution. Tarak fell asleep in his chair as it became clear that the guy was quite pathetically just in search of a market, a spot on the website, and access to a huge crowd so he could jizz his metaphysics on them and make a buck in the process. For the rest of the retreat they'd joke about this—"Are you grounded?" But a few weeks later, standing again and again before columns of angry cops, I've got to say that I fell back on what little I'd gleaned of his technique.

The rest of the retreat was far more reasonable. Sketching notes on giant sheets of paper on an easel, the organizers set out to assess what their proto-movement was up against and what its strengths and weaknesses were. While debate about the "one demand" had come to an impasse in Tompkins Square

Park, this group decided much more methodically not to state demands at the outset. For months already, they had been developing a fifteen-point set of proscriptions on issues ranging from military spending to public transportation, but now they started thinking that the group wasn't strong enough— not yet—to make such demands heard. They concluded from their discussion of Gene Sharp that there was no point in making a demand until they were in a position to force the system to accept it. Instead, their goal would be to host an open conversation at their occupation in the capital, to spread a culture of resistance to the illegitimate politics of Washington. Given where they were at the time, the first priority was to claim that space, cause a disruption, and grow.

The concluding topic of the retreat, after Goals and Strategy and Tactics were settled, was Message. Over wine that Saturday night, the group tripped and turned over words until finally landing on something that would let them go to bed satisfied: "It Starts Here." The slogan, however, was destined for obsolescence; by the time they pitched their tents in October, they would seem like latecomers.

Reports about the planned occupation of Wall Street trickled out slowly online, and consequently they betrayed the biases of the Internet: much discussion of *Adbusters,* US Day of Rage, and Anonymous, but hardly anything about the General Assembly—which, despite not having an active website, still constituted the closest thing to a guaranteed turnout on September 17.

Among the most prolific early chroniclers was Aaron Klein of the right-wing news website *WorldNetDaily.* His articles claimed that September 17 could bring "Britain-style riots," that "Day of Rage" was a reference to the terrorism of the Weather Underground, and that the billionaire George Soros—who else?—was behind it all. Because Stephen Lerner of the Service Employees International Union had been murmuring about wanting to see an uprising against banks, Klein concluded that the union was involved, together with the remnants of ACORN. None of it was true; when people from the General Assembly tried to reach out to unions and the like, none wanted to touch the idea of an occupation with a ten-foot pole. But Klein thought he saw exactly the kind of vast left-wing conspiracy he had been outlining in his book, *Red Army: The Radical Network That Must Be Defeated to Save America,* which was scheduled for release in October. Before most Americans had heard of #OCCUPYWALLSTREET, Klein's gumshoeing inspired a new fund-raising and lobbying campaign from the conservative AmeriPAC: "On September 17th," the title of one solicitation warned, "Socialists Will Riot Like Egyptians in All Fifty States."

My next chance to go to an NYC General Assembly meeting was on September 10, a week before the date *Adbusters* had named. The facilitators this time were especially expert—impatient with off-topic speeches and creative with synthesizing what was said into passable proposals. Things got done. But really, most of the work was already being handled by the various formal and informal committees that had grown out of the General Assembly. I was learning that the point of a consensus process like this is often less to make decisions than to hear one another out; individuals and subgroups can then act autonomously, respecting the assembly while sparing it the burden of micromanagement.

On September 1, nine people had been arrested while attempting to sleep legally on the sidewalk of Wall Street as a "test run," and a video of it was getting traction online. A student group was rehearsing a flash mob to Michael Jackson's "Thriller." The Food Committee had raised eight hundred dollars—the only funding that I heard mentioned—which was about a quarter of the goal for supplying water and peanut butter sandwiches. The National Lawyers Guild would be sending observers in green caps. More than any one plan, there were plans.

I didn't see Georgia Sagri there on September 10. Gary Roland showed up with an actress he'd met at Bloombergville; they had gone on a bike trip around the country but then decided to come back to see what would happen on the 17th. There was enough of a crowd that the facilitators had to demonstrate the "people's microphone," which would become a hallmark of the movement: the speaker addresses the audience in short phrases, and those who can hear repeat them in turn for the benefit of those who can't. Less can be said that way, and less quickly, but more actually tends to be heard.

In the three weeks since the previous GA meeting I had attended, the mess had congealed into common wisdom. Frustrations were past, folded into the present, and turned into lessons. Some of these planners would later be accused of belonging to a secret leadership cabal behind the leaderless movement; if they were, it was the result of nothing more mysterious than having come to know and trust one another after a month and a half of arguing, digressing, and, occasionally, achieving consensus.

The Tactics Committee gave its report. An occupation right in front of the Stock Exchange seemed unfeasible and overly vulnerable. The previous week, the GA had decided to convene an assembly on September 17 at Chase Manhattan Plaza. The committee was coming up with contingencies, and contingencies for contingencies, in case that plan didn't work. In all likelihood there would be a legal encampment along sidewalks, which many had done during Bloombergville. Despite *Adbusters*'s initial suggestion to "bring tent" and the rapper Lupe Fiasco's promise to donate fifty of them, tents would probably be too risky—though it all depended on how many people would be there and what those people would be willing to do. As in Cairo and Madrid, the encampment would have to form itself.

Keeping tactics loose might also be safer. Everyone assumed there were cops in the group—I, for one, had my short list of suspects—and the less you plan ahead, the less they can plan for you.

By this point, the idea of making a single demand had completely fallen out of fashion. After a month and a half of meetings, those in the General Assembly were getting addicted to listening to one another and being heard. Rather than discussing the Glass-Steagall Act or campaign-finance reform, they were talking about making assemblies like this one spread, around the city and around the country. The process of bottom-up direct democracy would be the occupation's chief message at first, not some call for legislation to be passed from on high. They'd figure out the rest from there.

I was still wrapping my head around this. Everyone was. This was a kind of politics most had never quite experienced, a kind apparently necessary even if its consequences seemed eternally obscure.

Drew Hornbein, who'd almost left the movement after how he'd been treated at the meeting three weeks earlier, was back. "What's really keeping me in this is the idea of a general assembly, of the horizontal power structure and decision making," he said. Mike Andrews—a tall, well-muscled book editor who usually spoke for the Tactics Committee—told me about how he felt after being at a GA meeting:

> It pushes you toward being more respectful of the people there. Even after General Assembly ends I find myself being very attentive in situations where I'm not normally so attentive. So if I go get some food after General Assembly, I find myself being very polite to the person I'm ordering from, and listening if they talk back to me.

Maybe assemblies like this could even become a new basis for organizing political power on a larger scale. Of course, in the months to come this would be exactly what happened; as the call to occupy spread, assemblies followed. From Boston to Oakland to Missoula, Montana, activists wiggled fingers in horizontally structured meetings, using a common language to discuss problems both local and global—just as was hoped for, just as was planned. But the fact that there was a plan doesn't mean that the plan was complete, or reassuring, or guaranteed to have the intended effect.

A spree of decisions passed by consensus the night of September 10. There would be no appointed marshals or police negotiators; if the police wanted to negotiate, it would have to be with the whole assembly. The General Assembly would start on the 17th at three o'clock—"and if we're in jail we start it there." A few rebellious minutes after ten, when the park was supposed to be closed, the meeting ended, and we huddled around tables at Odessa, a nearby diner, for drinks.

Throughout the week before September 17, there were committee meetings, civil-disobedience training sessions, and warm-ups. People from all over started sending pictures of themselves holding signs with their grievances against Wall Street, which were posted at wearethe99percent.tumblr.com. When the Arts & Culture Committee put on midday yoga classes and speakouts in front of the Stock Exchange, onlookers were baffled, but that didn't matter. "I've never felt so liberated, so free!" one of the planners told me, a Brazilian doctor studying for a master's in public health. He was carrying around with him a hefty copy of Peter Kropotkin's *Mutual Aid*.

Also in front of the Stock Exchange one of those days was a man in a giant white no. 4 lottery ball suit with an Uncle Sam hat on top that said "JUSTICE." The suit, he told me, had been created for a business of his then in litigation. Next to him his colleague held a sign that said "Please Re-Elect PRESIDENT OBAMA Or The little guy Has No Chance." I asked if they were involved in occupying Wall Street, and they informed me they weren't. For them, the choice of location was a practical matter.

"We were at Times Square once," the man with the sign said. "It was just too crowded."

That week, too, Anonymous threatened a fearsome attack on bank websites. And more. No one could know everything that was happening, much less whether it would work.

"Maybe the General Assembly has been the really big central planner, but I don't know," Drew Hornbein told me that week over lunch. "There might be a lot of other stuff going on." I mentioned the group organizing for October 6, and he asked me to send him some links. If Wall Street didn't work out he could help with that.

There was a small meeting a few days before the 17th in the back of a bar in the Bed-Stuy section of Brooklyn—for outreach, to talk about #OCCUPYWALLSTREET with some locals. It's a mostly black neighborhood, yet all but one of us—hip-hop elder Radio Rahim—were white. Still, "What a propitious moment this is!" predicted a retired schoolteacher. "This is the moment."

"This is fucking really new, this is the definition of a truly radical movement," said one of the graduate students from the General Assembly. "So, yeah, we're gonna win."

Occupation was on my mind constantly as the date approached, but it was still a mostly secret fixation. Norman Mailer's mesmeric account of the 1967 march on Washington, *Armies of the Night,* was on my nightstand. I saw "OCCUPY WALL STREET SEPTEMBER 17" scrawled in chalk near the fountain in Washington Square Park. On the whole, though, the city's landscape seemed innocent of what was being planned for it—if what was happening was really planning at all.

On September 16, the night before whatever it was was slated to begin, I opted to pass on covering a civil-disobedience training to satisfy my curiosity about an occupation-themed Critical Mass bike ride setting out from Tompkins Square Park. Online, Anonymous associated the ride with something called "Operation Lighthouse."

A critical mass there was not, unless you counted the police, who were stationed at every corner of the park and periodically motorcycled by to monitor the handful of bicyclists waiting in vain for more to turn up. The bicyclists accepted soup and coffee from enterprising evangelists and obtained a tepid blessing for the next day's undertaking. Rather than invite the police to form a motorcade around the group, those present decided to leave the park one at a time and reconvene downtown for a scouting mission.

After riding into the Financial District and passing by Wall Street, I stopped in front of a boxing match two blocks south of the New York Stock Exchange. Seeping out from the Broad Street Ballroom, an inexhaustible electronic beat surged under a looping bagpipe track. Well-decorated couples and gaggles paid their forty-five dollars per person to slip through the doors and into the crowd surrounding the ring, where two sinewy fighters were bouncing back and forth, punching and kicking each other. They were following Thai-style rules, but the scene looked more like the last days of Rome. Along the back wall stood a row of Doric columns.

On the sidewalk, looking in and around, I recognized Marisa Holmes from the General Assembly meetings as she veered away from the entrance to the boxing match. She looked worried, but she usually looked worried, so it was hard to be sure. We nodded to each other knowingly, like spies, and maybe for a moment even questioned whether to acknowledge each other publicly. But we did, and we exchanged our reconnaissance.

She had just been down at Bowling Green, where a Department of Homeland Security truck was parked. Barricades surrounded the *Charging Bull* statue like a cage. I told her I had been up at Chase Manhattan Plaza, north of Wall Street, and it was also completely closed off. A stack of barricades sat in wait just across a narrow street. We stood in silence and watched as the fight ended, the combatants making a gesture of good sportsmanship. Marisa continued north to Wall Street, and I got on my bicycle to go home.

Nights in the Financial District are desolate, even ones with scattered boxing fans and police officers preparing for God-knows-what. One can feel the weight of the buildings overhead, all the more because there are so few people around to help bear the load. The buildings seemed completely different, however, while I rode home over the Manhattan Bridge. They were distant, manageable, and light. Rolling high above the East River and looking back at them, I wondered if they had any idea what was coming.

TWO | NEW MESSIAH

When night fell on September 17, the Financial District had that feeling of loneliness about it again, of lifeless towers, of quiet. This night, though, it was at least somewhat less unoccupied.

One or two hundred people were huddled in circles, scattered around Zuccotti Park's stone floor. A little before 10 P.M., more than twenty empty police vans passed by them on Broadway in a solemn line, their flashing lights lighting up the empty buildings above. Soon, on that narrow end of the park, there formed two rows of officers with clubs drawn and plastic white handcuffs dangling from their trousers. Two more rows lined the park's longer northern and southern sidewalks. A trio of officers on horses stood in wait by a scaffold across Broadway. When a pack of boys on BMX bikes cruised past, officers mobbed them and told them to leave the area immediately. The boys tried to argue and tried to linger and witness what was or wasn't about to happen, but eventually they complied.

The day had begun around noon, when the NYC General Assembly's Arts & Culture Committee convened its "New York FUN Exchange" at Bowling Green. An anticlimactic crowd of a few hundred people marched for a while around the *Charging Bull,* which was still surrounded by barricades and a few police officers. "Protect us, not the bull!" the marchers chanted at them. There was yoga, and there was waiting. I talked with a hedge fund guy from New Jersey and a whole new crop of anarchists. Some planners from the October 2011 Coalition came to see how this attempt would go, hoping to learn from it for their own. Soon, the wandering crowd coalesced into a mass on the south end of Bowling Green to hear the performance artist Reverend

Billy, who was preaching through a bullhorn on the steps of the Museum of the American Indian.

Adbusters had initially called for twenty thousand people, but this was looking more like two thousand. A lot of them, too, were reporters, though it wasn't especially easy to tell the reporters apart from the protesters. "There are more cameras here than signs," I heard someone mutter. The Global Revolution channel, at least, had five thousand viewers online.

"What is this?" went a chant. "This is just practice!" They seemed to be saying it to console themselves.

Others gave short speeches after Reverend Billy finished—whoever wanted to give one. Meanwhile, the Tactics Committee huddled, trying to decide what to do next. Some were saying it was better to have the big assembly where they already were, while others said they should move. Maps were being passed through the crowd with several locations identified and numbered. Chase Manhattan Plaza, which the planners had agreed on for the three o'clock assembly, was obviously out of the running; it was gated shut, so Tactics had decided on Zuccotti Park as the first backup that morning. Gary Roland, who helped pick Zuccotti as the target for OpESR months before, was scouting there. He called another organizer down at Bowling Green to say that it was clear of cops. There were a few drops of rain, adding to the urgency.

And so Tactics made the announcement from the steps of the museum. Location number two: Zuccotti Park. Everyone should walk there, together—in pairs, like the Sand People in *Star Wars,* so they could go legally on the sidewalk. There was an argument about the wisdom of this choice among those gathered there around the steps, and there were speeches to the contrary, but by then it was too late. The crowd had already started to move.

Moving up Broadway felt slow and maddening, but it was only a few minutes before we were at Zuccotti, filling the space between the granite and the treetop canopy. There were no police blocking it. Actually, it was beautiful. As we poured in, the hard, gray, corporate plaza looked like a promised land.

There, a semblance of an assembly began. Before most people knew what hit them, the General Assembly from Tompkins Square Park had been reconstituted, and it promptly broke into smaller groups so that people could discuss with one another why they'd come. Many had shown up to what they thought was a protest, but what they got was a giant meeting. They took it in stride. Some people talked, while others started to work. Those so equipped pulled out their laptops to upload video, to check in on Internet relay chat channels, or to monitor police scanners.

I heard reporters complaining about how the energy was gone from the earlier chanting and marching. They were disappointed. This wasn't just a protest, but something subtler and longer, and it would take patience.

But it was still a protest, too. A group of people got restless and decided to go on a march to Wall Street, just a few blocks down Broadway. Led by social-ist signs and Anonymous's signature Guy Fawkes masks, they set off, already crying the chants that would soon be stuck in so many people's heads around the country: "We! Are! The 99 percent!" and "All day! All week! Occupy Wall Street!" Those who stayed behind were busy trying to figure out just exactly where they were and whether it made sense to stay.

With a smartphone's glance at Wikipedia, I noticed something interest-ing. Before 2006, when Brookfield Office Properties named the place after its chairman, Zuccotti Park had another name, which was still on the side of the building to the north: "Liberty Plaza." Kind of like Tahrir— "Liberation"—Square in Cairo. This fit. Some people said "Liberty Park," others said "Liberty Square," and others said "Liberty Plaza." Neither name would ever quite become standard. But when I told the Egyptian woman in the food cart on the corner that the place had been renamed "Liberty," she grinned.

I stood by while Lucas Vazquez called Brookfield on his cell phone. There were rumors that maybe the company had decided to allow the encampment to remain there. He asked if that was true.

"So," Lucas said, after hanging up, "he said they have not allowed us to sleep over. And he said that we'd be arrested for trespassing if we sleep over— his words."

Lucas was a high school senior from Long Island, which was hard to believe, except for the fact that he'd have to leave at night to catch the Long Island Rail Road for home. He'd already helped organize the May 12 march on Wall Street and Bloombergville, and then was part of the planning GAs for this. He was serious and smart, and game for anything—but stuck in educational servitude.

"I'd rather come here than school, but I wanna graduate," he said.

Across the park, the actress-turned-political-candidate Rosanne Barr was giving a speech through a megaphone demanding "the blessed and holy guillotine" for "guilty leaders" and "priests." The marchers returned, victorious. The Food Committee's peanut butter sandwiches were there to greet them.

As the sun set, just after seven o'clock, a facilitator from the planning meetings opened the evening session of the General Assembly. "You know what general assemblies are," he cried. "You've seen it in Tunisia. You've seen it in Egypt. You've seen it in Spain. And now you see it on Wall Street!"

The police presence was growing, with horses and plastic cuffs. This was foremost on people's minds, but it didn't stop a few from taking the opportunity of assembly to grandstand about whatever. A woman who'd called for a general strike earlier did so again, and another demanded the end of corporate personhood. "Buy physical silver!" someone advised—not the only one to do so that day. Across the plaza, a drum circle nearly drowned out their voices anyway.

The real substance of the discussion was simply about what to do. Some felt that they'd come to occupy *Wall Street,* and they wouldn't be satisfied except there. But Wall Street was completely barricaded off and surrounded by police. "I propose that we march to Wall Street and sleep on the people's sidewalk," said Lucas. A man in a suit and tie volunteered to "repair to Wall Street for repose," set up a tent, and see what would happen. It was a tough call.

"I love this space," another voice said. "It's very comfortable. But revolution is not about comfort!"

Finally, the assembly arrived at the decision to stay in Liberty Square indefinitely and to take good care of it. People split up into working and thematic groups to begin the business of doing so. One of the most tempting of these to join, given the circumstances, was the meditation and massage circle; already, the crowd had thinned from a couple thousand to a couple hundred, and it was thinning more, while the number of police grew. Some were saying that there had been an undercover cop in the Media Committee, and theories were circulating about others. A group returned with dumpster-dived cardboard for sleeping.

Looking around at who was there, I noticed also who was not. Nobody from *Adbusters;* Micah White, in Berkeley, had taken a vow against flying on planes for the year, and Kalle Lasn had an elderly mother-in-law to attend to in Canada. Georgia Sagri wasn't there either; "I wasn't and am still not interested in the metaphorics of the occupation," she would later tell me. Alexa O'Brien was "running the back end" for this and actions around the country that day. She brought supplies but would hardly be seen on the plaza thereafter.

I walked along the sidewalk to see what the police were doing. They seemed ready to move in and clear the park. A black Suburban drove up and stopped on the corner. Its window was rolled halfway down, and a small, older man with a bald head peered out and spoke to the commanders in white shirts. Not long after he pulled away, the second row of police disappeared, as well as the horses. The drumming quieted, and the newfound Occupiers started going to sleep.

There would be no raid that night. A dilemma had been posed to the powerful, and for the moment the powerful capitulated.

I saw Marisa Holmes. She was ecstatic, with the caveat of course that there were no guarantees. Along with some other organizers from the city, she left for the night. I prepared to go to a colleague's apartment to help edit the video he'd shot that day. As I left, I wrote to myself that I didn't think it would last. I didn't think it would change anything. I was tired, and all I could feel was the precariousness.

"They're so young, they think they know everything," one police officer said to another. I heard other cops talk about how much they take home after taxes.

Neither they nor anyone else seemed to grasp what was happening in front of them. How could they? It had taken the organizers long enough to begin to realize what they were organizing, and they still didn't really know. There would be time to start figuring it out, though, because the occupation was staying.

Sunday, day two, the Occupiers kept busy. There was such a barrage of details between them and what this could be. They were making signs, eating donated pizza, collecting trash, laying down sleeping bags and cardboard to sleep on, and running a media center on a few uncomfortable tables with a generator and a wifi hotspot. They conducted a large, loud march around the Financial District. But, mostly, they assembled. There were several hours of General Assembly meetings in the morning, and then an extended debate— from midafternoon until late at night—about what the plan of action would be for Monday, when the neighborhood's population would turn from tourists grazing for photogenic prey to those coming to do the very business that this occupation was there to oppose.

Early in the afternoon, it seemed that the chilly first night had taken a toll. Numbers in Liberty Square were lower than they had been the evening before. Those still around sang redemption songs a little behind the beat, or intently read texts of significance, or simply sat and waited. Others tried to confirm more rumors of police agents in their midst. But as evening fell, some of the previous day's energy returned, as did an influx of new people who'd heard about the occupation on the Internet or from friends—still only two or three hundred in all. Pizza kept arriving through the night, and through its little crisis.

At about 9:15 P.M., by way of Occupiers reporting to the General Assembly, the police demanded that all the signs that were beginning to proliferate on the park's walls and trees be taken down. There was a fractious reaction at first. Some thought it a reasonable request and wanted to comply. Others refused on principle, not wanting to be taking orders from the police. People on either side made speeches and tried to start chants. Some took it upon themselves to remove signs, and others moved to stop them. There were whispers that undercover cops were sowing divisions, though it hardly seemed like the Occupiers required any help with that. Just when unity was needed, it wasn't there. Officers started taking down signs themselves while Occupiers chanted, "Shame! Shame!"

The focal point of it all became a spot on the eastern edge of the park, along Broadway. Several protesters—women and men, young and older—decided to sit down there in front of a Socialist Workers Party poster (whose affiliation would later be stripped from it) that said, "A JOB IS A RIGHT! CAPITALISM DOESN'T WORK." Others tried to get them to move, but they wouldn't. The police didn't move them either. There were no gory arrests. The sign remained as long as they did. Police and fellow protesters withdrew, and the meeting continued.

Moments like these were messy and far from flattering, and there would be many more to come.

I slept my first night in Liberty Square without a sleeping bag, curled up on a few sheets of cardboard. There were people playing music quietly with guitars and drums in far corners of the park. Near me the medics were planning for the next day's action. A couple dozen Occupiers had just held a candlelight vigil by the barricades that were still surrounding the blocks around the Stock Exchange, mourning the death of capitalism. The barricades proved to them that they were winning. "Wall Street is already occupied," one person had said earlier. "We've already achieved our objective."

On Monday morning, I woke up just after sunrise with the shivers. My eyes opened to see polished shoes and suit pants and skirts passing all around me, walking from the subway to work. There were TV news trucks on the north edge of the park. A groggy woman near me cried, "Look at the news, guys!"

After overnighters groggily packed up their bedding and lined up for dumpster-dived bagels, an unplanned-for 7 A.M. General Assembly session began. Its purpose was a rundown of the day's events. Committees that met the night before had decided to have marches to Wall Street at 9:00, 11:30, and 3:30. But then somebody came to the front of the assembly and announced through the people's mic that he was going to march right then. Wall Street bankers were walking to work, and we were just sitting there. The commuters would already be at their desks by nine. He ran off and, promptly, more than a hundred others followed. They marched around the plaza first, chanting, "All Day! All Week! Occupy Wall Street!" and then set off heading south on Broadway. The occupation was starting the workweek early.

Upon arriving at Wall Street, the marchers found that the blocks around the New York Stock Exchange, which had been barricaded completely throughout the weekend, now had open sidewalks. After briefly massing at Wall and Broadway, they proceeded down the sidewalk on Wall Street, chanting and banging on the barricades that were still blocking off the street, making a mighty noise. They flooded the commuters trying to get to work in that area and clogged the way—which was the point. "We! Are! The 99 percent!" they chanted. To the large detachment of police alongside them, they'd sometimes replace "We" with "You."

For almost two hours the march went on, continually evading attempts by police to pin it into an enclosed space or guide it out of the area. When the barricades on Broad Street were opened in order to let the marchers out (and keep them out), they used hand signals to turn around and head back up toward Wall Street. The march morphed into a long, two-directional picket line along Wall Street itself, going back and forth and back and forth as the Stock Exchange's opening bell rang. "Ring! The! Bell!" they cried. With so many Occupiers out in the streets, scouts went back to make sure that there were still enough people in Liberty Square to hold it.

Most bystanders and commuters in the midst of the march weren't amused. (The goal wasn't to amuse them.) "Shit" was something I heard a lot. A bitter dog walker said to a security guard, "They say it's their street"—the chant was "Whose street? Our street!"—"but they don't even pay taxes." Along those lines, also, I heard the soon-to-be-ubiquitous "Get a job!" And then there was ambivalence: "I hope the police protect the financial ... bullshit."

A middle-aged woman from El Salvador with painted eyebrows and a coffee in her hand said, "We used to do this in my country in the '70s and '80s. They'd arrest all of us." She was on her way to work but took pictures of the police officers in charge and made sure I did too, just to have them on record.

When the "Let's! Go! Home!" chant finally came at around quarter after nine, the march returned victoriously to Liberty Square and took stock. There were four arrests over the course of it—for crimes such as stepping off the sidewalk and touching a barricade—followed by several more as the day went on. A meeting convened to talk about how to do it better next time. These people were not just there to march; they were there to occupy, to discuss, and to build a blessed community.

Over the course of the day, more and more reporters turned up. It was one thing to hang around a private park for the weekend, but it was another to stay into the workweek and disrupt the business of the Financial District with the intention of doing so for longer—all day, all week. The afternoon General Assembly meeting was full of new faces, and sign holders stood against a substantial line of police on the sidewalk along Broadway. People passing by snapped pictures of the vast spread of messages painted on cardboard that was becoming Zuccotti Park's new floor.

In the rupture of the ordinary that characterized those early days, everything felt in some sense religious, charged with a secret extremity and transcendence —secret, because the rest of the world hadn't yet become aware of what was happening down at Liberty Square. Whenever I came back to Liberty after some time away, there was a feeling of entering sacred ground. Yet the moment I arrived, I was suddenly in a whirl of frantic conversations about worldly things: squabbles, crises, food mishaps, small victories, marches, and so on. All those things were sacred too. Once enmeshed in this kind of talk, you couldn't escape the plaza if you tried, because someone else, and then someone else, would come up to you with some other fantastic question or need. It was a place especially conducive to those of us with obsessive tendencies, who like to be consumed in a given interest or project to the exclusion of all else. There, the god of ordinary life was dead, resurrected in the business of self-reliance.

Notwithstanding what Liberty Square would later devolve into, it had a Puritanical single-mindedness early on. One night, in the middle of a group cozying up to go to sleep, somebody slipped out a bottle of vodka. "What are you doing with that?" another whispered. Why bother with *that* when there's *this?* Chain-smoked, hand-rolled cigarettes were ubiquitous, but at first that was it. Some would confess to me that they were desperate for a joint, it had been so long. They hadn't been tending to their addictions.

I remember watching, one morning, a guy in glasses as he greeted the sunrise by putting out a small rug, alone, and beginning the morning *salat,* which Muslims pray five times daily. Just as he started, one of the food vendors on the plaza came out from his stand and interrupted him. He pointed eastward, correcting the Occupier's guess as to the direction of Mecca.

On Tuesday the sun rose—behind clouds—on a tent city. Although police had made clear they wouldn't tolerate any structures, the prospect of overnight rain made a group of Occupiers decide around midnight the night before to set up tarps over media and food supplies, as well as to erect some of the tents that had been donated by Lupe Fiasco to sleep in themselves. This would make for their roughest confrontation yet with those sworn to serve and protect them.

While few were yet awake, I got up out of the deluxe-sized tent where I slept with almost a dozen others and wandered around the plaza. I heard a motorcycle cop saying on his cell phone, "That's my plan—to have them down as soon as possible." On the north side of the park, where the morning before there had been three TV news trucks to serve as witnesses, there was now only an NYPD Communications Division Command Post truck. Inside I saw an officer with "COUNTERTERRORISM" on the back of his uniform.

At 6:58, a cop wearing a suit and tie began walking through the plaza, peering through the mesh into tents where Occupiers were sleeping, demanding, "The tents have to come down."

Those who spent the night woke up and sprang into various sorts of action. Some immediately began complying by pulling out tent poles—"for the good of the movement"—while others insisted that they should stop. Still more suggested a middle path: to hold up the tents and tarps by hand, rather than with poles. An ad hoc meeting started in the center of the plaza to discuss the matter, but in the course of it nearly all the tents and tarps were taken down by self-appointed volunteers. A lot of people were frantic. A lot of people were terrified.

The scattered arguments and confusion coalesced at the plaza's northern wall, where General Assembly meetings were being held. At around 7:20, Justin Wedes—a twenty-five-year-old, Twitter-savvy schoolteacher with close-cropped hair and thick black glasses—takes hold of the megaphone to speak. His words are echoed fervently but unnecessarily by the people's mic, and like many others he has nearly lost his voice from all the chanting.

"We derive strength from each other," he says, as the soon-to-be-notorious Captain Edward Winski walks up to him, followed by a posse of officers. Winski whispers something in Justin's ear, presumably an order to put down the megaphone. But Justin continues: "More important than that, though"—until Winski grabs him, throws him to the ground, folds his arms expertly around his back, and takes him away.

"Shame! Shame!" shout Occupiers, and, "The whole world is watching!" That was the last time I saw any of them with a megaphone on Liberty Square.

Ten minutes later, the police were back. A group of them approached an Occupier near the rear of the meeting. As he was accosted and cuffed, officers shoved others aside, who started chanting the NYPD's motto, "Courtesy, professionalism, respect!" In the scuffle, a guy who had been making peace signs with both hands high above his head was pushed to the ground and arrested as well.

The incursions seemed timed to prevent a repeat of the big march and picket at the Stock Exchange that had begun around that time the day before. But if that was the case, the police needn't have bothered; Tuesday's march was planned for 9:00, and I looked at my cell phone as it started and saw that the time was 9:00 on the dot. I don't recall, before or since, Occupiers ever doing anything quite so punctually.

As if in retaliation for the march, cops were back on the plaza again an hour later. This time the excuse was the tarp that had been laid over sensitive media equipment. By then it was raining, and nearly all the Occupiers' possessions had been collected under tarps, plastic bags, and unassembled tents. But the media area was what interested the police. A group of officers approached the tarp, and the officer in charge gave orders through a megaphone that it should be removed. An Occupier climbed on top of it, banging a drumstick against a pan lid. He was grabbed, but slipped away, and began drumming again. Then, several officers took him to the ground. While he was being cuffed and beaten, he cried out, "I can't breathe!" and called for his inhaler.

Another, Jason Ahmadi, then stepped up to hold the tarp in his place. Jason had already been arrested the day before for writing "Love" on the sidewalk, just after a woman had been arrested for sidewalk chalking as well. This time, going limp, he was pulled off the tarp by police officers, dragged, cuffed, and then dragged more across the plaza and the sidewalk on his back, with his hands trapped in plastic cuffs between the sidewalk and his back. By the end of it, they were discolored and bloody.

One other guy close to me was grabbed too, and the cops pushed his face into a flower bed while he was cuffed. As a woman was taken away to a police van, a man ran after her shouting that he loved her. She, like several other female protesters that week, was taken not just to jail but to a psychiatric evaluation, as if on suspicion of hysteria.

Officers finally removed the tarp from the media equipment, exposing it to the rain, and left the plaza with other tarps, tents, and trash bags still in place. There was a standoff on the edge of the sidewalk as protesters chanted, shouted, and stood silently before the police, who at last received the order to withdraw.

There were seven arrests that morning, in three incursions. Each of them, for the Occupiers, was a new trial. They warned each other of the next incursion with steady tom-tom beats and other loud noises. Some offered acts of dignified resistance, while others yelled angrily, or sang chants, or simply watched. At the end of the last incident, a group convened to discuss deescalation techniques.

By late morning in Liberty Square, under a light drizzle, there was a feeling of drifting, of lost cohesion. The holdouts tried to find things to do, like hold signs, or play music in their underwear for the police, or defiantly recline on tarps, or arrange for the next meal. There was serious talk about abandoning the plaza, about other places to go in the area: south to Battery Park or west to the Irish Hunger Memorial. Maybe that was the fear talking, or maybe it was undercover cops, or maybe it was sensible. But once again inertia carried the day. The occupation did what it did best: it stayed.

The Command Post truck pulled away at 11:42 and was replaced by vans full of officers on each of the four sides of the plaza. People whispered about whether a dispersal was imminent but then changed the subject and carried on with their business.

When a group of Danish students stopped to watch the underwear musicians, a bearded Occupier from Massachusetts took the opportunity to tell them about what was happening in the plaza. He did so while teaching them the people's mic—slowly, one phrase at a time, in rhythmic call-and-response, like he was reciting a fairy tale. "We are out here." (Repeat.) "Because we've had enough." (Repeat.) He talked about the bailouts, and the banks, and the General Assembly. After the morning the occupation had had, he told me, he had to remind himself of why his friends had been hurt and arrested and why he was still there.

The police vans drove away at 12:03, leaving the usual handful of officers and cars and the mobile observation tower on the northwest side. An hour later, in time for the General Assembly meeting, the whole place felt different. The rain had stopped, and there were perhaps three times as many people, with new faces as well as familiar ones. The sidewalk along Broadway was full of Occupiers holding signs again, and the GA process was gearing up. Videos of the morning's action were spreading on YouTube. I talked with a man from Washington Heights—on the far north end of Manhattan—who had come for the first time after learning about the occupation on the Internet. People seemed happy, and eager, and curious. The next morning, this little secret of a place was the cover story of the tabloid newspaper *Metro,* with pictures of the arrests.

Getting arrested, on purpose or otherwise, was new to a lot of these people, but not to Jason Ahmadi. Just days before the occupation he'd arrived in New York from a homeless, vagabonding life in the Bay Area, where over the years he was involved in tree sits, banner drops, Food Not Bombs groups, and hunger strikes—that is, after he got over playing lots of video games in college at Berkeley. He came to New York for a War Resisters League meeting and decided to stick around for the occupation. The city made him crazy, though, and he could take it for only so long at a time before he had to get out to swim in a lake somewhere.

He once authored a typewriter-and-handwriting zine, *Arlo's Cooking Corner,* a practical, scientific, and philosophical guide to wrapping heated pots in blankets for long periods of time. "i love experimenting," it says in type at the outset of the section on baking. "it is how i grow as an individual." Hand-written on the back cover: "figure it out yourself."

Jason had wild, dark hair and wore colorful secondhand sweaters. In ordinary conversation he was all over the place with his moods and convictions, but when talking to the press or facilitating a meeting, there was hardly any-one more sure with words. His skill as a slow cooker expressed itself in a contentious room, which he could let simmer as the hidden consensus slowly started to express itself, but then pluck out whatever nonsense might fall in and mess up the process.

While Jason was in police custody, I felt a special urge to keep an eye on his white poster-board sign to keep it from falling into a puddle or getting thrown out. This became my mission. "The world has enough for everyone's NEED but not for everyone's GREED," it said, in the words of Gandhi. NEED was in blue, GREED was in pink, and the rest was in black. A couple of times, when I felt tired of reporting or talking to people or worrying about the cops, I held that sign myself on Broadway, in a row with all the other sign holders, watching the reactions of the people passing by with a dull expression on my face. Doing so would send me into a kind of trance, a bliss, although tinged by journalistic guilt. Yet what was not objective about holding a message so damning and elegant and true, which nobody can really deny? Maybe report-ers should do this more often.

In the center of Liberty Square at any given time, a dozen or so people were huddled around computers in the media area, pushing out tweets, blog posts, and the (theoretically) twenty-four-hour streaming video—soon to sprout into many copycat channels. They could edit and post clips of arrests in no time flat, then bombard Twitter until the clips went viral. The Internet, in its own way, was becoming occupied by this movement. But for outsiders look-ing to understand even the basic facts about what was actually going on—before September 17 and after—the Internet was as much a source of confu-sion as anything else. Reporters would come looking for *Adbusters* staff, or US Day of Rage members, or Obama supporters, or hackers from Anonymous. The everpresent WikiLeaks truck—marked "Mobile Information Collection Unit," and with a bed inside for the artist who drove it—led some to wonder whether Julian Assange himself might miraculously appear. Reporters were briefly disappointed to find none of the above.

Because of the General Assembly's early hiccups in setting up a website during the planning process, the occupation's online presence was left to the whims of improvisation. A transgender Internet security expert, Justine Tunney, registered the OccupyWallSt.org web domain anonymously on July 14 and started assembling a team to populate it. The site became the main clearinghouse for information about the occupation's progress, and soon it was getting as many as fifty thousand visitors per day. That first week at Liberty Square, as I looked over Justine's shoulder at a laptop screen with an open Internet relay chat channel and a usage graph for the Iceland-based server (which needed monitoring in case of distributed-denial-of-service attacks), she explained:

> OccupyWallSt.org is all open source. It's under full revision control, so you can see every change I make, except to the articles. Go through this history, it's all up here. Right now I'm trying to get more developers to help me out with this. So far I'm the only person developing it, and that's bad. I'm a firm believer in collective responsibility, because if I get hit by a bus, people are screwed.

In Nebraska, a pair of web designers who couldn't make it to New York set up OccupyTogether.org to coordinate the occupations beginning to appear around the country. Less happily, a document called "Occupy Wall Street—Official Demands," eerily dated September 20, 2013, was being circulated and discussed online. It included detailed proposals for reforming the financial system, none of which had been approved by the GA. Speculation abounded on the Internet, too, about the occupation's institutional sponsors—big labor, the Democrats, and so forth—but five minutes at a GA meeting would have easily disabused one of such associations. The Occupiers had hardly any organizational friends yet. Besides the thousands upon thousands of dollars that were pouring into the food fund but were stuck in an inaccessible WePay account, the movement had almost no money. There were a handful of Occupiers with Guy Fawkes masks backward on their heads, suggesting to some that Anonymous might somehow be in charge, but they were just one cadre among many.

I was spending every minute I could moving from happening to happening in the park, an endless parade of encounters. I'd go on most marches and sleep little at night. But there were also people I knew who were stuck in offices all day, watching on Twitter and Livestream. We'd compare what we knew and what we'd seen. They, by the light of the Internet, had seen much that I had missed, which often had little to do with what had filled my days on the ground. They could follow news from the other occupations cropping up in other cities, for instance, but not always the latest drama at Liberty. There could be no one all-seeing eye—not in the news, not on the plaza, not over the Internet. There was so, so much that I missed.

What was actually under way at Liberty Square was both simpler and more complicated than anyone not there could imagine: talking, making, organizing, eating, marching, dancing, sparring with police, and (not enough) sleeping. Cops and Occupiers alike used the bathrooms at the nearby McDonald's. Nobody was exactly sure yet who was doing what, but it was more or less working, and they were learning. Everyone was doing something. Some, both women and men, were doing so topless.

In all sorts of subtle ways the occupation was riding the momentum that came from the GA meetings that had been going on for a month and a half before it began. Those meetings built a community of people who trusted one another, who had a sense of one another's skills, and who were in some basic agreement about ends and means. To survive, however, this community would have to grow. Whole swaths of Americans—from immigrants to day workers to children—were largely missing among the Occupiers. There was a lot of talk about doing real outreach—door to door, subway car to subway car—but the overeducated young radical set that was dominant tended to stick with clever tweets and viral videos for the time being. And at least they could march.

On Thursday evening, a vigil gathered at Union Square to mourn the execution of Troy Davis, a black man in Georgia, and Occupiers went up there to stir the vigil into a march toward Liberty. Police tried to stop them with barricades and clubs and arrests, but they couldn't; when the marchers arrived, the numbers in the plaza swelled like they never had before. There were a lot of new faces and new kinds of faces. It paid off to quit the Internet, to go where people actually were and bring them back.

At the GA that night, Ted Actie, a producer for a black-owned TV production company in Brooklyn, called on the protesters to speak more directly to the communities around them. "You do so much social networking," he said, "you forget how to socialize."

Overheard at a miscellaneous meeting:

Occupier 1: "I hate and love the Internet."
Occupier 2: "It's complicated with the Internet."

Some people muttered about whether all the outrage about Troy Davis's death, even if he was falsely convicted, really had anything to do with occupying Wall Street. Did JPMorgan Chase kill Troy Davis? Did Bank of America? One old socialist said they did. Really, though, the crowd that poured into the park from that march was answer enough. Those faces seemed to make clear that if these Occupiers were going to talk about inequality and corruption in the United States of America, and in New York, they couldn't just talk about high finance. They would have to talk about race and about inequality's ugliest consequences. The task of occupying Wall Street was starting to reveal itself as more bewildering a project than most people might have thought.

Maybe that's why, one afternoon, an Occupier with long blond hair and multicolored spandex leggings got up on a table in the middle of the park during a moment of despair, announcing that he was going to drive a nail through his hand "in solidarity with Jesus Christ," "in solidarity with Troy Davis." He was, however, dissuaded.

Marking the one-week anniversary of the beginning of the occupation, a large march was planned for noon on Saturday. It was September 24. Several hundred marchers paraded around the plaza to their favorite chant, "All Day! All Week! Occupy Wall Street!" and headed down to the Wall Street area, where police arrested several of them. The march kept going and continued up to Union Square. Upon arriving, there was some debate about what to do next, until finally most people turned south again for the two-and-a-half-mile journey back to Liberty Square. That was when the police attacked.

At around 3 P.M., near Fifth Avenue and Twelfth Street, officers began unrolling plastic orange barriers, isolating a crowd of marchers—along with reporters and onlookers—and began arresting everyone inside for blocking traffic. Caught on cameras were scenes of one protester being dragged by her hair, and others being slammed into the pavement. The most notorious scene of the day, though, was the video of a group of women, already trapped by the net, who were writhing and screaming as Deputy Inspector Anthony Bologna doused them in pepper spray.

In total, police arrested eighty people. With not enough room for them in vans, many were taken away in city buses. The march thereafter dispersed, and those who weren't arrested made their way back to the Financial District.

No one, afterward, felt safe. It seemed certain that a full-on police dispersal would come that night. Contingency plans were being discussed in the General Assembly. Those who would drop by days or weeks later never felt how uncertain everything was the first nights, when the village being built on the plaza seemed so fragile, so liable to be destroyed at any moment in a surprise police sweep, like a thief in the night.

A bit after ten, though, there was a celebration around the media tables. Photocopied facsimiles of Sunday's *New York Daily News* were being passed around and photographed. After having held the plaza with hundreds of protesters at any given time for a week and having kept the blocks surrounding the Stock Exchange barricaded by police all the while, the protest had finally caught a major paper's attention.

"The *Daily News!*" I heard someone say. "We've already won!"

In an article that recounts as many gory details as would fit, the *Daily News* devoted only two short paragraphs to what the occupation was actually about and what protesters had been doing all this time: "attempting to draw attention to what they believe is a dysfunctional economic system that unfairly benefits corporations and the mega-rich." The real story, rather, was not this unusual kind of protest, or how it functioned, or exactly what conditions provoked it, but the excuse to have the word *busted* on the cover next to the cleavage of a woman crying out in pain under a cop's knee.

The Occupiers didn't care. The *Daily News* and the presence of TV vans all around seemed like guardian angels, ensuring that the occupation would survive until morning.

Thanks to the activist habit of *ressentiment,* acquired by seeing protest after protest fail to make headlines, the Occupiers had planned for creating their own media much more than serving anyone else's. There was no place in the encampment more seemingly sophisticated and elite than the jumble of glowing laptops and indiscernible wires around the media center; visitors passed by it with awe for this physical manifestation of the age of the hashtag. To Occupiers it was the source of such precious commodities as wifi and outlets, which were available only to those who could appear to be doing official movement-media business. As time passed, the right to be inside its bounds—marked, at first, by a ring of parked bikes—was ever more jealously guarded. This was an important place.

The level of preparation was almost zero, however, for co-opting traditional news outlets. At the outset no official working group had the job of doing the press releases, the hand-holding, and the modicum of homage that the modern reporter expects. It was mainly just Patrick Bruner who was doling out interviews, posting "communiqués" at OccupyWallSt.org, keeping reporters informed, and, unintentionally, spreading false rumors. Many others at Liberty weren't even aware he was doing it.

Patrick was a valiant, lanky, always black-clad student studying writing at Skidmore College. He grew up in Tucson, the son of two lawyers—"well-to-do," he said, and with a "very strong social conscience." He'd never done PR in his life, at least on purpose or by name. He met Justine through the Anarchism section of the website Reddit, and on September 17 he showed up ready to go. Because he was working with her, and because she ran OccupyWallSt.org, and because OccupyWallSt.org had the only publicized phone number related to the movement, he found himself in the PR business.

"That's the best thing about this world, is that you just show up," he said.

After a week of exhausting himself, Patrick asked me to lend a hand with his nearly only one-man media operation. It was another sin against proper journalism, but letting him get some rest seemed more important, so I did. I let him forward the press phone number to my phone, which meant that it was ringing unceasingly for hours until I was finally able to get it switched back. I also drafted the daily communiqué for OccupyWallSt.org, trying my best to follow the prevailing style:

This is the ninth communiqué from the 99 percent. We are occupying Wall Street. The police barricades that have been surrounding the Stock Exchange help.

Sunday has been decreed, once again, a day of rest. We didn't march. We have made a new world, a new city within the city. We are working on a new sky for where the towers are now.

Throughout the day our sisters and brothers arrested yesterday came back home to Liberty Plaza. They greeted the new faces that have joined us here. They shared their stories of imprisonment, of medical care denied and delayed. We welcomed them and listened.

We had visitors. [embedded videos of Chris Hedges, Immortal Technique, and Reverend Billy]

Yesterday was a day of action, and today was one of healing, discussion, and preparation. Working groups met in small circles around the plaza, planning their work and preparing to report back to the General Assembly as a whole. The Assembly debated, as always, the hows and whys of being here. In the morning, we talked about the occupations rising up in cities around the United States, joining us in what we're doing, as people begin rediscovering the power in themselves against the powers looming over them in buildings.

We talked of calling still others to do what we're doing. In the evening we talked about staying, or leaving, and what this space means for us. We love it, we're almost addicted to it, but what we are is more than this.

We strolled around the plaza. We wrote songs with new friends. We argued about politics with each other, but not a politics of puppets: a politics for us. We fed the hungry and gave sleeping bags to the cold. We rough-housed. We talked to the world on our livestream. Most of all, we kept on organizing ourselves. Our library grew.

Drums blared for hours into the night when the assembly wasn't in session, until the time came for quiet. The drummers ended by reciting from the Principles of Solidarity we approved in Friday's General Assembly, in the rain. Before the police lined along the Broadway side of the plaza, they cried together, "We are daring to imagine a new socio-political and economic alternative that offers greater possibility of equality."

"Safety in numbers!" a sign by them says. "Join us."

That night, as I tucked myself in to sleep, there was paranoia in the air—fears that this would be the night of the shutdown, again. Someone said in the GA that all the discussion about every provocation from the cops made him feel like he was living in a police state. Others said that should've been obvious already. (A few hours earlier Commissioner Ray Kelly bragged on TV that the NYPD had the weaponry to shoot down an airplane.) One guy who had been arrested a few days before seemed shell-shocked and terrified; he worried that the news trucks would leave us to the mercy of the police. Every threat was existential.

"Occupy your heart," another voice proposed through the people's mic, "not with fear but with love!"

At 2 A.M., the media center was still busy and would be all night. The medics were debating remedies. The filmmakers were debating religion. Nick the meteorologist updated his prediction for the next day. It was starting to seem incredible how much trouble these few hundred Occupiers had already caused. But how long would this last? It was becoming hard to imagine life any other way. I started having fantasies about someday in the future coming back to this plaza, by then cleaned and recorporatized, and seeing the ghosts of these beloved people.

At least in the heads of the species of made-up, spotlessly dressed television news reporters who were swarming among the dirty and battle-worn Occupiers, something began to change over the course of the next day, the second Monday. In the morning—and their trucks were out bright and early—the reporters were after one thing and one thing only: "the pepper-spray girls." A mere witness wouldn't do, Mr. Channel 7 told me, gravely. His journalistic integrity forbade it. He had to have one of those poor girls, caught on by-then viral video, who had been pepper-sprayed with no apparent provocation by the police officer whom *The Daily Show* would soon dub "Tony Baloney."

By afternoon, though, the reporters' attention shifted. The "girls" were no longer around, and maybe the pepper-spraying was already old news. For whatever reason, the questions they asked started getting more interesting. Instead of gory details, they finally became curious about just what exactly all these people were doing in Zuccotti Park. And, after getting bored with asking sign holders, "Why are you here?" and ogling the generator-powered media center, they even asked about the General Assembly. It, however, was only one among many curiosities. On one end of the plaza, people from the Global Movement (preparing for "2012: the New Dawn") were doing a big happening of some sort. A guy dressed in all white was screaming in a cracking voice, convulsing. Union members began to appear with matching signs and T-shirts to show support—the CUNY professors and the nurses, for instance. Dinner was couscous and beans.

At the GA, there was a lot of talk about marginalized voices. Several caucuses convened, including one to prep non-male-identified Occupiers on how to do interviews with the media. However constitutionally hopeless the reporters seemed and however unhelpful the Occupiers often were to them, the stories trickling and then flooding out were getting better and truer. The *New York Times,* for its part, published a letter I'd written against some of its initial, dismissive coverage.

Celebrities like Michael Moore, Susan Sarandon, and Cornel West turned up. Their presence, and that of the cameras that followed them, increased the ecstatic air of safety from the police, almost lending an air of permanence. But they always came as supporters more than as participants, standing out from the unknown, unaffiliated Occupiers. The Occupy movement, unlike most other burgeoning media sensations, was not theirs.

From: Bryce Edge <brycepedge@gmail.com>
Date: Thursday, September 29, 2011
To: arts_culture@nycga.net

Subject: RE: Radiohead @ Occupy Wall Street

Dear Occupiers,

My name is Bryce Edge, and I'm one of the managers for the band Radiohead. The guys are really impressed with what you have managed to pull off, and they wanted to stop by and play a couple songs in support before leaving New York. I don't want to create a big media circus that might worry the police or endanger what you've built, plus the band wants to play for the people who have been camped out, not everyone in New York who didn't get a ticket for Thursday's show. I was told this was the committee to email—do you think this would be possible? They have some unscheduled time Friday afternoon between 4 and 6, would that work? I read that the police aren't allowing sound equipment, but they could do acoustic. Let me know.

> Best,
> Bryce Edge
> Courtyard Productions, Inc.
> 8383 Wilshire Boulevard #526
> Beverly Hills, CA 90211–2425

By this point, this kind of thing—that one of the biggest bands in the world would want to just show up at Liberty Square for the fun and solidarity of it—was perfectly plausible. When word started to spread on Friday the 30th, OccupyWallSt.org got so much traffic that it crashed. But neither Radiohead nor Mr. Edge ever showed.

Patrick Bruner called me, flustered and angry, after he realized that the announcement he'd broadcast to all the occupation's newly acquired press contacts was a hoax. "I got set up," he said. "I can't trust anyone ever again."

Liberty Square was so packed that afternoon that you couldn't move. The next morning, stories about the hoax were in all the papers. The perpetrator later revealed himself to be Malcolm Harris—an editor at a clever online magazine, the *New Inquiry*, whose personnel had been around since the planning meetings. It was Occupy Wall Street scamming itself, and to great effect. As a result, thousands of people had come to Occupy Wall Street for the first time.

From: Bryce Edge <brycepedge@gmail.com>

Date: October 1, 2011

Subject: We could have just as easily been cops.

??? [repeated × 15]

you could have done it without us.

Following their fateful excursion up to Union Square the week before, Occupiers decided that, for the occupation's two-week anniversary on October 1, they'd try presenting themselves to the inhabitants of a different borough. A few minutes after three o'clock, between one and two thousand marchers made their way toward the Brooklyn Bridge. Rather than scaring the public off, the last weekend's brutality attracted even more people this time. As the march neared the bridge, I heard a cop say, "Be nice to us, hear?"

Suddenly, the march split. Some followed the publicized route, up the elevated pedestrian walkway in the middle of the bridge. Another group, however, broke away and took to the Brooklyn-bound road on the bridge's south side, eventually filling the whole roadway so that no traffic could get through. The front row of them locked arms and proceeded. At first, police had blocked neither entrance, and, on the road, they actually seemed to be leading the march.

"That was not planned at all," Sandy Nurse, a member of the Direct Action Working Group, told me, looking down from the pedestrian walkway at those marching on the road. "I think there's a lot of people in that group that don't realize what they're getting into." At the head of the march on the road below, though, I saw other Direct Action organizers, along with one of my top candidates for being an undercover cop.

Before the marchers on the roadway reached the first stone tower, they were intercepted from the other side. Out came dozens of officers with cardboard boxes full of plastic cuffs. Some of them unrolled the same type of orange nets they had used the previous Saturday, while others lined up opposite the marchers, halted them, and began to apprehend and handcuff all seven hundred of them, one by one.

I watched from the pedestrian walkway directly overhead. Officers took the first row of marchers, and then the second, and then a little girl. "This Is a Peaceful Protest!" people chanted. And the Beastie Boys line: "No! Sleep! Till Brooklyn!" But soon the whole process assumed the appearance of routine and of solemn, stupid bureaucracy.

At the front and back, with the crowd on the roadway surrounded on three sides by nets, police continued cuffing people and leading them away. Most of the marchers sat down and waited. "If you sit down, there is no fear," cried one marcher through the people's mic. They talked, smoked cigarettes, sang songs, and chanted. Many smiled for the cameras as they were arrested and shouted their names and birth dates to the legal observers.

Keeping us under control on the pedestrian walkway were NYPD Community Affairs officers, who, with blue polo shirts and nearly genuine friendliness, tried to keep us from watching the arrests close up. This provided opportunities for confrontation. One among us was a middle-aged man who, along with his wife, introduced himself to me as the father of an Occupier who'd been beaten and arrested at Liberty Square a few days earlier. After saying so, he turned to the cops.

"Arrest me too!" he shouted. "Hurt me like you hurt my son!"

He was a nice man and didn't look accustomed to anger. He paced back and forth while his wife stood and watched. He didn't end up being arrested, at least as far as I saw.

More police arrived on the pedestrian walkway, and they used more nets to cordon off the area directly in front of where the arrests were happening. It went on and on that way over the course of hours, as police vans and city buses arrived to take away those arrested. It started raining—lightly, at first, and then hard.

The several hundred marchers who had been on the pedestrian walkway and had turned back to the Manhattan side rallied at the base of the bridge. They marched around in the rain, stopping at 1 Police Plaza to demand the release of their comrades. Then they debated where to go next and finally agreed to return to Liberty Square. On the way, they were joined by several hundred more, who had made it to Brooklyn on the pedestrian walkway and come back on the Manhattan Bridge. As a mass, together, they all returned to the plaza.

It was dark by then. Dinner was ready, and the General Assembly began discussing the next move. The unexpected mass arrest was starting to feel like another victory.

I wasn't satisfied that I understood what had just happened, or what was happening in general, or what all those arrests on the bridge had meant. Maybe creating such an obstruction at least did fulfill the purpose of occupation—it is a way of reclaiming public space, of being heard, and of stopping business as usual. But it also obstructed a lot of people who were not the protest's targets. Was disrupting the flow of traffic really shining a clear light on economic injustice? Anyway, it was the police who had closed the bridge for the whole afternoon; if they'd simply let the marchers cross, it would have been over within a few minutes.

That day, hundreds of people were arrested, many for the first time. More would follow. The world was watching, and what it saw were lots of peaceful protesters being treated like criminals en masse while crossing one of New York's most touristy landmarks. I've never been able to look at that bridge the same since.

Several days later, I was summoned to a little TV studio in Manhattan that Al Jazeera was using for remote interviews. There, in the waiting room, I exchanged remarks with a reporter from New Zealand, and the two of us realized that we knew each other, that we'd been introduced by a mutual friend at a bar a few years before. He asked me what I thought of Occupy Wall Street. That was too much to answer, so I asked what New Zealanders thought. He said that they had just started to hear about it—two weeks in, thanks to what had happened on the Brooklyn Bridge. By the middle of October, Auckland would have an occupation of its own.

I met Victoria Sobel one morning during the first week of the occupation. We were interviewed together on WBAI radio, after which we walked back to Liberty Square from the studio. An art student at Cooper Union, her dark, curly, close-cropped hair was streaked with a blond stripe. She exuded a combination of frenetic busyness and warmth that, despite her own state, would always put me at ease and make me feel a little guilty in turn.

The crisis bearing down on her that day was a crisis indeed: before the midday GA, she had to come up with a proposal for what would become the Finance Working Group (later renamed "Accounting"). There had to be some way to deal with all the donations that had been piling up and that remained inaccessible. Not many people around had dealt with hundreds of thousands of dollars before, so the whole proposition seemed disastrous, as it would in fact turn out to be. There wasn't much of a chance to think about how to be the change one wished to see in the world, at least in this respect.

It was fortuitous, at least, that at the very moment Victoria was running around the plaza trying to figure out the problem of a fiscal sponsor, I happened to see Tarak Kauff from the October 2011 Coalition, and Victoria and I asked him what he thought. Within minutes he'd set it up so that October 2011 Coalition's fiscal sponsor, the Alliance for Global Justice, would take on OWS as well. It was a convenient alliance between the well-connected October 2011-ers and the Occupiers, who didn't really know what they were doing but were doing it anyway.

Victoria would also assemble and circulate enormous lists of things that various working groups needed, which were posted on websites and e-mail groups and were tweeted, bit by bit, under the hashtag #needsoftheoccupiers. Comfort asked for sleeping bags and raincoats ("with zippers") and blankets—a hundred or more at a time—while Sanitation wanted brooms, contractor bags ("42 gallon+"), and boxes. The medics' needs were the most extensive, including fifty boxes of nonlatex gloves, ten pints of the topical antiseptic Betadine, five hundred hand warmers, ten blood pressure pumps, twenty bags of cotton balls, and many, many more such items. Food, at one point, requested ten thousand paper plates and the same number of cups, along with a multitude of knives, gloves, crates, and cutting boards. Everyone needed flashlights, lanterns, and batteries. Maybe even more amazing than the lists themselves was the fact that people would actually turn up at Liberty Square with the things that were listed.

The October 2011 Coalition's occupation of Freedom Plaza in Washington DC began as planned on October 6. Rather than relying on exuberance as the driving force, those in this group had thought through ahead of time a lot of the things that the Wall Street planners left to be worked out on the fly or not at all: arranging for portable toilets, securing a permit with the federal Park Police, and setting up a stage and a sound system. Key committees were already in place. More than thirty thousand dollars had been raised in advance. While those living at Liberty Square were predominantly in their twenties, most of those who converged on Freedom Plaza from around the country were grayed or graying.

I arrived in DC the night before the occupation began and came to Freedom Plaza to find the organizers, the folks I'd been attending meetings with since July, assembled in a circle and reviewing their plans. Something new was beginning, but something else was already under way. A few blocks north, along lobbyist-infested K Street, there was already an "Occupy DC" encampment up and running, modeled on Occupy Wall Street.

I compared notes from my experience at Liberty Square with the DC organizers. This group had always been more structured and more comfortable with leadership, but now, because of Occupy Wall Street, leaderlessness was in the air. I was talking about this and that in Liberty Square when Margaret Flowers cut me off. "I'm sick of being compared to Occupy Wall Street!" she said. "Why can't we just create our own kind of community here?"

That night, I slept on a church pew with others who'd come down from New York. After that, we slept on Freedom Plaza (though many of the organizers retired to their homes or a nearby hotel). I was out under the stars one night and another night in a big cardboard refrigerator box procured by Code Pink. There were daily marches, chanting, "We! Are! The 99 percent!" and "Whose streets? Our streets!" There was the same tension and anxiety about what the police would do next, though on the whole DC's cops seemed determined not to repeat the NYPD's mistakes. When a march set off, they actively cleared the streets and led marchers wherever they wanted to go. Despite threats, there were no arrests of Occupiers sleeping on U.S. Park Service land, upon which both of the city's occupations stood.

Compared to the Occupiers at Liberty Square, whose rampant volunteerism took hold from the first moment there, people at Freedom Plaza tended to expect directives to come from on high; yet, when such directives came, they grew resentful that the process wasn't democratic enough. These were not instinctive anarchists. There was a general assembly, but nobody seemed sure how to run it. Even when there were no speakers or performers on the stage, dozens of people still sat in chairs and looked at it, waiting for something to happen. The committees running the kitchen and the information booth were having a hard time getting people to sign up for shifts. (I heard someone say it outright: "I want to find a leader to tell us what to do!") Occupiers at K Street and Freedom Plaza didn't trust each other, and they sparred over Twitter about which hashtags each would use to distinguish one from the other.

If you had asked me on September 16 whether Occupy Wall Street or Freedom Plaza had a better chance of succeeding, I probably would have gone with the one that was better organized, more experienced, and had money in the bank. The contingent of disciplined elders from Veterans for Peace alone would've secured my confidence. But hard-won know-how does not seem to have been the principal criterion for making a movement. People around the country were rallying and occupying, not so much on behalf of the reasonable policy proposals being issued from Freedom Plaza as for the collective effervescence of the general assemblies, and the viral-ready art, and the unpredictable crudeness of the encampments appearing in cities and towns everywhere that Occupy Wall Street had unleashed.

Freedom Plaza had one especially effective disrupter who would hang around the plaza and accompany marches. He had a substantial Afro, gray sweatpants, a silver ear bud in one ear, and round, mirrored sunglasses. Through the red-and-white megaphone he held at an angle from his mouth, he muttered about the gospel in monotone against the protesters attempting to somehow deescalate him:

> God is, was, will be. Long after you and me have come and gone, long after today is just a memory, while God is the God of love, while God is eternal, God is, was, will be. *A*men. As was written in the Book of First Corinthians, though I speak in the tongues of men, and of angels, if I had no love in *me,* then I must be doing this for nothing, *see.* And though I have the gift of prophe*cy,* and understand all myster*ies,* and though I have all knowledge, and all faith, that I could move mountains out of their *place,* if I should say what will be will be. If I had no love in *me,* then I must be doing this for nothing, *see.*

A police officer came to talk with him, and the disrupter offered a fist-pump.

Stopping at my mother's house in Virginia, I slept for twelve hours, finally, evidently needing it. In my old bed, I dreamed of getting incredibly lost. A part of the city, some city, had been destroyed and then relocated inside a tower. I was carrying Marisa Holmes's camera. I was looking for the General Assembly. An airship exploded. A mysterious person was trying to kill me, possibly with a musket. It was always night.

Occupation was starting to disguise itself as normalcy. On the morning of October 10, the *Wall Street Journal* quoted New York mayor Michael Bloomberg talking about Occupy Wall Street as if it were a semipermanent fixture:

> "The bottom line is—people want to express themselves. And as long as they obey the laws, we'll allow them to," said Bloomberg as he prepared to march in the Columbus Day Parade on Fifth Avenue. "If they break the laws, then, we're going to do what we're supposed to do: enforce the laws."
>
> Bloomberg said he has "no idea" how much longer the Wall Street demonstration will last. "I think part of it has probably to do with the weather," he said.

That afternoon, DC's Park Police officials made an offer to the occupation at Freedom Plaza: a four-month permit to stay where they were. The Freedom Plaza General Assembly accepted. The Park Police reportedly expressed to the organizers in a private meeting their own support for the protest.

"Would it be helpful for you to have arrests?" they asked—nudge, wink.

After having spent a few weeks in Liberty Square under the panoptic eye of the NYPD and having heard untruth after untruth from them and threat after threat, it was hard to know how to take such kindness. As I watched three green helicopters taking off from the White House lawn that day—one of them surely Marine One—I couldn't help but wonder whether somebody from on high saw an opportunity for himself in the tent city now located a few blocks from his home, on federal property, with voices chanting dire slogans and trying to hold a meeting.

PART TWO

FALL TO WINTER

THREE | PLANET OCCUPY

#15M #1world1struggle #60WallSt #Consensus #DiversityOfTactics #GlobalRevolution #LibertySqGA #OccupyBoston #OccupyEverywhere #OccupyTheory

There was this moment, while I was standing on the steps of the New York County Supreme Court building overlooking Foley Square, when things came together right in front of me. It was October 5, the day of the first big march when organized labor turned out in support of Occupy Wall Street. A few thousand union members, students, and allies were rallying in the square when a few thousand marchers from Liberty Square poured in from the north end on Worth Street. They kept coming, riverlike, and it seemed as if they'd never stop.

In the union crowd, people held mainly matching, printed signs. Among the Occupiers, the signs were mostly hand-scrawled on the cardboard pizza boxes that were so plentiful at the plaza. The distinction couldn't have been clearer. Leading the way was a big banner that I'd seen arrive at Liberty fresh from the printer the night before: "OCCUPY EVERYTHING," it said.

There's a memory I have of being a little kid—sitting on one of those orange seats on the Metro in DC, I think—and wondering, *What will my generation do?* It seemed to me then, there, before that crowd, that I might be looking at the answer. The trouble was knowing what it really was, or what it meant.

What it meant should have been obvious: why do you think a bunch of angry Americans would be making a fuss at the exact center of their country's concentrated wealth and reckless corruption? Yet the more that pundits and their adherents on the outside talked about it, the more they kept harping on the absence of something like the "one demand" that *Adbusters* had initially recommended, especially one that would fit cleanly into the poisonous discourse in which politics supposedly begins and ends with what politicians are willing to talk about.

"How many politicians does it take to change a light bulb?" went a joke Jason Ahmadi told, with slurred words but clear meaning.

"Ha! Politicians don't change anything!"

The fact was, even though no single policy proposal had been raised by the Occupiers as a whole, by the end of September the General Assembly had approved two significant documents about what it stood for, which were also indicative of the experience of the occupation for those taking part. These were almost completely ignored, however, by the critics who kept demanding demands.

"This is not about the demands," said a facilitator at a GA meeting on September 26. "The demands will come. It's about the beautiful thing we're doing here." The demand, so far, was simply the right to carry out a process—one in which people could speak and money could not. You wouldn't hear people on the plaza discussing whatever bill happened to be before Congress or the latest presidential talking point. They were deciding not between choices presented by corporate-sponsored politicians but among choices that seemed reasonable to them, on their terms.

On September 23, a statement called Principles of Solidarity passed by consensus in the General Assembly as a working draft. (This qualification was important—again, process.) In its preamble, the Principles stated a complaint about "the blatant injustices of our times perpetuated by the economic and political elites." The principles themselves, though, were all matters of method:

- Engaging in direct and transparent participatory democracy;
- Exercising personal and collective responsibility;
- Recognizing individuals' inherent privilege and the influence it has on all interactions;
- Empowering one another against all forms of oppression;
- Redefining how labor is valued;
- The sanctity of individual privacy;
- The belief that education is a human right; and
- Endeavoring to practice and support wide application of open source.

Just as the planners at Tompkins Square Park had concluded, the occupation's first step was to make the experience an end in itself, while also prefigurative, while also inviting. These points outlined the kind of movement the Occupiers wanted to build, the kind they were already building in the encampment. They were practicing direct democracy in the General Assembly; they were talking a lot about privilege and oppression; nobody was being paid for work, but all were benefiting from it; teach-ins and a library provided for more education than anyone could hope to absorb; open-source software and practices were running the movement's websites and media. (With enough cameras around the plaza to make it feel like a nonstop press conference, privacy was still only an ideal.) At its end, the Principles of Solidarity promised, "Demands will follow." But not in any hurry.

The document that came after it was the Declaration of the Occupation of New York City, which passed with the usual cheers at the September 29 evening GA. The minutes recall:

THIS IS WHAT DEMOCRACY LOOKS LIKE!

We will vote on that now. Straw poll. Looks good!

CONSENSUS!

WOOT WOOT!

The Declaration contained no demand either; instead, it was a litany of injustices perpetrated by "corporations, which place profit over people, self-interest over justice, and oppression over equality" and which "run our government." More than that, though, the Declaration was a call to action, an insistence that "it is up to the individuals to protect their own rights, and those of their neighbors."

After the longish litany—which spoke to such crises as widespread foreclosures, forced dependency on fossil fuels, the corruption of the legal system, media manipulation, workplace discrimination, militarism, and more (footnote: "These grievances are not all-inclusive")—the Declaration addressed the "people of the world":

Exercise your right to peaceably assemble; occupy public space; create a process to address the problems we face, and generate solutions accessible to everyone.

To all communities that take action and form groups in the spirit of direct democracy, we offer support, documentation, and all of the resources at our disposal.

Join us and make your voices heard!

People did seem to be joining. By the end of September, OccupyTogether.org listed nearly a hundred cities and towns in the United States where occupations had begun or were in the works. From precarious little Liberty Square you could hardly believe it, but news arrived day after day of yet another encampment appearing in some far-flung place. In most of these cases, too, horizontal, directly democratic assemblies were being used to organize and self-govern, just like at Liberty, but also different. Rather than the big discrete action that *Adbusters* had recommended, Occupy Wall Street was swelling into an organism with many tendrils, each with its own means of being a nuisance.

Every day, crowds of bystanders would gather around the collage of hundreds of cardboard signs that lined the northern edge of the plaza, between the ceaseless drum circle and the media center. Each sign made its own separate demand, but together they had a certain coherence: "Peaceful Revolution." "Bail Out the People." "Wall Street Is Our Street." Those who stopped to read them did so transfixed, as if having a silent conversation with each other over the blaring of drums and the plucking of banjos. "One demand" or not, they seemed somehow satisfied.

My friend Adam Roberts, a poet who came to Liberty Square for a few days around this time, e-mailed me photos of some verses he'd written in blue ballpoint, on lined paper:

demand nothing
offer things

And:

demands
are directed
at authority
and help make that authority
real

our one demand
is instead
an offering

join us

The truth is, there *were* demands, when fitting and necessary. It wasn't long into the occupation before Gary Roland was running around the park agitating people into joining the actions he was helping to organize in support of locked-out Sotheby's art handlers, members of the International Brotherhood of Teamsters. He and other Occupiers were disrupting Sotheby's auctions and parties, risking arrest, while the union members picketed safely outside. In that case there were definitely demands—reasonable and achievable ones, in the short term, for the moment: the workers wanted a contract and decent wages. The following May, after months of lockout, with ongoing Occupy actions targeting Sotheby's higher-ups throughout the city, the workers eventually won; they got their contract and went back to work.

When the time comes to fight and win something, demand it. Why not? But when there are just a few hundred people precariously holding to a park, still only beginning to organize, still starting, still trying to shake off the habits of powerlessness, what they can offer and offer one another matters so much more than what they might demand.

Ted Actie came up to me one day in the plaza with something to say. Ted, recall, was a TV producer from Brooklyn. In the first days, he kept imploring the General Assembly to send a clear, relevant message that could reach the black community in New York. All the sitting around in meetings, he was saying, wouldn't do. But now he had an epiphany to share.

"It took me a while to figure it out," he said. "This isn't just about making your point out loud—it's about learning how to go back to your own community and organize there." The important thing wasn't necessarily to bring Brooklyn to Occupy Wall Street, he decided, but to occupy Brooklyn—or unoccupy it by resisting the gentrification and police violence pushing poor people out. Each community could organize in its own way with its own demands and draw support from the others. It was at about this time that Occupy the Hood was getting started in Queens, and it soon spread to cities across the country.

I'd just heard something similar from Bre Lembitz—a tall, Nordic college student who could speak Chinese. She first came to OWS the second week after watching the live-stream online and joined the Medics and Facilitation. After arriving, she told me, it took about a week before she stopped being frustrated by not having any big demand and embraced the process on its own terms.

And so on and so forth, for person after person, again and again. They came for a protest and arrived at a school, a school of the sort that they didn't know was a school until they started learning its lessons—the school of happenstance arrests, the school of endless meetings, the school of many voices, the school of changing faces, the school the whole world is watching, the school that could close at any minute, the school that could save the world, the school that is mocked and slandered, the school without a name, the school with no degrees, the school that is outside and under trees, the school that may betray you, the school that's your only hope.

Or maybe the proper metaphor was that of a therapy session. People who'd never felt listened to in their lives got the cathartic opportunity to alternate between unloading long-pent-up polemics in the General Assembly and expending their rage at the cops' provocations, often teetering on the edge of a riot. They were rediscovering the social, rediscovering the satisfaction of ordinary conversations and interactions, as if waking up from a nightmare of isolation, frustration, and the Internet. Perhaps never having really had their political voices heard outside the comments on a blog, newcomers would interrupt the agenda and turn the people's mic into a soapbox. With practice, though, that would change. They'd usually find that hewing to the process was better than making off-topic speeches. Some passions would be soothed, while others became even more stoked.

"The starting point of theoretical reflection is opposition, negativity, struggle," writes John Holloway in the first lines of *Change the World without Taking Power,* a book one would occasionally hear mentioned by Occupiers. "It is from rage that thought is born, not from the pose of reason, not from the reasoned sitting-back and reflecting-on-the-mysteries-of-existence that is the conventional image of the thinker." And, amid all the acting out, there really was reflection.

Each night at Liberty Square, a few hundred people would cluster in loose, semicircular rows. The meetings always began with a primer—amplified, like every other public pronouncement at the plaza, through the people's mic. One of the facilitators would explain the hand signals: flutter your fingers upward for applause and downward for discontent; touch your index fingers and thumbs in a diamond for a point of order; hold up an index finger for a point of information. New signals could be added or old ones changed as needed.

The meetings proceeded with oral report-backs from the occupation's various working groups—Kitchen, Direct Action, Sanitation, Labor Outreach, Arts & Culture, Finance, and more, with new ones invented daily—then general announcements of a minute or two each, then agenda items and proposals, which could be anything from schedule changes to drafts of public declarations. Throughout, someone took stack—a list of those who wished to speak—and adjusted its order, if necessary, to favor those representing traditionally marginalized races, genders, and ages, as well as those who hadn't spoken yet. When someone made a proposal, others could counter with questions, amendments, concerns, and, finally and most seriously, blocks—vetoes, essentially. In the absence of a serious concern or a block, the assembly reached consensus (or a 90 percent "modified consensus"), and the proposal passed. When that happened, the human amphitheater would burst into applause and perhaps a triumphant chant in celebration of the wonder that hundreds of people had just managed to agree about something.

The GA meetings lasted a couple of hours, but they could just as easily go on all night. A good discussion usually took a lot of time, stretching over many days, which is part of why duration seemed so crucial to the occupation's success; it was not only a sign of commitment but a practical necessity.

Anarchic open assemblies like the GA trace their roots (more or less fictitiously) to indigenous tribal councils, ancient Athens, Quakerism, feminism, the New Left of the early 1960s, the civil rights movement, the antiwar movement, and human nature itself. The collective memory at OWS, however, tended to be a whole lot shorter or nonexistent. If you were to ask those who had been around since the planning meetings, you'd probably hear about the assembly-based 15M movement in Spain.

Several Spaniards were there helping out at the plaza, especially at the media center—watching, offering advice, and reaching out to other movements around the world. A slogan of the Spanish Indignados, "Real Democracy Now," spoke to how these interconnected movements were enunciating a demand by carrying it out for themselves. Monica López, a Spanish journalist who was traveling back and forth between Liberty Square and Madrid, laughed and cringed as she watched Americans repeat a trial-and-error process like what the 15M movement had gone through, only worse. Even the beloved people's mic, she prophesied, would get old before long and need to be replaced.

One of the General Assembly's more direct antecedents was the spokescouncil structure used to organize the mobilization against the 1999 Seattle WTO summit, as well as subsequent mobilizations during that phase of the global justice movement. Marina Sitrin, a lawyer and activist who was a facilitator at the last planning meeting and the inaugural GA on September 17, first encountered consensus process in Seattle, and she became addicted. She went on to compile a book of oral history, *Horizontalism,* about the assemblies that formed in factories, neighborhoods, and occupied spaces after the 2001 economic collapse in Argentina. These assemblies scrupulously rejected the hierarchies that had helped lead to the crash, and they became—and in some cases, remain—a political force there.

In an alluringly titled book, *Freedom Is an Endless Meeting,* sociologist Francesca Polletta argues that movements adopt assemblies not simply out of utopianist principle but because they're actually well suited to managing this kind of loose organization. An assembly's egalitarianism fosters individual initiative, she says, while its emphasis on consensus helps to secure everyone's full commitment, which is especially important when there is risk of arrest or injury. Assemblies are also flexible, allowing for division into independent but cohesive assemblies of assemblies. A spokes council, for instance, is a body designed for coordinating among a number of consensus-based groups, each of which puts forward a "spoke"—sort of a representative, but not quite—to articulate the positions of the group to the other groups. By emphasizing participation over privilege, directly democratic structures like these have the benefit of innate resistance to being co-opted by charismatic individuals or sold out to moneyed interests. They're more likely to break down and do nothing than to bow to corruption.

The most experienced facilitators recognized that Occupy Wall Street's beloved assembly process would have to adapt over time. "It's untenable, especially with so many new people, to have both real consensus and the possibility of a block," Marina Sitrin told me early on. A spokes council of some sort among the various working groups would be a logical next step. But with just a few weeks of practice, most people in general assemblies in New York and across the country were still just getting the hang of it, and they wouldn't let it go easily. Once one became converted to the GA's power, once one had twinkled one's fingers with so many hundreds of others, the process became a precious ritual, the performance of which came before all else, because it was a harbinger of the future, a bulwark against compromises with the past.

Rachel Signer, whom I have known since we went to elementary school together in Virginia, wrote about the GA this way in November, in an essay that appeared on the website *Killing the Buddha:*

There are meetings, and they both excite you and fill you with impatience. The General Assembly seems to drag on and on, and you think to yourself that this system is so flawed, so confusing and bureaucratic. A small spark inside you goes off, a secret hope that this will all end, will fail, the kids will go home and go back to hacking or running info-shops or whatever they do, and you can continue on with movies and online dating and re-reading *Milles Plateaux*. But then you can't help yourself and you start asking questions, start mic checking at assembly meetings, start going to working group meetings and using the consensus process like it's a language you were born knowing. You finally sit through almost an entire—painfully long, frustrating, argumentative—General Assembly, and come to appreciate that it's really fucking hard to keep this movement going. You see the tent city slowly emerge and the problems it causes, and the Comfort people and the Sanitation crew and the Medics working their asses off to mitigate issues that come up. You ask yourself if you would be able to sacrifice comfort and ownership to sleep here. You are not sure.

She ended like this:

It's only temporary, anyway; you'll be back tomorrow at your real home, this weird place that has come to occupy your heart, this place that holds you close and tells you that you're beautiful just the way you are, that understands you and sees how amazing you can be, this place that was made for you, that you helped to make, this place where you can never be alone, can never be lost, can never be afraid as long as you can make it work, can work with each other and respect each other's sacrifices and needs and human imperfections, this place where there is nothing to do but occupy, which is really everything we need to do and everything you want to be; it's everything.

There was a sing-song cadence that would come out in people's voices, especially through the people's mic when the facilitators needed to make some particularly sensitive point of process in the GA. It could sound a bit like talking down, but in a lullaby sort of way—that is, genuine and well intentioned, while always provisional in deference to process. Phrases would end in high-rising terminals, as linguists call them, raising the pitch so as to submit the words for repetition to the people's mic. This melody would make the words stick in your head all day and as you lay down on the granite at night. Perhaps these words from the GA on September 24 can be transcribed:

We have this prócess / and sýmbols / to hear éveryone équally.

The cadence accompanied another verbal practice—harder than you might think—of trying to go through the day without telling anybody what to do, out of respect for their sacred autonomy. For instance, at a Jewish prayer service in the park one night the officiants avoided uttering even a simple command like "Turn to page 22." Instead, they simply noted, "We're on page 22, and you can turn there if you like."

Groups proliferated more quickly than anyone could keep track of them. At first, they'd meet in a circle somewhere on Liberty Square. But as the drummers became more and more incessant, and as there was less and less space in which to gather, meetings began happening elsewhere in the neighborhood and even elsewhere in the city. Times and locations were posted more or less methodically on a giant chalkboard at Liberty, or on nycga.net, a busy BuddyPress site that for a few weeks at least gave a decent impression of what was happening on any given day. The most popular meeting spot was Deutsche Bank's private/public atrium at 60 Wall Street, a bizarre, high-ceilinged house of mirrors with vaguely treelike columns, a rock face on one side, and plenty of movable tables and chairs. By mid-October, a dozen groups could've been meeting there at a given time, huddled around a table with a sign in the middle indicating the group's name—which didn't stop people from passing by and interrupting the discussion to ask, "Is this the Tech Ops meeting?" "Is this Global Justice?" There were working groups, which tended to have some sanction from the General Assembly, as well as more ad hoc project groups, autonomous affinity groups, and a profusion of others whose members neither knew nor cared how to categorize themselves.

The way you could tell whether a given group of people sitting around a circle meant to constitute itself as part of Occupy Wall Street, though, was the determination to be attentive at every turn to matters of voice, voices, hearing, and listening. Marginalized voices, come forward; ones that society normally privileges, step back. It was an obsession with the structure of conversations that one could decry as a particularly extreme form of political correctness. But, like all so-called political correctness, it was merely an attempt to manifest in ordinary language and habits what we all claim to stand for anyway, against the casual racism and sexism and other -isms that normally go unnoticed by their beneficiaries and that their victims resign themselves to enduring. Movement time would not tolerate such endurance any longer. The trouble was, this sometimes turned the movement against its own favorite features.

On a break from the plaza during the first week, when I and seemingly everyone else were thrilled with the people's mic and the supposed horizontality of the General Assembly, I was surprised to learn how oppressive even the GA could seem.

"I hate it," an Occupier in her early twenties told me over a beer. "Can't you tell that it's always the loudest men who can get the people's mic to amplify them?"

No, I hadn't noticed that. For a moment, I even took offense on behalf of the beloved technique. But then I thought about it, and paid closer attention.

When a big guy wanted to get people to listen on the plaza, he just had to start shouting, "Mic check! Mic check!" Those with quieter voices, though, would have to round up a few friends first and secure their support and their vocal chords just to have a chance of possibly being heard.

In the media, it was people who looked like me who tended to be interviewed, and celebrated, and picked out as leaders. We were the ones with access, with connections, and with a perceived air of respectability. We were more likely to be on some nonprofit's payroll. It was true enough already that the occupation had trouble attracting the very people whose concerns it sought to uplift, but on the news, the faces of the movement were even more white and male than those on the plaza.

In the shared almost-utopia of the occupation, there was no ghetto into which the silenced could take cover. They had to stand their ground and fight for their dignity, not just as part of the movement, but also within it. Nor could they just fight; they also had to educate.

Identity groups formed, with names like Safer Spaces and the People of Color Caucus and the Feminist General Assembly and OWS in Español. First, they argued over who could join. Would white, male-bodied people be allowed to attend? Could they speak? And then there was the paradox of isolation: the more marginalized voices sequestered themselves, the less they would be a part of the main assemblies and working groups. They had to do both at once. They had to create spaces for themselves while also trying to be heard in the movement at large. Thus, another burden: in the name of diversity, certain visible people of color became especially sought-after as organizers or spokespeople, putting overwhelming demands on their time and making them feel tokenized in the end. You couldn't win.

White Americans tend to be shocked upon discovering what most people of color in this country are reminded of every day—that racism still runs rampant and that those of us who don't notice it are either secluding ourselves or somehow perpetuating it. In Occupy's movement time and movement space, those with a lot of privilege got a taste of the discomfort others experience regularly, even if just by being told that they'd said something offensive out of ignorance or talked over someone else. They'd often react with anger. For those used to benefiting from the order of things, having this pointed out could seem very, very radical, and frustrating, and like a waste of time. But if this movement was going to be any better than just an outburst of privileged people scared of losing their privilege, nothing could be more important. Those used to talking had to learn to listen more, and those used to shutting up had to learn how to teach.

We'd been taught for decades, after all, that racism was mostly solved by Martin Luther King Jr., that capitalism is not only good but inevitable, that there is no class war, that discrimination over sexuality is finished because President Obama let gay people come out in the military. As a result, most of us didn't know how to think or talk about race, or the war on the poor, or alternatives to corporate rule, or gender queerness. It was the queerest spaces of all sorts that needed this movement most.

Here, the unassailable spell protecting capitalism from criticism was broken, and the rest of the status quo was vulnerable too. Language had been stunted. Polls say, for instance, that young people in the United States are accepting of a much wider range of gender and sexual identities than their parents are, even if their words and assumptions rarely catch up to the aspiration. This was the leading edge of sexual revolution in 2011. In Occupy, people were learning not to think they knew someone's gender from appearance alone. They had to practice not speaking of straight, cisgendered existence as normal and of everything else as an aberration, even if a tolerated one. They had to work out the consequences of what they already claimed to think.

You might have expected to hear a lot of conversations at Occupy Wall Street about things like banks and financial regulations and maybe campaign finance reform. And they were happening all the time. But that was only one part of the noise. Some people would beg for unity and forward momentum: "Why can't we return to our focus, to the banks, to Wall Street?" Others would call this racist, and classist, and bourgeois. Both were right, I think. In the United States of America, there can be no real revolution against Wall

Street or anything else unless people of color, and the homeless, and queer folks, and natives, and so many more of those normally left out are at the front of it.

When diversity of any kind is real, it gets uncomfortable. "Diversity of tactics," in the context of political protests, is often treated as essentially a byword for condoning acts of property destruction and violence. The phrase emerged about a decade ago at the height of the global justice movement, especially after window-smashing antics during the 1999 WTO demonstrations in Seattle. While any serious civil resistance movement will inevitably rely on a variety of nonviolent tactics—the theorist Gene Sharp famously listed 198 of them—in this case the word *diversity* was a kind of attempted détente between those committed to staying peaceful and those who weren't. The way that the Occupiers were carrying out this policy, however, made me start to think of its meaning and implications differently. Process was not just what Occupy Wall Street was doing in meetings; it had also been happening in the streets.

The main points of the march guidelines promulgated by the occupation's Direct Action Working Group in the first week were as follows:

1. Stay together and KEEP MOVING!
2. Don't instigate cops or pedestrians with physical violence.
3. Use basic hand signals.
4. Empowered pace keeps at the front, back, and middle of every march. These folks are empowered to make directional decisions and guide the march.
5. We respect diversity of tactics, but consider how our actions may affect the entire group.

Many who (like myself) extolled the need for nonviolent discipline were disappointed to learn that Occupy Wall Street had made "diversity of tactics" its official modus operandi. But in practice the Occupiers were keeping non-violent discipline relatively well, even if they didn't always preach it. What "diversity of tactics" actually seemed to mean for them had a lot less to do with violence than with a broader philosophy of self-organizing and direct action. In this, "diversity of tactics" shares the same heritage and logic of the open assemblies. A passage from a pamphlet on hand at Liberty Square, *Anarchist Basics,* explains:

Affinity groups [elsewhere said to be "of 5 to 20 people"] decide on their own what they want to do and how they want to do it, and aren't obliged to take orders from any person on top. As such, they challenge top-down decision-making and organizing, and empower those involved to take direct action in the world around them. Affinity groups can make decisions in whatever way they see fit, but they generally use some form of consensus or direct democracy to decide on goals and tactics. Affinity groups by nature are decentralized and non-hierarchical, two important principles of anarchist organizing and action.

Operating this way reflects values that many in the emerging Occupy movement insisted on: individual autonomy, consensus decision making, mutual responsibility, decentralization, and equality. Small groups acting more or less autonomously toward common goals is a matter of principle as well as of pragmatism. These groups, ideally, coordinate with one another. Incompatible actions should be planned so as to take place in separate times and spaces. Properly understood, diversity of tactics should be a means for collaboration, not an excuse for recklessness. Sparrow Ingersoll, an Occupier in Direct Action, explained:

> A diversity-of-tactics framework just says, "Let's have a conversation that's critical about what we're doing and also respect that other people in other places need to make different choices." That's it. It's a position of compromise. It's not demanding a totalizing strategy or demanding that everyone have the same opinion about anything—but it's treated as a full-frontal attack against liberals. It's absurd. This was actually designed so that we can work together. That's what this framework was created to do: to enable liberals and reformists and radicals to work together.

It's a philosophy of organizing, primarily, not a fixed position on violence or nonviolence. It's a means of flourishing when no one's in charge.

Consider, for instance, the two main events that brought public attention and sympathy to the movement: the arrest of almost a hundred people on the march near Union Square on September 24—precipitating the infamous pepper-spraying incident—and the arrest of more than seven hundred a week later on the Brooklyn Bridge. In both cases, the arrests directly followed instances of autonomous action by small groups, which improvised on the plan established by Direct Action. At Union Square, marchers differed about whether to take the march back to Liberty Plaza or to the United Nations; at the Brooklyn Bridge, hundreds of marchers chose to spill onto the road rather than remain on the narrow pedestrian walkway. The moment things got unpredictable, the police overreacted and showed the violence of the system with its pants down, and the Occupiers came out on top.

The NYPD, as a hierarchical, highly structured organization, operated according to certain plans and procedures arranged in advance. Its commanders gained whatever intelligence they could about what protesters intended to do and acted accordingly. When the protesters didn't follow the plans police had prepared for, or when their plans weren't unified, the police resorted to a violent crackdown, which in turn highlighted the protesters' own nonviolence in the media reports. Their movement grew. The net effect was that it almost seemed as if the police were intentionally trying to help the Occupiers, for that was what their every action seemed to do.

At the time, I was writing articles that suggested the movement might adopt more orderly kinds of civil disobedience actions, ones targeted specifically at the laws they oppose—on the model of lunch-counter sit-ins in the civil rights movement, for instance. But I was forced to recognize that the chaotic stuff worked.

A formal sit-in or a well-planned Freedom Ride had the capacity to confront the Jim Crow system in a very direct way, presenting a dilemma between violent overreaction and capitulation. But such tactics have tended to become ritualized and ineffective in American protest movements; the police adapted to them, and activists let them lose their teeth. Occupy Wall Street made civil disobedience interesting again by showing how vulnerable hierarchical command structures were to nonhierarchical action.

If this is true, the real strength of the successful 1999 Seattle WTO mobilization was not so much the particular tactics used—whether turtle costumes or window breaking—as the decentralized way in which activists organized and deployed them. (A subsequent RAND Corporation study on such "swarming" made note of this, alongside the strategies of Al Qaeda.) Nonviolence trainer Betsy Raasch-Hilman wrote in mid 2000:

> In terms of numbers, many demonstrations have been larger than the actions in Seattle. The difference between the WTO protests and the Million Man March on Washington, DC, (for example) was that people did not all do the same thing at the same time in Seattle. Spontaneity ruled the day(s). As in the physics of chaos, seemingly random events emerged into a pattern, and almost as quickly dissolved into a less-identifiable pattern.

One reason that traditional forms of civil disobedience weren't well-suited to Occupy Wall Street, also, was that the Occupiers weren't even capable of breaking many of the laws they opposed in the first place. While those in the civil rights movement could sit in the wrong part of a segregated bus, the Occupiers at Liberty Square couldn't exactly flout campaign finance regulations or laws regarding the behavior of banks. Such laws were simply beyond the reach of most Americans—which was exactly the problem. Consequently, the movement resorted not to civil disobedience but to what political scientist Bernard Harcourt proposed at the time that we call "political disobedience":

> Civil disobedience accepted the legitimacy of political institutions, but resisted the moral authority of resulting laws. Political disobedience, by contrast, resists the very way in which we are governed: it resists the structure of partisan politics, the demand for policy reforms, the call for party identification, and the very ideologies that dominated the post-War period.

Diversity of tactics is a form of political disobedience par excellence. Its emphasis on autonomy, as opposed to authority, stands in contradiction to the kind of order that ordinary politics presupposes. But a month into the occupation, and less than three months since planning began in earnest, Occupy Wall Street was just beginning to have the robust affinity groups that a diversity-of-tactics approach requires. Chaotic marches were still the movement's mainstay. And while a diversity of tactics presumes some means of coordinating among the groups planning them and allowing for separate times and spaces when necessary, these were rarely happening in practice.

The Press Relations Working Group began preparing language to use in case things got ugly—including specific tweets:

> Perspective: broken windows vs. broken financial system, broken politics, broken promises, broken priorities. #OccupyWallStreet still inspires!

> It would be nice if the media paid so much attention to the violence happening on Wall Street every day. #OccupyWallStreet #OWS

> Don't get distracted by a few angry people breaking things. There are millions of angry people working to change things! #OccupyWallStreet

Most people probably hoped those tweets wouldn't be needed, though some looked forward to when they would be.

What was it, exactly, that made the police in New York so cruel toward these protesters so consistently? We all had our theories. I recall one night talking with a policewoman along the north edge of Liberty Square, which was lined from end to end with cops while the people inside quietly went about their business. She said she had family in London but had never been there. She had a vague idea of wanting to take her next vacation in Spain but had never heard of the Indignados in Madrid. She did, however, know about the riots that had taken place a few months earlier across Britain. She asked me point-edly what I thought caused them. Poverty and police brutality, I said. Same as what always causes riots.

"Hmm," she muttered, then she looked off in the distance, as cops do, as if you're not there.

And then I wondered: Is that what they've been told? That this is another Tottenham, and that the point is to burn buildings and turn over cars? And they'd been told nothing about Madrid's peaceful Indignados?

A revolutionist pamphlet that appeared out of the Spanish movement around this time, *La carta de los comunes,* begins with an intriguing conceit. Set in a magical-realist Madrid of 2033, it tells of a population whose bodies had become physically hunched over in submission to a wealthy few. Then, at last, with their livelihoods nearly eviscerated, the people rise up and take over their city. They resurrect the medieval notion of the commons, creating a domain of shared resources apart from markets and bureaucratic oversight. They learn to stand upright again. The pamphlet then presents a Magna Carta for their new society.

I can't resist wanting to try out a similar futurism for Occupy Wall Street.

The small canon of texts that managed to withstand the consensus-building process at various general assemblies across the movement, inter-preted in light of the praxis in the occupations, provided no quick-and-easy legislative, executive, or judicial patches for the problems the protests meant to confront. Instead, the Occupiers set themselves on a path substantially more ambitious: a wholesale rethinking of political life, more akin to the promulgation of the Declaration of the Rights of Man and of the Citizen in revolutionary France than, say, to the introduction of a financial-transaction tax or the revocation of the Supreme Court's *Citizens United* decision.

It isn't crazy to think that the time had come to go back to the drawing board, politically. The constitutions of most countries today derive from ideas dreamed up during the late Enlightenment, long before anyone could foresee such realities as the global brands unceasingly present in our lives, or undeclared wars being fought by drone aircraft, or megacorporations profiting from credit default swaps and cataclysmic climate change. Our familiar, Lockean governments seem inept, powerless to oppose the incorporeal profit machines that, as the Declaration of the Occupation of New York City noted, can "achieve the same rights as people, with none of the culpability or responsibility." Unlike the Declaration of the Rights of Man, the Occupy documents rarely refer to property or patriotic sentiment. They don't even mention borders.

"We are creating an exemplar society," said Occupy Boston's Declaration of Occupation. That being the case, let's attempt some Occupy sci-fi: what would the world look like if it were remade in the image of Occupy?

"No one's human needs go unmet," continued the Boston declaration. Our imaginary planet Occupy, just as the actual occupations set out to do, provides food and shelter for everyone, no questions asked. Its inhabitants ensure one another's health care, education, child care, and sanitation. There is a large, meticulously cataloged library. Although this might sound like an ordinary social democracy, decisions about resources are made not through the ballot box but, in the words of Occupy Wall Street's Principles of Solidarity, by "autonomous political beings engaging in direct and transparent participatory democracy." They might be wired to the teeth, but the political beings of planet Occupy carry out their democracy face-to-face as well as online, in well-coordinated small groups that operate through an interplay of consensus and initiative. It's "participatory as opposed to partisan," added the Statement of Autonomy, passed by the OWS General Assembly on November 1; the aim on planet Occupy is for all voices to be heard, rather than for one party to shout down the others. Those with "inherent privilege" defer to those with less. The consolidation of power is discouraged rather than celebrated and is resisted when necessary.

Representation, the basic mechanism of the post-Enlightenment political order, had no currency in the occupations. The OWS Declaration was addressed not to governments—no hope there—but rather "to the people of the world," urging communities everywhere to "assert your power." Even in the most ordinary of interactions, but especially in the assemblies, representation was both a dirty word and an unwelcome practice. "I am here to represent—" someone might begin but then cut himself or herself off and start saying much the same thing again, except this time in terms of speaking-with rather than speaking-for. Politics was a matter not of who represented whom but of who contributed what and participated how in the utopia under way.

Planet Occupy's economy is just as upside down as its politics. Organizations exist for the public good, not for private gain. Participatory democracy prevails in workplaces, neighborhoods, and other productive groupings. Many aspects of the economy—food, especially—remain local, both to preserve community control and to sustain the natural environment; if this means living more simply and producing less than the dim memory of the American Dream promised us, so be it. Everyone on planet Occupy knows, after all, that if they don't protect the planet, there will be nothing left to occupy.

The Principles of Solidarity called for "redefining how labor is valued." Work at OWS had a different definition from that of most on planet Earth—or at least in New York City. You did what was needed or what presented itself as worthwhile or interesting, and work got done. Thus, OccuCopy, a worker-owned cooperative, arose to serve Occupy Wall Street's printing needs. Students became leaders, and elders turned into students. A scientist did a lot of social media and logistics and coordinating of artists. Artists did everything. The more wholly you gave yourself over to what was taking place, the less likely it was that you would be doing what was normally considered to be your job before the movement. On planet Occupy, a person is a person and a community member before being any particular kind of worker. People work less, acquire less, and live more.

Even with its inhabitants' passion for local communities, planet Occupy is a globalized place. People and their ideas travel freely, creating new opportunities and connections wherever they go. It's like how the Book of Revelation imagines the New Jerusalem: "During the day its gates will never be shut, and there will be no night." Assemblies share their plans and innovations over networks that have supplanted the original Internet, overrun as it became by corporate advertising. Following the urge in the Principles for "the broad application of open source," all ideas are common property, and, according to the Statement of Autonomy, they're valued more highly than money—which in turn takes the form of open-source currencies. Censorship in the name of ownership is not okay.

Also not okay is amassing armies of killers to resolve conflicts between groups. Almost every Occupy document made some statement to this effect. Occupy Boston's Memorandum of Solidarity with Indigenous Peoples envisioned "a new era of peace and cooperation that will work for everyone." When injustice occurs, as is inevitable, people resist through the "non-violent civil disobedience and building solidarity based on mutual respect, acceptance, and love," described in the Principles. Deescalating conflict is the job not of militarized cops but of the whole community, especially its most patient listeners.

An anarchist utopia like this might be hard to take seriously. But the Declaration of the Rights of Man, drafted while Louis XVI still had his head, wasn't easy to comprehend in its time either. The circumstances of our world exceed the politics we're used to imagining for it, and the politics that are really necessary will therefore seem a little impossible—even to the revolutionaries. As Sparrow Ingersoll told me:

> I don't believe that we're in a position to say, if we're able to overturn capitalism or the state, what would come next, because we've been diseased by those power systems. I have the disease of capitalism. So I am in no position to tell anyone else what the world without it would look like or how it should work because I don't know. I don't think we're actually in any position to say that. We can imagine forward and hope and think creatively about what that might look like, but I think to reify it in any sort of program is a really terrible idea.

The occupation was an eddy of grace amid the Fall, one that for its own good would have to pass away—a "temporary autonomous zone" of the kind imagined by the anarchist writer Hakim Bey. "The TAZ," Bey writes, "is a guerrilla operation which liberates an area (of land, of time, of imagination) and then dissolves itself to re-form elsewhere/elsewhen." Yet few people there dared speak of the occupation ever ending; who could imagine going back to the lives they'd lived before, to planet Earth?

"We have come to Wall Street as refugees from this native dreamland, seeking asylum in the actual," says "Communiqué 1" in the movement journal *Tidal*. "We seek to rediscover and reclaim the world."

One seemingly important element mostly missing from the documents that describe planet Occupy is family. What would families look like there? The only occasional appearance of the Parents for Occupy Wall Street group suggests that its members constituted just a fringe identity rather than one of the movement's basic constituents, as parents are in most contexts. Family rarely came up in conversation; even serious couples in the movement, when organizing together, often didn't publicly identify themselves as couples, either by words—*partner* was always the accepted term, if they did—or by signs of special affection. They were the exception. But reasons for this aren't too hard to guess. The immediate target of the whole protest, after all, was an austerity economy that encourages putting off parenthood as long as physically possible (or longer) and provides decent housing, education, and health care to children only at the cost of debt servitude.

One might have thought that family was entirely distant from these busy radicals' minds, until you got to know some of them well enough to catch them in moments of thinking beyond the immediacy of the movement, when they would stare into nowhere and start wondering to one another how they could ever bring children into the world and raise them decently, the way things were going. It was common to think of the people at the center of this movement as being overly radical in one way or another, when really the problem was more a matter of the world just not being habitable enough.

The more that well-meaning multitudes were being energized by Occupy Wall Street, the more one heard from them that the movement needed to shed its radical origins so as to actually get something done. "If they can avoid fetishizing the demand for consensus," New School professor James Miller wrote in the *New York Times* on October 25, "they may be able to forge a broader coalition that includes friends and allies within the Democratic Party and the union movement." Especially as the 2012 election season got going, the thinking went, it would be time for Occupy to quit the anarchy and get real.

It was the same phenomenon I'd been observing on the ground since before September 17 and again and again during the early days of the occupation; people arrived with some preconceived agenda about what needed to be done given the current political situation and complained that the anarchists were hijacking the movement's progress by bogging it down in process. But, after a while, after enough long meetings, a lot of them would start to come around, to speak the exploratory language of process themselves. Helping shape the daily decisions of the occupation actually started to seem more empowering for the moment than trying to tell President Obama what to do.

The anarchists' way of operating was exhilarating, and when occupations spread around the country, the horizontal assemblies spread too. These were not subsidiaries of OWS, or chapters, but distinct and interconnected groups using a common process to confront their local manifestations of global capitalism. It was an amazing isomorphism—similar forms spontaneously arising in all sorts of different contexts. A lot of newly politicized people were suddenly feeling anarcho-curious.

The anarchism they were discovering wasn't simply a negative political philosophy or an excuse for window breaking, as many people tend to assume anarchism is. Even while calling for an end to the rule of coercive states backed by military bases, prison industries, and wage servitude, anarchists try to build a culture in which people can take care of themselves and each other through healthy, sustainable communities. Many are resolutely nonviolent. Drawing on modes of organizing both radical and ancient, they insist on using forms of participatory direct democracy that naturally resist corruption by money, status, and privilege. Everyone's basic needs should take precedence over anyone's greed.

The Occupy assemblies were opening tremendous space in American political discourse. They had started new conversations about what people really want for their communities, conversations that amazingly still hadn't been hijacked by celebrities or special interests. Soon, economic inequality and corporate power and police violence were beginning to be talked about by politicians, where before they'd seemed unutterable. But before anything meaningful could happen through the politicians, ordinary people had to remind themselves who they were and what they stood for. By mid-October, Occupy Wall Street had an approval rating of more than 50 percent—higher than President Obama or Congress.

The radicals who lent this movement so much of its character offered American political life a gift, should we choose to accept it. They reminded us that we don't have to rely on Republicans or Democrats, or Clintons, Bushes, or Sarah Palin, to do our politics for us. With the assemblies, they bestowed a refreshing form of popular organizing that, if it could last, might help keep the rest of the system a bit more honest.

The Occupiers knew, though, that more traditional political organizations, such as labor unions, political parties, and advocacy groups, would be critical to making their message heard. Yet such organizations aren't the coziest of bedfellows for assemblies. They are financed by, and dirty their hands with, hierarchical politics, which a horizontal assembly must avoid like the plague. It is by nature a wildcat.

But the traditional organizations that found new momentum in the Occupy movement didn't need to sit around and wait for the assemblies to come up with demands or certain types of actions. They too could act autonomously, so to speak, doing what they do best with the good of the broader movement in mind: pressuring lawmakers, mobilizing their memberships, and pushing for change in the short term while the getting was good. They could even build coalitions on civil liberties and campaign finance with the Tea Party. The Occupy assemblies wouldn't do these things for them, and it was a mistake to wish they would.

"Any organization is welcome to support us," warned the OWS Statement of Autonomy, "with the knowledge that doing so will mean questioning your own institutional frameworks of work and hierarchy and integrating our principles into your modes of action."

As assemblies entered U.S. politics through the Occupy movement, one had to take care to recognize what they were not and would never be. Even more important, though, was what they'd already done. They reminded this country that politics is not a matter of choosing among what we're offered but of fighting for what we actually need, not to mention what we hope for. And for this, in large part, we had anarchy to thank.

FOUR | NO BORDERS, NO BOSSES

#Anonymous #Horizontalism #lulz #OccupiedWSJ
#MediaBlackout #N17 #O14 #p2 #SpokesCouncil
#Syntagma #TeaParty #WeAreLegion

If there was one apotheosis of Occupy Wall Street atop all the others, surely it was the early morning of October 14, just before dawn. A few days earlier, Mayor Bloomberg had made a surprise visit to the occupation to announce that the park needed to be cleaned. Police would help clear it in stages to allow sanitation workers to come through. Not coincidentally, the cleaning was to be on the eve of the global day of action planned for October 15, first called for months earlier by the Indignados in Spain, but now poised to be a worldwide coming-out party for the Occupy movement, a huge convergence at Times Square. Nobody believed for a second that the mayor's real concern was cleanliness.

On the 13th, vast quantities of supplies appeared at Liberty Square and, led by the Sanitation Working Group, a rigorous cleaning took place both actually and symbolically as Occupiers swept through their park with industrial brooms and mops. Computers and equipment and precious cardboard signs were piled into a nearby indoor storage space, just in case. Preparations would go on until morning. "Let's stay the fuck up tonight," said a voice in the General Assembly. "This is our home. This is our community. This is our revolution!"

At a time when Occupy Wall Street had become a household name, when half of Americans supported the movement, whatever it was, thousands of New Yorkers turned out to defend it. There were elected officials and hipsters and grandmothers. Even MoveOn.org, the dreaded progressive establishmentarian co-opter, dispatched its army of e-mail recipients to Liberty Square in a rare departure from pure clicktivism. The park was full as it had never been before—even more so than for the promise of Radiohead. The sky was still dark.

The people's mic had to be three or four or five generations long just for everyone to hear. "The people!" cried the inner circle, and then "The people!" outside of it, and then "The people!" again outside that. While those at the extremities were still crying, "The people!" and then "United!" those at the center called out, "Will never be defeated!" and those words, too, propagated outward. The effect was more like that of a song sung as a round than of an assembly—or like the sound one might expect to find in the heart of a bee-hive, by which each person's thoughts fall into synchrony with the whole. At around 6:30 A.M., word came through the hive that the cleaning had been postponed, that the mayor and the police had backed down. The cascading voices cried to one another, "Let this moment be seared in our minds!"

A march was called for, and when the sun rose it began much as marches always did, circumambulating the park on the sidewalk clockwise, gathering marchers and making noise. A press release had earlier promised they'd go "with brooms and mops to Wall Street to do a massive #wallstcleanup march, where the real mess is!"—and so they did. It was a celebration. A brass band played the tune of "We Shall Overcome." The police, defeated and unpre-pared, seemed especially vengeful.

As marchers and cops snaked through the Financial District streets, the marchers would at times surround and overtake the cops and pass through them unhindered. At other times the cops fought back. One marcher was punched by a deputy inspector. A legal observer was hit by a police scooter, which pinned down his writhing legs. Marchers who stepped off the sidewalk were grabbed and arrested. On Pine Street, half a block ahead of the main march, an Occupier near me danced through the road with a broom, brush-ing away trash. A mob of cops tackled him and took him away. He only wanted to clean.

Occupy Wall Street had won. The occupation had turned the city against the mayor and against the police, and its contagion kept spreading. "Because it started here" was one of *New York Magazine*'s 2011 "Reasons to Love New York." When I went to a free clinic in Brooklyn a few days after October 14, the first thing the West Indian nurse said when I sat down was, "You know who I'm thinking about today?" She pointed out the window, into the rain. "The kids down at Wall Street." She complained that her unemployed hus-band didn't go down there as he should and resolved, on her next day off, to go make them breakfast.

The occupation that, weeks earlier, had been so fragile and so lonesome was now a cup overflowing outward, over the walls between itself and the world it had set out to alter. New faces were on the plaza all the time, making their way into doing the work of its little village, or just passing through. I'd run into friends I never would've expected to see at a protest. Old people wandering around would start talking to me out of nowhere just to tell me that this was the best thing they'd seen for decades. The children's crusade was becoming everyone else's. Revolution, maybe, was just a matter of time, and maybe not even very much.

The Occupiers who'd been around all along couldn't quite believe what had grown out of their creation. Sometimes a few of them would huddle together away from the massive GA of strangers—"that fucking beast," as one of the North Dakotans referred to it—and sigh in relief at one another's familiar presence. News passed from ear to ear around Liberty Square: thirty-five thousand dollars more in donations. Deepak Chopra came to visit. Problems with drugs. Another arrest. Breathe.

You couldn't keep track of it all, or even start. There was always something new: a water-saving dishwashing system at the kitchen, a bicycle-powered generator, another celebrity visitor, another person shouting nonsense, a dozen new websites, a dozen new posters. The skill and imagination on display—constantly, unpredictably—mounted ever more as an indictment of the alienated world outside that before had kept us from sharing what we could do with one another, that had tricked us into selling our time and talents for money. There was so much. There was too much. There was always, also, a crisis.

"Welcome to the media blackout," said a sign that hung for a time near Liberty Square's media center, the cramped enclosure surrounded by a wall of bikes, wires, and a humming red generator. This was a complaint one heard a lot. The blackout may have been real early on, while the major papers weren't giving the occupation headlines and the national news networks weren't picking up the stories being gathered by the cameras of their local affiliates. Online, there were accusations of outright censorship. Yahoo admitted to the "not intentional" blocking of e-mails with links to OccupyWallSt.org, blaming the spam filter. Twitter similarly seemed to block #occupywallstreet from being listed as a trending topic. This may have been because it kept being throttled by Anonymous bots—or maybe, more conspiratorially, because JPMorgan Chase owned a stake in the company.

By the time the police violence and mass arrests kicked into gear, though, Liberty Square was a nonstop media frenzy, teeming with reporters willing to talk to anyone and willing to take any utterance as authoritative. It is rare, to say the least, to find a place so full of people under thirty for whom appearing on national television had so quickly become commonplace.

After reporters got over the initial skepticism that a non–Tea Party protest in the United States could possibly be worth their time, they found that the world of Liberty Square, with all the little pockets of worlds going on inside it, was the ultimate playground. It was a contained space but one full of stories. No one person knew or claimed to know all that was going on, and there was something for every interest or expertise. Food writers could write about the kitchen, and financial reporters could go to the wonky meetings of Occupy the SEC. Lit critics could thumb through the library, and tech bloggers could spread rumors about the Occupiers' promised replacement-in-progress for Facebook. Together, they could team up and compare notes while secretly competing to get one little step closer to ascertaining and articulating just what this whole crazy thing was about and what was to be done about it. A bloc of radical journalists organized their own shadow "assembly" on an e-mail list and in bars to support one another's work. The lack of any single authority or intention in the movement, though the reporters assiduously complained about it, was partly what made Occupy Wall Street such an attractive and inexhaustible subject.

I remember one day in late fall picking up the *Wall Street Journal* and finding in it a tick that seemed peculiar, especially for a paper of that political orientation: just about half the articles, whether they had anything to do with Occupy Wall Street or not, saw fit to at least mention the movement in passing, as if in necessary deference to the story of the moment. Far from a media blackout, Occupy became a media obsession and an excuse for a momentarily endless profusion of content, whether it was a wire service report, or an Andrew Breitbart hatchet job, or the live-stream from Tim Pool's mythical flying OccuCopter. "Zuccotti Park may well be the most intensely scrutinized landscape in recent journalistic history," Thomas Frank later observed, disapprovingly.

Occupy Wall Street coincided with a period when the sales of newspapers and print books were rapidly declining, together with the stores that tried to sell them. Yet one of the respects in which the movement may have actually represented a glimpse of the world to come was in its relationship to physical publication. For a phenomenon that began with a hashtag from

Adbusters, and spread by social media online, and was persistently broadcast by the various live-streamers, the printed word had a surprisingly decisive role to play. The most celebrated example was the People's Library, which began with a pile of free books at the northeast corner of the park in the first days of the occupation, sprouted under donated tents and tender care, and eventually met a gruesome end. The friendly anarchists of A New World in Our Hearts staffed a folding table covered with a generous supply of free-to-take, photocopied-and-stapled pamphlet editions of radical classics, along with Occupy-specific manuals on direct action and direct democracy; I collected these like treasures, for in their light the mysteries of the movement would make a clearer kind of sense. Catholic Workers handed out the latest issue of their paper, too, with polemics against usury among Dorothy Day's greatest hits. And so much more. At the People's Library, editorial assistants from the top magazines and publishers in New York were depositing sample copies of their wares at what had become the hottest literary showcase in town. The movement was also a prodigious publisher in its own right.

OWS's print publications carried a kind of authority, and legitimacy, and pride that no website or Twitter account ever quite could. Thanks to thousands of dollars from supporters inundating a Kickstarter campaign, stacks of the *Occupied Wall Street Journal* would arrive on Liberty Square as proof that there was in fact a message for all to see—read all about it. The publication's significance was all the more reason that the entirely male first issue (including an article of mine) aroused so much anger for its gross demographic oversight. Arun Gupta, the veteran movement journalist who helped start the *Journal,* subsequently traveled around the country to help other occupations get their papers going too. Then in New York came *Tidal,* a magazine of speculative theory and strategy by which organizers tried to explain what they were doing to themselves.

Print could do what the Internet alone could not. The occupation's most important position paper, the Declaration of the Occupation of New York City, had been almost entirely ignored by the outside world until it appeared as a handsome pamphlet. Longer booklets were commissioned and published under the auspices of Zuccotti Park Press. A whole issue of the *Occupied Wall Street Journal* was devoted to the movement's poster art, and much, much more could be downloaded from Occuprint.org. Everything printed had to be beautiful, to justify the necessity of printing and to announce its authority to a skeptical world, and just about without exception it was.

Gatekeepers like the *New York Times* and the *New York Review of Books* looked down from on high with amusement at this Internet-age movement's output in print. It could be mistaken for retro, or quaint, but in fact print was plainly necessary. When passersby asked, "Yes, but what do you want?" they could be handed a piece of printed matter and let that settle that. Once I even saw a cop give a copy of the *Journal* to satisfy a curious tourist. Physical print, like the physical occupation itself, like pinching yourself in a dream, was also a special kind of assurance that this was really happening.

Liberty had become a society of spectacle—a place to be seen, and to be recorded, and to be famous. But fame could get you in trouble, too.

One night, the hip-hop mogul Russell Simmons was allowed to speak during a General Assembly meeting. He interrupted the discussion at hand and gave his two cents about what, in general, the movement should do concerning the by-then-tabled question of demands. He received applause and thanks. But a few minutes later, after the scheduled discussion continued about how white, male-bodied people on the plaza needed to "check their privilege," a white, male-bodied young man got up and said something like, "Perhaps celebrities should check their privilege, too." At Occupy Atlanta, civil rights veteran Congressman John Lewis was denied the chance to speak at the GA on that same basis, and scandal ensued.

These incidents represented the effort on the part of Occupiers to smash the idol of celebrity in society, even well-earned celebrity. The implementation of this aspiration, though, was uneven, and it didn't reflect well that both Simmons and Lewis were black. Some notable people got essentially no attention during their visits to the occupation, while others got mobbed, for better or worse.

Once, at a meeting in a dilapidated church, Michael Moore sat behind me. He remained there all evening, listening and whispering with people he knew. As the meeting wound down, a facilitator started querying the group, "Michael Moore is here. Should we invite Michael Moore to speak?" This caught Moore off guard.

"I didn't come to speak. I really didn't," he kept saying to those of us around him. Then he stood up and said the same to the whole room.

The facilitator quieted him for the sake of process, though, and he kept the discussion going: "Should we invite Michael Moore to speak?" Some spoke for, some spoke against. Several trying minutes later, with Moore himself squirming in his seat the whole time, a decision was made to invite him—and he indeed spoke, pretty rousingly, for fifteen minutes. The young facilitator, whom I'd never seen before, thanked Moore and welcomed him to Occupy Wall Street, apparently unaware that Moore had been a frequent visitor since the first week. Moore, in turn, welcomed the facilitator to the struggle against corporate rule, which he'd been fighting in for decades.

I ran into Moore some weeks later in an airport security line in California and, when I reminded him of that meeting, he insisted again, "I didn't come to speak!"

One night in early October the occupation had a visit from Jeff Mangum, the reclusive singer of the band Neutral Milk Hotel. It was carefully timed for the end of the evening, when the GA was over and pretty much just those spending the night were left. There was a modest mic-checked announcement, and people started to gather around him and a pair of acoustic guitars. He played his songs like lullabies on the steps along Broadway, surrounded by a chorus of a hundred Occupiers, huddled close together, quietly singing along: "Know all your enemies—we know who our enemies are." Ketchup, a facilitator with big red glasses and long, straight red hair, knew every word. It was the first time I'd ever seen her seem other than agitated.

The more that was happening in Liberty Square, the less I wanted to be there. By late October there were so many tents—mostly a hodgepodge of ordinary camping tents—that it was hard to walk anywhere without stepping on one or on someone sleeping or passed out. Since there was no place to congregate, the working groups were all meeting at the 60 Wall Street atrium or elsewhere. During the day, whatever human variety and inexplicability that New York City could muster lined the edges of that one square block of park. Everyone with some invention or act or need descended there. At night, fights and raving individuals, trailed by the crowds failing to deescalate them, became an ordinary part of the soundscape. People who'd been living on the streets already, not by choice, took refuge in the park from the city's punitive and inadequate provisions for them. They brought new challenges. Liberty still felt to me like the sole sliver of reality in the whole universe, but when a week or two passed since I'd slept on its granite floor I was starting to lose my sense that I belonged there or even recognized it.

While wandering around aimlessly one night I found Victoria Sobel, the Cooper Union art student who'd first cobbled together the Finance Working Group weeks before. She looked even busier and more exhausted and frustrated than usual, but it was good to see her. We made our way around the park for a little while and then crouched inside a tent that had been commandeered for the purposes of Media—specifically, for one of the several live-streaming teams. A man was sleeping inside, but we went in anyway, and Victoria started showing me the financial spreadsheets. Pretty quickly, though, our attention turned to the screens of a pair of laptops lying on the floor, which were playing live video from Oakland. It was the night after Occupy Oakland's first eviction, and there was a huge protest in response. The police brought out tear gas and guns. We'd later learn that Iraq War veteran Scott Olson was nearly killed that night after being shot by police with a beanbag round. On our screens, though, it was all just flashes of light and smoke and shadows in the streets.

After who knows how long watching those scenes and whispering, trying not to wake up the sleeping person, and trying to figure out the right stream to follow and which tweets to trust, I got tired, said good night to Victoria, and went back to Brooklyn.

I was fielding a lot of radio interviews throughout the fall—sometimes several per day—and in the course of discovering the interviewers' various levels of familiarity with Occupy, or those of Occupiers themselves with their own movement, or even the process of education that I was going through myself, I devised a sequence of grand epiphanies by which to phrase my explanations of how the movement understood itself. If the interviewer or caller seemed to already be at Stage One, I could focus on Stage Two. And I wouldn't bother trying to mention Stage Three if they didn't seem to have a good grasp of One and Two. And so forth.

None of these stages, as it turned out, was "wealth inequality," the complaint most commonly associated with the Occupy movement in the media. I suppose that association was correct, but strangely it wasn't talked about very much among the organizers I spent most of my time with. On this scale, maybe, the fact that there is gross wealth inequality would rank around Stage One-Half, or possibly lower, somewhere between complete ignorance and Stage One. Named after common slogans, the stages were roughly as follows:

Stage One: Shit is fucked up and bullshit—which meant grasping wholly and deeply the brokenness of "the system" that had been sold to the highest bidders and that rigged economic life, despite certain appearances of prosperity, as an illusion meant to keep us taking on perpetual debt in order to buy the products that were destroying our minds, bodies, communities, and planet.

Stage Two: This is not a protest, this is a process—a process through which, by occupying space and deliberating together, people recovered their capacity to think beyond the constraints that Stage One's corruption imposed on them and remembered how politics and economy were really supposed to work in the first place: from the ground up, not from the top down.

Stage Three: The only solution is global revolution—which expressed the recognition that because the crisis of capital was global, the movements had to be global, and that the real, reasonable reason there was no demand for the U.S. government was that there was nothing it alone could do.

There was surely a fourth stage as well, though it was harder to place in the order of the sequence, depending as it did on a given person's predisposition and experience: *Fuck the police.* A fifth, oppositely, and also difficult to place: *Occupy your heart.* This had to do with some kind of inner work and how people could relate to one another. It complicated, but didn't necessarily exclude, the fourth stage; perhaps these two belonged on a different, parallel spectrum or sequence from the others. In practice, they were just about always a cacophony.

As Liberty Square swirled on around me, I could sense that there were surely other stages, too, ones that I had not begun to fathom. The more time passed, the more I came to think that it all boiled down to the name of the place—to liberty, to liberation, to making this taste of freedom spread as widely and unpredictably as possible. But while I was willing to spend day after day taking in these inexhaustible mysteries, others understandably wanted answers.

As a general rule Occupy resisted the impulse to classify. Even the idea of belonging to the left, as such, was something that the typical young Occupier was not especially comfortable with, except when there appeared to be no other way of identifying the movement's populist blend of anticapitalist and anti-oppressive commitments. There was reason to think that a glitch in the normal political spectrum might be revealing itself in the consistent presence early on of libertarians and others typically associated with the political right. They could agree, for instance, about the need to get big money out of elections and to stop bailing out banks—thus opposing practices that both main political parties pursued with nearly equal vigor.

In some curious ways, Occupy resembled the early formations of the right-wing Tea Party that had flourished in the preceding years—its base among the sinking middle class, its nostalgia for preindustrial life, its aversion to the idea that salvation would come from government on high. Decades before either movement, libertarian prophet and *National Review* cofounder Karl Hess used the language of the 99 percent and the 1 percent. One could even find in Tea Party literature paeans to process and decentralization and prefigurative communities. What these movements had in common, whether expressed through gun-toting nativism or artsy civil disobedience, reflected the basic deceptiveness of the standard political spectrum, which persists in order to divide majority opinion for a minority's ends. This might have been an opportunity for an unstoppable coalition.

"See, here's why I want the libertarians and not the liberals first—," one hot-shot organizer began saying during the first week on the plaza, before he made me turn off my recorder. But his dangerous vision for a right-left alliance was not to be. As time went on and the culture of the occupations hardened, right-wing libertarians had a harder and harder time taking part.

The notion that the Occupy movement was dedicated to Marxism or communism or socialism—promulgated on Fox News to its constituency of McCarthyite holdouts—was a half truth at best. When I spoke on a panel hosted by a group of rather doctrinaire Marxist students at NYU, they seemed just as uneasy with the new movement as the Democrats were. It was doing everything wrong. There needed to be clearer ideas, clearer class analysis, clearer strategies. There needed to be a formal structure, and a party, and an apparatus for agitating workers. Occupy was way too anarchist-y for the true socialists, but of course never enough so for the anarchists themselves.

Sometimes it seemed like nobody understood the movement quite as well as the Fox-style right-wing media. They—unlike those on the institutional left trying to claim this uprising for themselves—were at least willing to say outright that the young Occupiers habitually denounced capitalism and the American way of life, which was true. But rather than accompanying reports with scenes of the devastation wrought by that capitalism and that American way of life, Fox showed scenes of scary protesters in black masks or some Occupier somewhere defecating on a police car.

Also confounding to potential allies on the left were the Occupiers' dueling desires for an anarchist utopia, on the one hand, and a beneficent welfare state, on the other. In the language of conventional politics: Did they want a bigger government or a smaller one? One would hear this paradox in the slogans and signs of Liberty Square: "Fight! Fight! Education is a right!" followed by "Two! Four! Six! Eight! Eat the rich and smash the state!" Pleas for federal regulation of finance accompanied teach-ins on alternative currencies.

For a century and a half, the left has been arguing over whether the stateless workers' paradise requires first seizing control of the state or eviscerating it; Marx and Bakunin squabble on. But I found a bit of a clue about this dilemma when I asked a Norwegian anthropologist what she thought had led to the development of her country's social democracy. To my surprise, she started talking about eighteenth-century pietists—religious reformers who questioned elites, prized equality, and created self-sufficient communities. By fostering a subculture apart from the state's reach, they started building what would evolve into powerful populist movements. Similar things happened with the wave of unionism that led to the New Deal in the United States and with the rise of Islamist movements in the Middle East. By doing the state's job better than it does, you make it pony up to demonstrate its worth, to prove its right to exist.

All the rationalization I could muster, anyway, still failed to produce a ready-made ideology for Occupy's particular mix of overeducated, underemployed, postindustrial technoprimitivism. Insofar as this was an organic expression of the moment, it proved as confounding as the present always seems to be at the time. Thus the Occupiers might be forgiven for the extent to which they were bold enough to think that they were not representing any tradition or lineage at all and that what they were doing was entirely new, free from the various missteps of movements past. There are respects in which, I suppose, any emerging movement must wrongly believe this to be true and other respects in which it actually is.

One by one, people I knew, or people I didn't, kept asking me to tell Occupy Wall Street what to do. They'd come with a framework, or a strategy, or a demand that those hapless Occupiers allegedly, sorely needed. It was hard to know what to say, since the movement didn't take advice from me anyway. How could it? Calling the movement leaderless, or participatory, was not just a gimmick. No one person really was in control, so it wasn't like I could pass some nugget of wisdom on to the secret leader. (I tried.) If you wanted a certain idea to get internalized in the movement, the best advice I could give you was to take part yourself. Join relevant committees or start an Occupy _____ of your own, then be patient and try to persuade people to agree with you. Form an affinity group with friends. Enjoy. But be warned: if you were to do it right, you'd probably change your mind in the process.

Considering the corrupt and backward ways in which we're used to the world working, I suppose this was less obvious than it should have been. Occupy was regularly faulted, for instance, for failing to follow the Tea Party pattern of orchestrating a lightning electoral coup in Congress. But there's something to be said for the movement not having cast its lot with super-rich financiers like those who eventually drowned out just about all of the Tea Party's meaningfully populist impulses with the exact opposite. Besides, quite a few Occupiers did run for offices around the country, but by eschewing big money, they couldn't stand a chance. At the very least, a common and almost messianic refrain among sympathetic outsiders was that leaders in the traditional Gandhi-King-Chávez mold would be necessary and inevitable.

But it was fitting, so far as Occupy Wall Street was concerned, that the expression "take me to your leader" is conventionally said by a space alien. It would have been that hard to process. Within OWS, leaderlessness—or, as it was sometimes said, being "leader*ful*"—was a big part of why Occupiers were finding the movement so revolutionary, and so empowering, and so right.

It's a time-tested rule of thumb that the outcomes of social movements generally resemble the structure of the movements themselves—from the for-profit governance of the Tea Party to the vanguardist Bolsheviks. The way a movement organizes itself can be a playground of the impossible, but it's also a chance to craft what eventually emerges in the movement's wake. Further raising the stakes, too, was the fact that this leaderless thing was not merely the idea of a few influential anarchists in the Occupy movement—though it was that too. Among the popular uprisings that were spreading around the world, leaderlessness was the rule, not the exception.

When Mohamed ElBaradei turned up at occupied Tahrir Square, the people's overall reply was, "Thanks, but we don't need you"; as the Egyptian social media wizard Wael Ghonim traveled the world collecting laurels afterward, even he was chastened enough to say on the BBC, "I don't want to take much credit—the revolution was leaderless." When Romania flared up against corruption over the winter, one of the movement's participants, a professor named Claudiu Craciun, stood before the European Parliament and said, "I am here not as a leader or as a representative. There is not such a thing in the public square. Please accept me here as a storyteller."

Leaderlessness was becoming the dominant mode of popular political organizing the world over. It seemed to suggest a common search for stark alternatives to the business of politicians—plutocrats in the guise of representatives. Undoubtedly, too, it stemmed at least in part from the fact that so many people were spending so much of their lives online, connected to one another through decentralized, ostensibly self-governing networks, where some of them had been causing a lot of trouble.

Anonymous, thank goodness, has had an anthropologist in its midst. Gabriella Coleman, who teaches at McGill, was a participant-observer in Internet relay chat channels and Twitter exchanges as a community devoted to crude inside jokes grew into a herd of vigilante hackers for global justice. In an essay for *Triple Canopy*, "Our Weirdness Is Free," she summarizes what Anonymous is all about:

> Beyond a foundational commitment to anonymity and the free flow of information, Anonymous has no consistent philosophy or political program. Though Anonymous has increasingly devoted its energies to (and become known for) digital dissent and direct action around various "ops," it has no definite trajectory. Sometimes coy and playful, sometimes macabre and sinister, often all at once, Anonymous is still animated by a collective will toward mischief—toward "lulz," a plural bastardization of the portmanteau LOL (laugh out loud). Lulz represent an ethos as much as an objective.

Over several years, Anons became lulled—so to speak—from trolling pranks and porno on the website 4chan into dabbling in politics through their operations against Scientology, in defense of WikiLeaks, and on behalf of the Arab Spring. At Occupy camps everywhere their Guy Fawkes masks were a ubiquitous minority. The lulz ethos turned into a mode of movement building, and, combined with a few skilled hackers, it became singularly scary to such evildoers as secretive corporations and oppressive governments; several top Anons were busted, with formidable charges, just before Occupy Wall Street hit the ground. But swashbuckling for justice wasn't allowed to get too much in the way of fun. As if to ensure a modicum of chaos, Anons who seemed too much focused on do-gooding and not enough on sowing lulz risked being denounced as "moralfags."

One winter night I watched Anons chatting in an IRC channel as they launched distributed-denial-of-service (DDoS) attacks that took down the websites of government ministries in Bashar Assad's Syria, one after another—under orders from no one, just for the fun and rightness of doing so. Even when the effectiveness of DDoS attacks really depended on just a few Anons with access to large botnets of enslaved computers, the chief perpetrators handed credit to the thousands of rank-and-file participants. The fact that so many people took part in these virtual sit-ins conveyed the impression of a leaderless mass uprising. "We are legion," the accompanying propaganda would declare, in a biblical allusion to demonic possession.

"Acting 'on the wing,'" writes Coleman, "leverages Anonymous' fluid structure, giving Anons an advantage, however temporary, over traditional institutions—corporations, states, political parties—that function according to unified plans." Anonymous's allergy to top-down planning, furthermore, wasn't limited to tactics; as in Occupy, it was a way of life:

> While Anonymous has not put forward any programmatic plan to topple institutions or change unjust laws, it has made evading them seem easy and desirable. To those donning the Guy Fawkes mask associated with Anonymous, this—and not the commercialized, "transparent" social networking of Facebook—is the promise of the Internet, and it entails trading individualism for collectivism.

Anonymous shared the analysis that was motivating uprisings from Tunis to Moscow to Oakland: the kinds of governments that hung over our societies couldn't fulfill their own promises of freedom and transparency and justice. The reason both Anonymous and Occupy Wall Street didn't put forward any programmatic plan that existing institutions could follow was that there couldn't possibly be one. Rather, the movements themselves were their own programmatic plan, worlds unto themselves.

It was always a bit of a mystery how, as the Occupy movement spread around the country and the globe, the occupations all took direct democracy as the basic unit of political legitimacy, prided themselves on a decentralized structure, and discouraged credit taking and self-aggrandizement. How did people all over the United States and the world know how to Occupy so quickly? Their preparedness could be attributed at least partly to the veterans of the global justice movement of a decade earlier, who flocked to the occupations. But probably even more significant among the younger Occupiers was the experience many of them had had online with Anonymous and groups like it.

I kept trying to figure out who in OWS was an Anon and who wasn't. Some would admit it. Some would not but would then proceed to talk about 4chan the way only an Anon could. Other times I'd just try to avoid the Anon stuff altogether; both the occupations and Anonymous attracted more than their share of audacious adolescent boredom, which was just stupid and creepy. Take, for instance, this e-mail, which I lost a few hours' sleep over before learning how many others in the movement had been getting it too:

> From: nobody@smtp.remailer.dyndns.org
> Subject: We Are Legion.
> Date: October 15, 2011
>
> We don't appreciate being double-crossed.
>
> Soon you will feel the measure of our anger.
>
> The movement will fall.
>
> You will be the prime suspect.
>
> We Are Anonymous.
> We Are Legion.
> We Do not Forgive.
> We do not Forget.

Run-ins like this made me less sanguine, even if no less certain, that Anonymous's way of doing things was a kind of prefigurative politics in its own right.

You couldn't pull the wool of leaderlessness over some reporters' eyes. *Time* magazine would declare "the Protester" its Person of the Year and meanwhile identify David Graeber and live-streamer Tim Pool as Occupy Wall Street's figureheads—notwithstanding that neither regularly took part in organizing meetings during the occupation. (Bloomberg's *Businessweek* at least had the savvy to call Graeber an "anti-leader.") Other reporters chose Patrick Bruner, since he was often the first to pick up the phone when they called. The *New Yorker* focused its major article on Kalle Lasn and Micah White of *Adbusters,* who never visited Liberty Square. Dan Rather identified Priscilla Grim, one of the creators of the We Are the 99 Percent Tumblr website, as the real leader behind OWS: "She's brilliant with the Internet," he reasoned. At least *Fast Company*'s list of nine prospective leaders ended with the one candidate that at least some Occupiers might have identified as such, at least some of the time: the General Assembly.

Hapless media interventions didn't make OWS internal politics any less prickly. As Occupiers spread out from Wall Street through local neighborhood assemblies, or cross-country road trips, or the trove of online organizing tools, the problem of leadership was an undercurrent all along. It wasn't entirely clear how best to behave in a leaderless movement, much less how those putting their time and energy into it would ever pay rent. Talented and well-connected organizers had to navigate a precarious line between taking the lead on certain initiatives and "stepping back" so as not to accumulate too much power or appear too visible. A false move could risk endangering the fragile universe they'd created.

If the demand had once been a process, the process started seriously breaking down. As the fall wore on, fewer and fewer people attended the General Assembly, and attempts to start up the more streamlined Spokes Council were on the rocks. Some thought the Spokes Council was a ruse among the "organizers" to shut the true, overnight "occupiers" out of decision making or that it was a sin against direct democracy, the only legitimate form of which was the General Assembly. It was perhaps a symptom of the failure of horizontalism that people more and more often prefaced their speeches in meetings with the declaration that they were "day-one Occupiers" or that they'd been around since the first week or some other such claim to special authority, for fear that special authority was being exercised by others. Even the most obvious cop infiltrators knew this trick and used it shamelessly.

Day after day for a week, Marisa Holmes sat in the atrium at 60 Wall Street with her hands at her temples, explaining how a spokes council works and that it was a time-tested form of direct democracy in radical movements. Her patience belied, but also grew out from, her stubbornness; eventually she and her allies succeeded. When the OWS Spokes Council finally did get up and running on October 28, though, it was the target of wrenching and persistent disruption by those who, while dominating the proceedings, insisted they were being excluded. Some of these were from the growing population of homeless Occupiers who couldn't as easily leave the park to attend off-site Spokes Council meetings. But several of the disrupters were simply determined to make Spokes fail; at least a couple of them had been doing much the same thing, suspiciously enough, at Bloombergville the previous summer. Georgia Sagri, who had rarely been seen since the Tompkins Square Park planning meetings, reappeared for the assault on the Spokes Council. The discussions online at nycga.net were so overrun with trolls, meanwhile, that the occupation's main logistical website became unusable.

Neither the GA nor the Spokes Council was producing much of the collective effervescence that had been the GA's primary benefit early on. The constantly deferred promise that direct democracy would be a means of agreeing on shared political values and strategies kept losing out to daily minutiae and bookkeeping. OWS was sitting on hundreds of thousands of dollars in donations, and the incessant business of these deliberative bodies became the dispersal of it—for MetroCards, for direct actions, for printing, and for everything else. A few working groups were still trying to draft demands—or, more cautiously, "visions and goals"—that could be passed through the GA. The GA and the Spokes Council thus became treated as if they were legislative organs for some kind of haphazard government, even though such assemblies are premised on the prior rejection of any such thing. So goes a refrain of utopian politics: the movement replicates within itself the very habits of power that it set out to oppose. Eventually, the Facilitation Working Group, which was tasked with leading the meetings, became fed up and went on strike.

Not inclined to waste their time in the GA or Spokes, by November many of the most effective organizers were doing what they needed to do in independent, ad hoc project groups, further and further from the allegedly legitimate deliberative bodies. Groups like these were free to develop their own decision-making structures, and they found informal ways of coordinating with the movement as a whole, mainly through social media and word of mouth. Some groups were being formed by religious leaders and celebrities and rich supporters, whose usual specialness had been lost in the multitude of the movement. Some ambitious young nonprofiteers surely had future job prospects in mind as they found their way into these backroom networks. Students took time off to do so, deftly recognizing in OWS the makings of the ultimate internship.

Ad hoc affinity groups had been a part of the movement since the beginning, being responsible for such public-facing projects as OccupyWallSt.org and the *Occupied Wall Street Journal*. But now this was starting to be the main way of getting things done. More was happening than ever but with less transparency and less accountability. It wasn't entirely clear who or what was part of the movement and who or what was not. A basic commitment to leaderlessness, though, to practicing democracy directly, was almost always a prerequisite.

Older folks, in particular, would get fed up the most quickly with the fixation on leaderlessness. One, a Tiananmen Square veteran named Shen Tong, blasted a memo to fellow organizers insisting on the need to appoint particular people to particular leadership roles. "If OWS does not have effective interfaces to the outside world of the equivalent set of faces and leaders," he wrote, "the outside world will choose for OWS."

The response to his memo made clear, though, that his was a minority view. His younger comrades had no interest in making accommodations for those in power and redoubled their commitment to undoing the hierarchies that they believed society leverages in order to marginalize and oppress. But the urge to leaderlessness was aesthetic as much as it was political. At stake was not simply a model of governance, but a culture, a recognizable mode of being and acting. Leaderlessness was simply more beautiful. It was their way.

In the midst of the discussions about structure, which would ensue over the winter, this is a primer—"Be a Leader in OWS"—that Justin Wedes posted in a Pastebin online:

1. Start an open collective, affinity group, Working Group, whatever.
2. Be open, inviting, non-exclusionary.
3. Build consensus. Slowly, or quickly, but intentionally.

4. Don't talk shit.
5. Listen a lot.
6. Don't expect fame or glory. If you're doing things right, you won't get it. If you do, you won't like it.
7. When you get frustrated, take a break. Leave town for a few days. Don't burn out.
8. Don't speak for the movement, speak WITH it.
9. Make your intentions absolutely clear. And your actions. Report-back often to your group and to the broader community (GA).
10. Have fun. Laugh. Don't take yourself too seriously.

Justin himself was at times accused of violating such principles—which perhaps explains why @FakeJustinWedes was one of a handful of Twitter accounts that arose to troll organizers who had assumed leading roles.

A website called Occupy the Stack meanwhile presented a guide under the headline "Overcoming Male Supremacy (or White, or Wealth, or Hetero, etc.)," based on a list by the late activist trainer Bill Moyers. It warned against such pretensions as these:

- Hogging the show: talking too much, too long, too loud.
- Problem solver: continually giving the answer or solution before others have had much chance to contribute.
- Restating: saying in another way what someone else, especially a woman, has just said.
- Putdowns and one-upsmanship: "I used to believe that, but now . . ." or "How can you possibly say that?"
- Self-listening: formulating a response after the first few sentences, not listening to anything from that point on, and leaping in at the first pause.
- Avoiding feelings: intellectualizing, withdrawing into passivity, or making jokes when it's time to share personal feelings.
- Seeking attention and support from women while competing with men.
- Speaking for others: "What so and so really meant was . . ."

You had to watch yourself. You had to check your privilege. And it mattered, too, that these were not solely suggestions for some particular species of Occupy junkies. These were the habits of mind and practice that were cropping up wherever occupations and assemblies did. As movement after movement around the world seemed to be telling us, a different way of doing politics was ascendant.

The land that gave birth to European civilization seemed, by early November, on the brink of sinking the whole continent's economy. From a glance at the front page of a newspaper at the time, one might have guessed that a political meeting in Athens would have been full of talk about the resigning prime minister, the bitter bailout deals, and the euro. But among those I joined in a basement in the neighborhood of Exarcheia—a kind of Haight-Ashbury for Athenian radicals, full of coffee shops and walls covered with political posters—the agenda was completely different. They talked instead about parks, public kitchens, and barter bazaars. They actually seemed hopeful.

The lack of concern for political figureheads, in retrospect, was to be expected. These Greek autonomists—assorted anarchists, libertarian socialists, and so forth—had no more reason to care about whether Prime Minister George Papandreou went or stayed than those in Occupy Wall Street had reason to agonize over Republican presidential hopeful Herman Cain's sexual foibles. They had another kind of politics in mind.

The meeting, convened by a group called Assembly for the Circulation of Struggles, consisted of progress reports from neighborhood assemblies around Athens. Located down some stairs under a graffiti black cat, the basement included a ping-pong table, a kitchen, a bar, and a selection of political books in Greek. ("If the books do better than the bar," said a woman who offered me tea, "we consider that a good night.") For five hours, fifty or so people sat in an oblong jumble of plastic chairs and café tables, smoking hand-rolled cigarettes and nursing beers. Among them were the Argentine activist Claudia Acuña and Marina Sitrin from OWS. The Assembly for the Circulation of Struggles had just published a Greek translation of Marina's book about Argentina, *Horizontalism*. Thanks to Claudia and Marina, the Greeks' conversation about neighborhoods got a little more global—a spitting image of the new global justice movement, one focused less on shuttling around to economic summits, as was common a decade earlier, than on occupying public spaces everywhere.

"In New York, we're still the baby movement in the world," said Marina. Since Occupy Wall Street began on September 17, occupations and open assemblies had spread all over the country and beyond. But assemblies were only starting to find their way from the central squares into neighborhoods and workplaces, where most people spend most of their time and where many of their most vital concerns lie.

The Argentines and the Greeks had been at it longer. Both had shaken off dictatorships only a few decades before. In Greece, the most recent iteration of resistance dated back to the riots that followed the shooting of a teenage boy by police in 2008. The country's subsequent economic disaster and the government's effort to respond with austerity measures only strengthened the movement. There were enormous, volatile protests and occupations in Athens's Syntagma Square, which international papers portrayed with images of Molotov cocktails and broken windows. But those protests also gave birth to assemblies, where people revived the terminology of ancient Athenian democracy to explain their participatory, nonhierarchical decision-making process. After the demonstrations at Syntagma, activists from around Greece took assemblies home with them.

Like those in the United States, Greek protesters were blamed for being immature, impractical, and short on clear demands. But to those who gathered with the Assembly for the Circulation of Struggles, such complaints rang hollow. Rather than demanding particular reforms of the government, they focused on creating alternative institutions for themselves to resist it. Graffiti on the metal sheets protecting the windows of a post office on Syntagma Square asked in quasi-English, rhetorically: "CAN A REVOLUTION BE SELLFISH."

When assemblies took hold in Greek neighborhoods, as in Argentina, they were concerned less with ideology than with finding creative, unsanctioned means of survival. One man with long, curly hair running down his back reported on how his assembly built a park on a block that was slated to become a parking lot, while another described efforts to save preschools and public entertainment from being lost to privatization. These were very ordinary struggles. But everyone who was using a rescued park or sending a child to a reclaimed school was taking part in an act of political resistance. They were being radicalized by implication, by necessity.

Both the Greek and the Argentine movements had to deal with various leftist political parties that tried to use the assemblies to win recruits and parliamentary votes, distracting from the assemblies' own agendas. To protect against this, some organizers started smaller, closed assemblies with more rigid philosophical boundaries—like the one I attended in Exarcheia.

What worried Marina especially about Occupy Wall Street at the time was another form of co-option. The Greeks smiled half enviously when she said, "Only in the U.S. do you start a movement and people give you money." But Marina wasn't bragging. "As a movement, we can't have money. It's a massive problem." When supporters donated large quantities of cash—as opposed to actual supplies like food and blankets—they were helping to turn the movement into a bureaucracy.

The Greek activists said they were similarly worried that aid money pouring in would enrich the NGOs and further accustom people to taking handouts rather than providing for themselves. Claudia nodded knowingly. The Greek autonomists were trying to create alternative economies for sharing food, clothing, and other necessities. Doing so wasn't easy; it meant weaning people away from the taboo on using secondhand goods or accepting food when one can't afford it—a taboo the activists blamed on the capitalist state's false promises of luxury for all.

As the evening went on, people from the various neighborhood assemblies described their plans for the future. One was organizing a demonstration on motorcycles. (Motorcycle helmets and leather jackets were as common among Greek radicals as messenger bags and fixed-gear bicycles among their U.S. counterparts.) A union of delivery workers was trying to agitate for a four-hour workday. Through assemblies of assemblies, neighborhoods were taking part in mass disobedience campaigns, including ones against a new tax on electricity and the privatization of public transit.

Around two in the morning, a pair from the Assembly for the Circulation of Struggles finally drove Marina and Claudia and me back to where our hotels were, roughly tracing the marching route from Exarcheia to Syntagma Square. We passed a bank that was once torched by Molotov cocktails, killing three people inside. Though earlier the Greeks had been joking about which beer bottles make the best Molotovs, this time they spoke mournfully of the bomb throwers as uncontrollable kids, as "not even really anarchists." We passed the columns around the square where marble had been torn off to be thrown at riot police. A handful of police with shields were still stationed nearby, just in case.

Scrawled in graffiti on the floor of Syntagma, under a tree: "WE ARE 99%."

Just a few days earlier, I'd been on the Greek island of Santorini. It is shaped like a crescent, consisting of the rim around the crater of a gigantic sunken volcano. From Santorini, in the middle of the second millennium B.C., a dark cloud of noxious falling ash and a tsunami came forth and spread across the Mediterranean. This left in ruins the then-dominant Minoan civilization—that of the Minotaur, of the bare-breasted snake goddess, of the palace at Knossos. Some say the eruption might also have caused the ten plagues Pharaoh endured in the Book of Exodus. What remained was a monument to flux. The structures and orders and principalities that we inhabit seem invulnerable, as King Minos must have seemed once, until suddenly they aren't, and they fall.

FIVE | SANCTUARY

#D17 #D6 #Eviction #N17 #OccupyAdvent #OccupyCatholics
#OccupyFaith #OccupyJudaism #OccupyOurHomes
#ProtestChaplain #TrinityWallSt

All things must come to an end, but not necessarily like this.

When the sun rose on November 15, Liberty Square looked an awful lot like Zuccotti Park again—aside from the damaged flower beds and a broken plastic peace sign lying in the gutter. It was blocked off with barricades even though there'd been a court order that people should be allowed to return. The place had been completely cleared and power-washed, bare and dead except for the trees, whose leaves had turned a bright yellow for autumn. I don't think I noticed that they'd turned before; there was too much human commotion.

At one in the morning, hundreds of police in riot gear had stormed the plaza, shining floodlights and tearing down tents. Sanitation workers loaded Occupiers' belongings into garbage trucks, including thousands of books from the People's Library. Truck-mounted, "less-lethal" LRAD sound cannons were on the scene, and five police helicopters hovered high overhead, where airspace was closed to media aircraft. Occupiers locked arms around the kitchen area, facing pepper spray and batons for doing so. Reporters and elected officials who managed to get into the middle of it came out bloody with the rest.

I arrived about an hour after it began. Text messages from friends woke me, and I biked across the Brooklyn Bridge, the main road of which was closed to Manhattan-bound traffic. By that time, rows of police in riot gear were preventing anyone, including reporters, from getting closer than a block away from the site. On Broadway, at either end of the blockade, crowds gathered through the early hours of the morning. Those on the north side tended to be mournful, and in shock, and pleading before the unresponsive officers blocking the way. On the south side, at Pine Street, the shock expressed itself as anger, as shouting, as jumping on a parked police car and taunting the phalanx of officers.

Hours passed, and bands of Occupiers dotted Lower Manhattan with stray marches and spontaneous assemblies and affinity groups meeting in circles in the deserted streets. Text-message alerts about where to go conflicted with one another. People gradually began gathering at Foley Square; the strangeness of the movement's internal architecture manifested itself in simultaneous attempts to convene the General Assembly and the Spokes Council, though nobody was sure what legitimacy either might have now. I fell asleep for a little while as the sun rose over the General Assembly, with the sound of the people's mic in my dreams.

The idea that prevailed from the discussions was to set off on a midmorning march to Duarte Square, up on Canal Street, a mile north of Wall Street. It's not a place most New Yorkers know about or go to—a smallish plot inundated with the noise and fumes of cars charging for the Holland Tunnel. But adjoining it is another privately owned public space like Zuccotti, with an owner that Occupiers hoped might be more welcoming than Brookfield Properties: Trinity Church, an ancient Episcopal parish on Broadway, facing the entrance to Wall Street, which doubles as a massive real estate corporation and a soother of executive consciences through its charities.

The part of Duarte Square that Trinity owns was surrounded by a chain-link fence and plywood boards. Yellow and black "OCCUPY WALL STREET" banners had been hung along the fence. But the police were intent on preventing anything that would require a repeat of the morning's shock-and-awe operation. Still in their riot helmets, they blocked those trying to get through the fence and finally dispersed the tired, bruised, defeated crowd.

With remarkable timing if nothing else, *Adbusters* promulgated "Tactical Briefing #18: Occupy the High Ground" just hours before the eviction. Perhaps the time had passed for the movement to be so focused on encampments, the communiqué suggested, and it might be better to move on to bigger and better things instead. Although *Adbusters*'s scattershot advice had long since been ignored or ridiculed by most people in OWS, the idea of such a shift had been coming up repeatedly in conversations among organizers; after almost two months, they felt, the movement was starting to outgrow the occupation. The working groups, websites, and other infrastructure were already at such a point that most of the movement's political business had been happening outside the crowded plaza for weeks. Occupy actions were taking place around the country without being specifically tied to occupation sites. More and more people started to realize that encampments alone really posed little threat to the pillars upholding the power of the corporate elite. Even the encampment in Cairo's Tahrir Square probably couldn't have brought down Hosni Mubarak without the general strike that threatened to bring down the Egyptian economy. If focusing too much on encampments was going to distract the movement from posing an actual threat, maybe the encampments would be better left behind.

It was also true that the camps suffered from poor health, filth, and sexual harassment and assault. These were the stated justifications for the evictions of occupations throughout the country, coordinated nationally by Homeland Security, of which Liberty Square's eviction was only one. Some of these problems had been caused by the police themselves, who made a habit of dropping off offenders and addicts they'd apprehended at Liberty Square. Occupiers tried to provide an alternative for those people to the cycle of criminalization that the state had to offer, but mostly, increasingly, they didn't do so very well.

During the first week at Liberty Square, Monica López, from the 15M movement in Spain, reminded me that this occupation wouldn't last forever. It shouldn't. Don't expect it to. The time eventually came in Madrid when the Indignados decided they would be better off closing down their occupation—on June 12, less than a month after it began. They ended the world they'd created on their own terms. After that, the Spanish movement shifted its attention to projects like preventing evictions and organizing assemblies in neighborhoods. For the Occupy movement so far, though, the tactic of occupation felt indispensable. It was the name of the movement.

Mayor Bloomberg tried to present his surprise police raid as an opportunity for Occupy to turn a new page. "Protesters have had two months to occupy the park with tents and sleeping bags," he judged. "Now they will have to occupy the space with the power of their arguments."

As if to rise to his challenge, a forward-looking message came out from the Press Relations team and spread across the country: "You can't evict an idea whose time has come." Some Occupiers were already talking about "Occupy

2.0" or "Phase II" like they'd planned for it all along. But another contingent continued to insist that this movement was fundamentally about reclaiming space—space for assembly, space for autonomy, space for providing for one another, space for staging the struggle against those who claim to own that space. Seizing space and time, and holding them, was how Occupy caused its rupture. That's how it spread everywhere. For them, if there was no space, and no time in which to inhabit it, there was no Occupy.

The day after the eviction, I flew across the country to San Francisco. During the three-month anniversary day of action on November 17, I had to follow the sequence of events over Twitter and over the phone with friends. There were morning affinity group actions that tried to block streets and buildings around Wall Street, and a midday gathering at Union Square, and tens of thousands of people who marched across the Brooklyn Bridge while "WE ARE THE 99%" was projected onto the Verizon building overhead. I was absent from New York but present for a few days at Occupy Oakland, Occupy San Francisco, and Occupy Cal in Berkeley.

At Cal, the students had just undergone an eviction and some arrests. On the steps of Sproul Hall they held a General Assembly under a giant sign held up by black and white balloons that read "OUR SPACE." Occupy Oakland had already endured a couple of especially violent evictions, but on they occupied. I marched with thousands there against a school closure.

San Francisco still had an encampment at the end of Market Street, with lots of tents and pot smoking and dogs. A man at the information table was helpful and pointed me toward the GA already in progress and the kitchen where I could grab half a roll of bread to eat. The discussion in the assembly was principally about how to deal with the authorities, because the mayor had made certain demands regarding the Occupiers' behavior and how many inches there should be between tents. As had happened so many times when I was in New York and DC, a bottomless discussion unfolded about how to respond when the police came to clear the camp, which could happen at any time. The appointed liaison advocated that the group follow the mayor's "suggestions," as liaisons generally do, and others asked why they should care. Some even proposed moving the camp preemptively to another site, but that didn't pass consensus. Once again, a perfectly good opportunity for self-governance and self-organization seemed to be getting lost in reaction, in acting out of fear or out of hope that the powerful might be satisfied with good behavior. These sorts of discussions always happened, though there never seemed to be any point.

Police crackdowns were sweeping Occupy sites around the United States in those days, and all the horror stories made it hard to remember the euphoria with which the movement had begun in September. To return there, I'd sometimes rewatch Iva Radivojevic and Martyna Starosta's short online video *We the People Have Found Our Voice,* filmed during the General Assembly meeting at Liberty Plaza on the evening of September 27.

Over the din of voices, the roving focus of Radivojevic and Starosta's lens passes across nighttime scenes of Occupiers sleeping in bags, of drums, of eating, of hundreds gathered together in one conversation. Then we hear those words through the people's mic: "We the people. *We the people!* Have found our voice. *Have found our voice!*"

The thought of court-approved riot police demolishing encampments, juxtaposed with the Occupiers' constitutional cry of self-empowerment, suggests the extent to which Occupy Wall Street was posing legal, moral, strategic, and political dilemmas about the meaning of free speech. This tension birthed a minor growth industry, especially among legal working groups and activist lawyers at the various occupations, who sought to cast indefinite encampments as a right protected by the First Amendment. But legal justifications were not the only way to rationalize the kind of free speech the occupations represented. They may not even have been honest.

During the planning meetings for OWS, participants expected that setting up camp and sleeping in a public space would not be welcomed by law enforcement and that they would probably have to be arrested to make their point. Civil-disobedience trainings were held to teach people how to manage these engagements as safely as possible.

The prevailing feeling in those meetings at Tompkins Square Park was that they'd have to wait and see whether the occupation could "hold the space," as the planners put it. The outcome would depend on how many people showed up. If there were the twenty thousand people that *Adbusters* had called for, their chances of being able to stand their ground would be high. If it was only the sixty to a hundred people who had been coming to the meetings each week, the odds were slimmer. In other words, while legality was a concern, it wasn't the only one. Most planners hoped that the occupation would challenge the authorities' willingness to enforce the expected interpretation of the law.

Sure enough, on the night of September 17, the NYPD was ready to clear the park but got the order to stand down. That victory was not a legal one; it was tactical.

As the movement matured, it became common practice for Occupiers to make reference to the First Amendment's "right of the people peaceably to assemble" as they justified their actions to the public. The Declaration of the Occupation of New York City stated, "We have peaceably assembled here, as is our right." It further called on "the people of the world" to "exercise your right to peaceably assemble; occupy public space; create a process to address the problems we face, and generate solutions accessible to everyone." The Statement of Autonomy described the occupation as "a forum for peaceful assembly." Even as lawyers working on behalf of the movement were trying to establish the occupations' legal right to exist on First Amendment grounds, the constant police presence around Liberty Square suggested that they had none. The "right" that the OWS documents spoke of was more an aspiration than a reality.

Ultimately, the struggle didn't play out in court; Zuccotti Park remained occupied mostly thanks to extralegal pressures. When the city proposed to clean the park on October 14—effectively a forcible removal—thousands of people arrived before dawn to stand in the way. A month later, when the eviction finally came, it was as a surprise in the middle of the night. Again, the difference was tactical, not legal.

Mayor Bloomberg nevertheless defended his decision to clear the park in legal terms:

> No right is absolute and with every right comes responsibilities. The First Amendment gives every New Yorker the right to speak out—but it does not give anyone the right to sleep in a park or otherwise take it over to the exclusion of others—nor does it permit anyone in our society to live outside the law. There is no ambiguity in the law here—the First Amendment protects speech—it does not protect the use of tents and sleeping bags to take over a public space.

One can see the logic in this posture. In a perfect world, nobody would want freedom of speech to extend to the point that it overly obstructs the lives of others. We wouldn't, for instance, condone freelance roadblocks or preachers sermonizing in our backyards. (We might similarly object to free speech as grounds for unlimited and unaccountable political donations by those in Bloomberg's income bracket, but the Supreme Court doesn't agree.) While a violent nighttime raid was hardly the most humane way of enforcing the city's concern for law and order, its motivation was exactly what is to be expected of those in power. A New York City judge thought so, too, and upheld Bloomberg's eviction. Days later, the mayor affectionately referred to the NYPD as "my own army."

From the outset, Occupiers were intent on undermining that very law and order, protected by soldiers posing as police, rigged by and for corporate profits. Appeals to the law were therefore always at least partly a ruse. The call to occupy was meant to be adjudicated not so much by the legal right to free speech as by the one inscribed in conscience.

Occupy Wall Street found a new home on December 6—not a new park, plaza, or square, but a house. Just weeks after the movement's eviction from its encampment in the Financial District, a thousand Occupiers and locals braved the on-and-off rain to take a foreclosure tour of the East New York neighborhood in Brooklyn. It concluded with a celebratory block party as a once-homeless community organizer, together with his wife and two children, reclaimed a vacant home. It was one of many anti-foreclosure and anti-eviction actions taking place across the United States that day.

As the march through East New York passed by, I heard a local woman say, "This was a long time coming."

The afternoon was a reunion of familiar faces, of people who used to see one another daily at Liberty Square. But more visible than usual at Occupy Wall Street actions were collared clergy and elected officeholders. They were leading the marches and calling out the chants—all through the people's mic, of course. Staffers from unions and political groups that had once anticipated from afar what Occupy Wall Street would do were now busily coordinating the action. The day was also a launching pad for a new organization, Occupy Our Homes, hatched out of the Citizen Engagement Lab in Washington to coordinate housing actions nationwide.

During the march I heard grumbling among some who'd had bad experiences with this or that public figure or were suspicious of outside organizations as a whole. A City Council member might stand with the movement one day, but what will she expect from it on election day? And how far will a nonprofit go with civil disobedience before it starts to scare away funders? Without an encampment and needing to rely more on outside support, the now-homeless movement would increasingly have to face questions such as these.

As we approached the soon-to-be-reclaimed house at 702 Vermont Avenue, an Occupier ran past me with a drill in his hand. The march soon arrived, along with a team from Occupy Wall Street's Sanitation Working Group, to clean up inside the house. Outside, the occupation's old library and kitchen set up shop, along with teach-ins and a piñata. As long as the movement kept these myriad forms of direct action at its center, it still felt like a movement; it could still be Occupy. Politicians and nonprofits might join the cause not so much because they saw a comfortable opportunity for themselves but because they couldn't afford not to.

David DeGraw, who had led the ill-fated attempt to occupy Zuccotti Park back in June, told me that he was getting messages like the following from all over the country that day: "I just removed a newly changed lock off of a house to let the original owner back in. My Leatherman rules!"

As the action in East New York was winding down, I ran into Monica, the journalist from Spain. The Spaniards had been doing anti-eviction work almost since their movement began, helping out their comrades who were facing eviction. "As soon as a family got a notice that they were going to be evicted, we would all get ready to make an appointment for where we were supposed to go," she said, flashing a devious smile. "We showed up, hundreds of people, every single day that it was happening."

I asked whether this helped the Spanish movement grow after it was no longer occupying public squares. "Yeah—how can it not keep growing? I mean, this is for everybody," she said.

New communities and new organizations meant new complications. But if Occupiers could keep building momentum this way, by speaking and acting on behalf of people's actual needs, maybe they would always have a home somewhere.

Cracks in the Occupy Our Homes plan started becoming apparent when, after the first stop on the foreclosure tour, a woman came out of the supposedly foreclosed-upon house, screaming, "I live here! What are you doing?" The adaptations of East New York residents to the crises they faced were more than organizers had prepared for. The situation only became more complicated from there, as Rupert Murdoch was happy to report:

- "'They Took My Place!' Single Dad Trying to Take Back Home Occupied by OWS," *New York Post,* January 15, 2012
- "Occupy Squatters Finally Flushed from B'klyn Home," *New York Post,* April 29, 2012

The Occupiers were only trying to be helpful.

As Occupy Wall Street's three-month birthday party got going at midday on December 17, the mood was mixed—not unlike the mood with which, in a series of improvisations, the movement had begun in September. The party took us back to Duarte Square, the same spot along Canal Street where Occupiers had gone after the eviction a month earlier. At noon the square was full; lots of music, planning, anticipating, sign making, puppeteering, the works. Usual protest stuff. But uncertain.

The imperative for the day was to "Reoccupy"—specifically, to occupy the empty lot next to Duarte, the one owned by Trinity Wall Street. After a fifteen-day hunger strike, failed negotiations with Trinity, and even a letter from Desmond Tutu calling on the church to let the Occupiers use the lot (and another one that stated his opposition to trespassing), they were back. They wanted a place to build a new encampment, a new headquarters for the movement. Trinity, for its part, gave no sign that it would budge. Some weren't sure it made sense to keep pushing.

"When it comes to space, Trinity has been pretty good to us," one Occupier told me. The church had already allowed the movement to use its indoor spaces downtown for meetings, wifi, bathrooms, and breaks from the cold.

I repeated this to Father Paul Mayer, a Catholic priest—albeit formerly married and thus noncanonical—with silver hair under a black beret. The memoir manuscript he later gave me would relate that he had fled Nazi Germany as a child, a Jewish refugee, and as an adult entered a Benedictine monastery. His life of radicalism dated back to the civil rights movement and included just about every other movement since. Now he was a yoga teacher and had a busy schedule presiding at weddings. "No, Trinity hasn't done enough," he replied. When people are crying out in need, he thought, churches can't go on with business as usual.

As I stood waiting for the action against Trinity Church to begin, I asked Father Paul what he thought we Catholics would do if OWS were making a demand like this of us. It wasn't merely a theoretical question; the Catholic Church is the largest landholder in New York City, and Occupy groups in other places had already targeted Catholic sites (as well as saving a Catholic homeless shelter in Providence from closure). There were even rumors that New York priests had been warned from on high against supporting Occupy.

"We'd be worse," he replied.

In the days leading up to so-called D17, the demands upon Trinity's benevolence mounted, and the Occupiers' request sounded more desperate than strategic. *Trinity Church,* they seemed to be saying, *act like a church.*

Befitting the Advent season, during the week before, a little red tent appeared near the front door of Trinity with nativity figurines inside: Mary, Joseph, and animals praying over the baby Jesus. Behind them, an angel held a tiny cardboard sign:

LUKE 2:7
THERE WAS NO ROOM FOR THEM AT THE INN.

A larger, more legible sign on top added:

BUT WITH $10 billion in real estate, trinity has plenty of room. #occupyfaith
#ows

Out on the sidewalk, a collared clergyman from Occupy Faith sparred with a collared clergyman from Trinity. One spoke like a prophet, and the other like a politician. Artfully bringing their argument to a close, the one from Trinity insisted on leading the gathered protesters and reporters in prayer. The nativity tent was soon removed by a man from the church, accompanied by a police officer. One of the Occupiers on hunger strike, Diego Ibañez, stopped the man to shake his hand before letting him go about his work.

A 1910 polemical book by Ray Stannard Baker, *The Spiritual Unrest,* begins with "A Study of Trinity—the Richest Church in America," a reminder that Trinity Church has a long tradition of service to the 1 percent. Queen Anne's 1705 land grant to the church, which is the basis of its vast wealth, was originally meant for all "of the inhabitants of our said city of New York"—at least those of Anglican persuasion. Yet Trinity held on tightly to what it claimed as private property, which was precisely the legal language it would later use against the Occupiers. In the 1880s, Trinity resisted following a city law that required running water to be installed on every floor of its tenement buildings. During a prolonged court battle, Trinity argued its case against the city again on the basis of private property. Though it ultimately lost the case, the church managed to defy the law and keep running water from its poorest tenants for nearly a decade. The tenants' rents, meanwhile, went to support Trinity's cultural programming, as the rents of its corporate tenants do today.

Baker concludes:

> They are very far away from life, these poor [by which he means rich] men of Trinity; they have not felt the thrill and inspiration of the new time. By and by they will find it impossible to listen to beautiful and costly music, which they have not paid for, without thinking of the people of the tenements, and of the men and women and little children there who must work long hours at low wages, and out of whose small earnings comes the money to pay for that music.

Again: "They have not felt the thrill and inspiration of the new time."

The idea of going to Duarte Square actually dated back to well before the raid. It was to be a way of creating a new satellite occupation, one more orderly and disciplined than the free-for-all at Liberty. Plans spread quietly among OWS organizers. The expansion was slated to begin the very day that the city made its assault on Liberty Square, November 15. Those who had been planning the expansion to Duarte concluded that the timing of the eviction was not an accident—it was coordinated and preemptive. Thus they felt all the more defiant and determined, rhapsodizing to one another about space, space, space. The movement needed to decolonize space from capitalism and to open it up for people to come and fill and bring it to life. They weren't ready to give up on Duarte yet, and they lunged toward D17.

That day, I and a thousand others watched as George Packard, a retired Episcopal bishop dressed in a purple cassock, was the first to mount a makeshift wooden ladder over the fence around Trinity's lot. He climbed up and jumped down—a trespasser on the land of his own church. Father Paul soon followed, as did Sister Susan Wilcox, a Catholic nun, along with a handful of other clergy and several dozen Occupiers, who then called on others to join, to come in, to climb the fence and give them strength in numbers. Some did. But before long the police were in there with them too, arresting everyone inside, clergy and all.

As usual, the crowd reacted angrily against the police officers, shouting "Shame!" and "Who do you serve?" Some outside the fence began rocking it back and forth, trying to bring it down, and this caused the police to charge, to push people back, to clear the area around the perimeter. The protesters retreated to Duarte Square, where a dance party was already starting. As they did, they cried a chant from the occupation's uneasy first days: "This is just a practice!"

Walking around the fenced-in lot, I found Astra Taylor, a filmmaker and writer who had recently articulated her doubts about this action in the third *OWS-Inspired Gazette* put out by the literary magazine *n+1*. Despite a few moments of excitement as the ladder went up and the bishop went over, her fears were confirmed by what took place. "What is this going to look like?" she asked. To her mind, the movement wasn't strong enough to be targeting lukewarm friends like Trinity.

Astra and I watched as police took George Packard away in plastic cuffs and as protesters ran by, shouting. Recalling a silent vigil that followed the November 18 pepper-spray attack on Occupiers at UC Davis, she added, "Sometimes restraint is a good thing."

I could understand where she was coming from. I felt awkward about the whole thing myself. As publicity stunts go, there are more straightforwardly nefarious targets imaginable than a church whose holdings go to fund art and charity—even an especially well-endowed and Wall Street–friendly church like Trinity. For a movement that still struggled to make its goals clear to the public, putting the focus on a church like this, rather than on a bank or an appendage of government, could further muddy the message and provide kindling to critics. As a churchgoer, also, I was tempted to take the invasion personally, until remembering that being offended is part of what our religion calls on us to be. I meanwhile began to realize that what would appear to have been a strategic faux pas for the movement actually had a certain logic—even if it wasn't always very well articulated.

The movement had lent U.S. society so much energy, rage, and creativity. It jolted political imaginations; it broke a spell. But, after more than a month without Liberty Square as a home base, the movement had lost its center; meetings often went nowhere, and those who'd given themselves to activism full-time, without escape or enough rest, were showing signs of wear. As the initial euphoria of the movement wore off, its crisis was in no small part a spiritual one.

Now, it needed the very institutions that had been the mortar of complacency to follow suit, to take risks. It wasn't enough to simply applaud the movement and then keep keeping on. The unions needed to endanger their pacts with politicians and big business, to actually shut down the engines of an unjust economy. The nonprofits also needed to mobilize their resources and knowledge in more decisive ways. And the religious communities needed to offer their spaces, their networks, their moral leadership. Perhaps most of all what was needed was their wells of hope, their rubrics of ritual, their songs, their techniques of perseverance.

"Sanctuary for Assembly," read one of the banners that protesters carried on D17. "Assembly," of course, was the movement's insistence that it needed physical, in-person, public spaces to conduct its slow experiments in direct democracy. This was the method by which Occupy caught fire. It was familiar. Maybe it was even constitutional. But the word *sanctuary* was something new, with the first day of winter just a few days away. It was a cry, a plea, for the institutions that uphold the way of things to no longer stand aside but to join in making the rupture grow—to radicalize and to Occupy.

The stories have been rarely told in this way, but religious people and symbols and institutions played important roles in Occupy Wall Street since the beginning. The first thing I noticed as I biked into the Financial District on the morning of September 17 was a group of "Protest Chaplains" from Boston in their inaugural action. Standing at the corner of Wall Street and Broadway, facing Trinity Church, they were dressed in white robes, singing hymns and carrying a cardboard cross. Throughout the day, they were a favorite of reporters—a little more approachable than the average crusty protester, a little less weird than the LaRouchePAC choir.

That day's first substantial assembly took place at Bowling Green, on the steps of the National Museum of the American Indian, where people gathered to hear an impromptu sermon by Reverend Billy, the quasi-preacher performance artist. It was there, recall, that the decision was made to march a few blocks north to Zuccotti Park.

In the harrowing early days of the occupation, with Occupiers facing constant police intimidation, prayer and meditation and chanting and yoga were commonplace for those who wanted or needed them. Once, I remember, a few Occupiers spontaneously decided to take a silent walk to a nearby church to pray, which I joined, and on the way we discovered that each of us was carrying a rosary. For me, at least, this was unusual; I had only begun keeping one with me on the night of September 16, feeling the need for special protection for my new friends. The park, for many of us, became sacred ground. As Jeff Mangum sang during his visit in October, "God is a place where some holy spectacle lies."

Such ad hoc religion soon became more organized. For the holy day of Yom Kippur, hundreds of Jews held a Kol Nidre service across the street from Liberty Square. The following Sunday, Christians and allies marched from Judson Church at Washington Square Park to Liberty carrying a gold-painted replica of the *Charging Bull,* inscribed with "GREED" and "FALSE IDOL"; a photo of it appeared on the front page of the *Washington Post.* The clergy-driven Occupy Faith network became an interface between the leaderless movement and professional religious leaders. Around the country, they worked to serve the physical, psychological, and spiritual needs of Occupiers, while also launching campaigns of their own, including a "people's investigation" to study the human impact of the financial crisis. The Town Planning Working Group designated the northwest corner of the park "sacred space," and it became home to a jumble of statuettes, effigies, and shrines.

It was through a religious ritual, in fact, that the tents first went up at Liberty Square in mid-October. From the beginning, police had prevented anything resembling a tent from being erected. But Occupy Judaism coordinated with people in the Direct Action Working Group to raise a special tent in the park for Sukkot, the Festival of Booths, which Jews celebrate by building temporary structures. When police officers came to take it down, a crowd gathered around and a standoff ensued. The cops, spooked by the thought of disturbing a religious observance, backed down, and the sukkah stood.

"Tonight we're all Jews," cried a voice in the people's mic as it began to rain. "Build yourself a sukkah!" The park became a tent city, and so it would remain.

When eviction finally came, it was to churches around New York that Occupiers fled and took refuge. There they stayed, and met, and ate through the winter. This became an awkward arrangement in many cases, and eventually having pews full of homeless activists overtaxed the congregations' resources. But at just the moment when so much of the city turned its back on the movement, religious communities took Occupiers in.

There was potential for much more. The movement had yet to organize eviction-defense and anti-foreclosure actions on a mass scale, and religious communities could have been ideal platforms for doing so. Equipped with the right tools and strategies, church members might have rallied to save the homes of their fellow faithful that had been threatened with foreclosure—not merely on the basis of political ideology, but with the far more powerful motivation of looking out for one's own. Inventiveness, suspicion of authority, and autonomy are actually right in the mainstream of American religion, however cleverly disguised for the sake of bourgeois decency. Want to see mutual aid? Look no further than the nearest suburban megachurch, where members find free day care, credit unions, employment services, good works for the poor, support in times of crisis, and access to a political machine. Every time I set foot in one of these places, it strikes me how they put radicals to shame.

While religious communities have tended of late to be co-opted by the 1 percent, in the past they were engines that helped drive—as well as suppress—the early labor movement and women's suffrage, together with just about every other political movement with any major impact on U.S. history, from independence to civil rights. And how could they not? About 14 million people in the United States belonged to labor unions in 2011; closer to 120 million attended religious services regularly. Religion, by and large, is how Americans organize and imagine their way toward a different kind of world.

Besides, opposing predatory greed has special resonance in religious traditions, from the debt-forgiving Jubilee of the Hebrew scriptures, to the aid for those in need taught and practiced by Jesus of Nazareth, to the bans on usury in Islamic, Jewish, and Christian theology. An act may be civil disobedience by temporal standards, but to a higher standard, resisting oppression should be a basic requirement.

The night after S17, fresh out of jail, Father Paul and Sister Susan joined me and a lapsed cradle Catholic, a theologian, and a sociology student at a bar near Zuccotti Park for the first meeting of what would become Occupy Catholics. Already, a few of us had been finding one another online, testing out memes and slogans. Without our even asking, a friend in Baltimore sent block-cut logos she'd made for us to use: a single candle burning and a bird with a halo occupying a nest. Another in Virginia composed prayers for Occupy days of action, which we put on our website.

We came together in person with the common but still not-quite-clarified desire to create a group of Catholics who supported the movement, as well as to take what the movement was teaching us and bring it to our church. Maybe, someday, we could help Catholic churches respond better to Occupiers than Trinity did, and vice versa. The connection between Occupy and the calling to justice in our faith was so obvious that we couldn't ignore it. We needed this movement, and we knew that the movement no less needed us. I felt it needed me. Never more fully than that night had I crossed the line between observer and instigator.

When the occupation first began, I found that going to church was harder than it ever had been before. It wasn't because I believed less but because I believed more. Rather than just the priest's sermon, I wanted to hear from the old Caribbean women sitting around me, and from the children, and from the blind man in front. I wanted to know what *they* thought of the gospel reading. I'd sit in the pews and fantasize about mic-checking the liturgy, about setting the good news free. Occupy Catholics was a group of people who'd been having similar fantasies. Some hadn't gone to church for years, but when they got involved with Occupy, it reminded them of the social justice tradition they'd learned from nuns growing up. In Occupy Catholics, they found a community that was welcoming in ways Catholic churches themselves have so often failed to be. Some in the group even started going to Mass again. It became easier for me to keep going just by knowing that this group existed and that we weren't alone. On our subway rides back to Brooklyn from meetings at 60 Wall Street, Sister Susan would whisper to me about her latest experiments in mysticism. Together we conspired and commiserated.

We began by reaching out to laypeople, online and through the social justice ministries of local churches. We held an assembly at Maryhouse Catholic Worker, part of the organization Dorothy Day cofounded with Christian-anarchist principles to serve the poor and agitate for justice and peace. For months our group continued slowly growing, planning, and praying about how to encourage our church to understand Occupy's call. We brought buckets, water, and packages full of new socks to actions and washed the feet of dirty Occupiers. We arranged for organizers visiting from out of town to sleep in a Catholic school building. When the Vatican started cracking down on U.S. nuns for paying too much attention to the poor and for the "radical feminist themes" in their theology, we picketed in defense of the sisters and started a #radicalfeministthemes hashtag on Twitter. As the trial of those arrested on December 17 approached, we helped organize solidarity actions, and when it finally came, Occupy Catholics were sitting in the courtroom.

On Good Friday, the most solemn day of the Christian year, we stood in front of St. Patrick's Cathedral and sang, "Were you there when they crucified the poor?" against the bishops' silence on Paul Ryan's budget in Congress, poised to slash services upon which the 99 percent depends. "We love our church," we cried through the people's mic, "and right now the church needs to speak." So we did, and within weeks the bishops themselves actually voiced these concerns as well. When we returned to St. Patrick's again a few months later, we held an assembly out front on the sidewalk. We slept there that night, along with our handmade signs, our OWS allies, a homeless guitar player, and a cage of police barricades. Yet our favorite sign insisted, "WE ARE'NT PROTESTING WE ARE ADVERTISING LOVE."

An hour before the action at St. Patrick's on Good Friday, a member of Occupy Catholics read the following as part of the church peace groups' annual Way of the Cross procession, standing on a truck bed on Forty-Second Street, half a block from Times Square:

> In the early morning of last November 15, the legions of this principality swarmed the people's tent city in Liberty Square, a place that was real in every way that what surrounds us here is not. A month before, thousands of people had come to protect our tents, but this time most stood by in silence, letting our Zion fall. With helicopters overhead and shields, the legions kept those of us outside away from where they were beating our friends, destroying our library, our food, our medicine. All night we marched through the streets, not knowing where was safe, until finally, as sunrise approached, we collected ourselves under the looming buildings that had been issuing Pilate's justifications and decrees. We held a General Assembly. We heard each other's voices, and echoed them, and our fingers wiggled above our heads in unity. That night, by the thousands, we returned to Zion, and beheld it, destroyed and cleared and resanitized, made safe for the corporate kingdom. Again, we heard each other's voices, and echoed them, and our fingers wiggled above our heads in unity. The principality could evict our bodies and our tents, but it cannot evict our spirit.

Just when you think it's over, there is so much further to go. Back on October 5, a few minutes before the big march to Foley Square began, I ran into Daniel Berrigan and some of his fellow elder Jesuit priests at Liberty Square, all in plainclothes. This was a wonderful surprise. The plaza was overflowing with new faces that day, and I was happy to see some familiar ones. I generally have dinner with Dan and the others once a month, and I felt that I could stand a little taller than I ever had around them before because now my generation had its movement, too.

After I cajoled the Jesuits into posing for a picture with me, we were approached by a man who introduced himself as a TV reporter from Greece. He had a cameraman waiting a few paces behind him. I nodded a hello, but he went straight for Dan.

"Can I interview you?" he asked. "I'd like to show the world that it isn't just a bunch of radicals here."

What he was referring to, of course, was the widespread perception that this occupation was a mob of mischief-making kids, and surely an old man would prove otherwise. The reporter had no idea whom he was talking to, that this old man was possibly the most radical person on the whole plaza. Dan, ninety years old at the time, had spent a lifetime in resistance against war and empire. For his trouble, he served years in prison—not just a few hours in a holding cell.

Sacrifices were only starting to be made, and the powers that be had only begun to feel the least bit threatened, if they did at all. The protomovement still could have faded away with little harm done. To me, and to most of the young people there who were doing this for more or less the first time, these had been among the longest, best, and most sleep-deprived two-and-a-half weeks of our lives. But seeing Dan there put those weeks in perspective. They were just a practice.

PART THREE

WINTER TO SPRING

SIX | DIVERSITY OF TACTICS

#ACAB #BlackBloc #ChrisHedges #J28 #JustPlayin #M17 #M24
#Nonviolence #Occupy2012 #OccupyOakland #OccupyUnionSq
#PlusBrigades #StopAndFrisk

Protest in 2012 was no longer so legal as it had been in 2011. On New Year's Eve, President Obama signed into law the latest National Defense Authorization Act, which included new powers for indefinitely detaining U.S. citizens, and on March 9, he would sign the Federal Restricted Buildings and Grounds Improvement Act, which heightened penalties and limits for protests near Secret Service–protected people or events "of national significance." To add insult to injury, on April 9, the Supreme Court went on to rule that invasive strip searches were permissible for any arrest, no matter what the cause.

Occupy Wall Street, anyway, celebrated New Year's with a party in Zuccotti Park. Enraging the police, revelers pulled apart the barricades then surrounding the park and piled them in the center. The next morning, in the backseat of a car traveling from Kentucky to Ohio, I pulled up tweets from the night before on my phone.

@Newyorkist Barricades in a pile on ground inside Zuccotti. A few dozen for sure

@ProtestChaplain LOL from livefeed "Movement hungry . . . feed more barricades" http://www.ustream.tv/timcast #OWS #occupy2012

@NYC_GA Trusty #Ows medics tend to pepper spray victims

@jesselagreca This is one of the most beautiful things I've ever witnessed. People dancing on pile of barricades at liberty square #ows #occupy2012

It sounded like fun, though from so far away it was hard to see the point.

Marisa Holmes and I met for coffee on New Year's Day in the Columbus airport. Columbus was where she had grown up, and we were both passing through that day. We talked about where things were in Occupy the best we knew, and the madness of the Spokes Council. But we kept trailing off as we did, then forced ourselves to continue. There was none of the usual urgency. In the strict sterility of the airport we could've been mistaken for people of that world, rather than of the occupation and its world to come; we blended in, and it blended into us.

Occupy Fresno was one of the only twenty-four-hour occupations still standing in 2012, holding firmly on to a corner of Courthouse Park in the sleepy, conservative city of half a million near the exact center of California. They'd begun the occupation on October 9 and learned how to conduct an assembly by reading the minutes on the NYC General Assembly's website. By New Year's, they'd endured several police raids and a total of ninety-nine arrests—a number that, for its symbolic value as well as for their own sanity, they were trying not to make larger. The dozen or so Occupiers who turned out for the Fresno General Assembly the day after Christmas had the look of refugees from a lost civilization, hardy but a little nuts.

They stood around their lone remaining tent, in front of a piece of artwork depicting an octopus named "Mr. Greed," as they described to me their efforts in recent months to resist cuts to the education budget and fight the city ordinances against the homeless that were now being used against their occupation. They'd even had some wins in court. They prodded me for stories about Occupy Wall Street and other occupations I'd seen, and what stories I could offer seemed to be a much-needed reminder for them that they were more than just this, that they were part of a larger whole, that they were not alone.

Back in New York, drifting among the meetings under the columns of the 60 Wall Street atrium, I looked for familiar faces. One of them, who'd been around since the first planning meetings, seemed especially lost in euphoria. His hair was wild, shaved like a medieval monk in reverse, a halo of scalp. He talked on and on, about what I can't remember—some wild plan for some wild experience. It seemed like he was living faster, bigger, more than he could handle.

During an un-conference for the movement a few days before the new year, a blank time line was laid out across yards and yards of an enormous roll of paper, along with markers and pens. The collaborative result charted a long prehistory through the centuries of events that led to Occupy Wall Street, then the proximate causes, and then a sequence of the movement's highlights over the course of the fall. From "TODAY (YOU ARE HERE)" it set off on a projection into the months and years to come. Some highlights of that future, transcribed:

- 2012 is significant (Aliens!)
- 2012 is a huge Disappointment (No Aliens :( )
- * Miley Cyrus gets Stockholm syndrome *
- Stop public school closings
- National Student Strike
- Boycott all corporations who don't pay taxes. A17: TAX DAY
- May Day! what happens? whatever?
- BANK SHAREHOLDER MTG
- ¡REVOLUTION! (AFTER DETENTION CAMPS AND SHOOTING OF PROTESTERS)
- March on Washington—Resurrection City
- NYPD-BPA votes to support OWS and stand in solidarity against oppression in all forms.
- Occupy The National Elections
- OCCU-Π Apple
- Dec. 21st 2012: Mayan Calendar ends = Apocalypse
- 2015—End of Nation States
- 2025—No more corporate food!
- RESTORE BILL OF RIGHTS. NEW CONSTITUTION
- Death & Destruction
- Ⓐ LIVE

The die-hard OWS subculture had winnowed down over the winter. The troublemakers of Direct Action had held on and kept going with a vitality that most sub-subcultures in the movement had lost, so they were the ones setting the tone for the spring. That word, *spring*, had a magical sound to it in those months, like a spell that, if invoked enough times by enough people, would bring back what had been lost, and more. There really wasn't any reason to doubt that it would work; with the warm weather, people would come back, and they'd find an OWS more radical and thrilling than ever, and together they'd start bringing state and capital to their knees. It was only a matter of time.

Some of the specific projects being talked about in the winter months, for example:

- "Occupy the Courts" against the *Citizens United* decision
- "Occupy the Dream" and "Occupy 4 Jobs"—actions for Martin Luther King Jr. Day
- The destruction of Bank of America by midsummer
- A "national occupation" in DC starting in late March, led by the Freedom Plaza group
- A "national gathering" in Philadelphia for July 4 (*not* the one already called for by the "99% Declaration" people)
- Various ideas for reoccupying public space, at Zuccotti Park and elsewhere
- "Revolutionary Games"
- The organization of assemblies in neighborhoods across New York City
- Actions in Chicago in mid-May surrounding the NATO and G8 summits
- A May Day general strike

The return of what the winter had repressed began in earnest on January 28. Occupy Oakland set out on a quixotic attempt to occupy a vacant convention center, led by a phalanx of homemade plastic shields. Police fought them with tear gas, rubber bullets, and kettling. Some of the most widely circulated photos depicted the burning of an American flag that had been removed from Oakland's City Hall. Others showed the ironic "armchair radical" among the black-masked ranks at the front lines, behind an actual armchair. The next day, Occupy groups around the country took to the streets in solidarity marches. In New York, marchers raged through Greenwich Village at night, throwing bottles at police and turning against one another. Live-streamer Tim Pool had his smartphone grabbed, thrown to the ground, and broken by someone dressed in black.

Those who had been at the afternoon's Occupy Town Square gathering beforehand, at Washington Square Park, might have seen this coming. There, members of OWS's Direct Action Working Group held an impromptu teach-in on a section of grass about the idea of diversity of tactics. The villains of the presentation, perhaps even more so than actual police, were the "peace police"—those within the movement who might try to stop others who want to do things like damage property or fight back against cops. Insisting on nonviolent discipline was described as not only oppressive of one's comrades in general but probably sexist and racist as well.

The teach-in also revealed differences of understanding among participants. Several of them indicated that they thought Occupy was supposed to be a nonviolent movement. And to an extent this was true; just about every major document passed by the General Assembly included some mention of nonviolence, and other Occupy camps around the country had issued much more explicit commitments to nonviolence for themselves. But New York's Direct Action group, of course, had in its GA-passed guidelines a nod to respecting a diversity of tactics—which opened the floodgates. The organizers at the teach-in explained that in an Occupy Wall Street action, you couldn't assume that whatever you happen to consider to count as nonviolent discipline would be maintained by everyone in the movement. The big takeaway was that this was a good thing, that people should support one another's various styles of struggle. A lot of the movement's success, we were reminded, stemmed from creating a framework that smaller, autonomous subgroups could fill with their own creativity and instincts and their sense of what tactics were appropriate.

But some of those at the teach-in raised concerns. The prospect of small subgroups doing dangerous things on behalf of a larger crowd could make even fewer people feel safe while taking part in the movement. It could also mean that the media attention would be unduly monopolized by a rowdy minority, rather than the combined effect of a peaceful many.

When the afternoon teach-in was over, a small group of participants stuck around, many of whom seemed to be troubled by what they'd just heard— that Direct Action might not be planning marches and demonstrations with nonviolent discipline in mind. They felt that nonviolent action and destructive tactics don't mix.

You could feel the tension building and bursting and then building even more. A report I wrote about the teach-in won me such epithets as "dirtbag" and "racist, sexist asshole." February, it turned out, would be Violence vs. Nonviolence Month at OWS.

Let's be clear: Occupy Wall Street wasn't stashing weapons, or making bombs, or anything close. Direct Action wasn't making plans to injure anyone. Part of the problem was that talk of violence and nonviolence was still mainly in the abstract, pivoting on words that are hard to define and incidents of property destruction or in-the-moment reaction that most people had seen only filtered through the agendas of the media.

Since the earliest stages of the movement, those taking part were in a deadlock about the question of committing to nonviolence. At one of the planning meetings in Tompkins Square Park prior to September 17, one guy in dark sunglasses said, knowingly, "There is a danger of fetishizing nonviolence to the point that it becomes a dogma." In response, a young artist added a rather misleading "point of information": "Nonviolence just means not *initiating* violence." The question of nonviolence was tabled that night and thereafter. "This discussion is a complete waste of time," another speaker concluded. Property damage and self-defense thus remained on the table from the start, though few seemed especially inclined to practice them.

The Occupiers' main self-defense against police violence was with cameras, not physical force. There were no cases of intentional property destruction that I knew of in the early weeks. One reason for this was surely the Occupiers' common sense; when facing an essentially paramilitary institution like the NYPD—which nobody held to a standard of nonviolence, of course—there was little hope that a few hundred or a few thousand protesters could stand much of a chance by fighting. Another reason was the Occupiers' awareness that any act of violence would reflect on everyone in the movement, most of whose participants wouldn't want it. The Principles of Solidarity described Occupiers as "engaged in non-violent civil disobedience and building solidarity based on mutual respect, acceptance, and love," and the Declaration of the Occupation of New York City said, "We have peaceably assembled here, as is our right." When Naomi Klein spoke at Liberty Square on October 6, this was the part that earned the loudest applause:

> Something else this movement is doing right: You have committed yourselves to nonviolence. You have refused to give the media the images of broken windows and street fights it craves so desperately. And that tremendous discipline

has meant that, again and again, the story has been the disgraceful and unprovoked police brutality.

As winter came and the encampments were systematically destroyed, the movement's outdoor presence hit a lull. The conventional wisdom came to be that Occupy might be dying out for good. The exception—which, for some, proved the rule—was what happened in Oakland on January 28. On a national conference call after that, one concerned voice said, "The diversity-of-tactics message in New York City is spreading very, very quickly—and it's a sexy message, and we need to counter it."

Enter Chris Hedges, the battle-worn war reporter-turned-apocalyptic polemicist, a supporter of Occupy since the beginning. On February 6, at the news website *Truthdig,* he published an article called "The Cancer in Occupy," which immediately began making the rounds on organizers' e-mail lists. "Chris Hedges nails it," said the subject line of one long-running thread. The article was a broadside against "Black Bloc anarchists," whom Hedges perceived to be a disease at the fringes of the movement threatening to destroy it with an anti-agenda of adolescent violence and criminality. His article resonated with a lot of people in the movement, who echoed his denunciations to their comrades. Others denounced the ignorance he displayed about anarchist culture, repeating again and again the semantic point that a black bloc is not an ideology or a sect but a tactic that some people sometimes choose to employ—dressing in all black, that is, to mask their identity while taking coordinated and risky action at a protest. Hedges's words conjured the fearful specter of anarchists in the shadows. His polemic seemed to hark back to a century earlier when, at Ellis Island, "Whether an Anarchist?" was among the twenty-nine questions asked in order to weed through new arrivals, right after "Whether a Polygamist?"

The effect in OWS's Direct Action Working Group, which had lately been the movement's most vibrant quarter, was catastrophic. "Chris Hedges really screwed us," said Chris Longenecker, who had been with Direct Action since day one. "It's anarchists that are driving this movement." So many of OWS's most cherished institutions—the general assemblies, the leaderless structure, the diversity of tactics—had roots in anarchism and were being maintained by anarchists who'd been practicing them long before the movement began. They included both pacifists and insurrectionists. Within a few days of

Hedges's article, there was a proposal at the General Assembly to create an anarchist caucus, a measure usually reserved for marginalized identity groups. It failed to reach consensus. Some people quit the movement in frustration, others in tears. To Sandy Nurse from Direct Action, it felt like a "witch hunt" against her friends. "A kind of hysteria happened," she said.

Suzahn Ebrahimian, who had been one of the organizers of the January 29 teach-in I attended, was twenty-three years old, with short, dark hair and dimples when she smiled. She was starting to think seriously about leaving OWS for good. "I woke up the morning of September 18 and felt so invested and got right to work," she said. "I literally changed my entire life—like almost everybody else who was there that day. To feel pushed out like this is so crappy."

Some weeks after the teach-in, I sat with Suzahn and Sparrow Ingersoll on a bench back in Washington Square Park. It was a delicate meeting; the present crisis placed me and the two of them in allegedly opposing camps, and we each overacted our roles. They schemed about turning over cars, and I played the aloof pacifist. But actually we got along fine, and it wasn't long before Suzahn was telling me where she learned how to do hard-locks, a trick in which activists attach themselves to one another as part of a blockade.

> Greenpeace. A totally nonviolent organization—which was my first official foray into radicalism. It's definitely not where I stopped. At this point, I've moved beyond NGOs completely, and I've felt that their perception of nonviolence was in order to protect their corporate image, which turned me off a lot.

She told me about her grandmother's funeral in Iran, which she and her father couldn't attend because of the Patriot Act and the saber-rattling of governments. Over the years, experiences like these pushed her further and further.

"And you identify as an anarchist?" I asked.

> I guess so. That's really complicated for me, though. My personal assessment is that I have to identify as an anarchist. Based on my existence in society as is, if I don't want to identify with anything that's presented to me, I have to call myself the "anti," which isn't necessarily the position that I want to be in. I would like to say that I am just a human being and that I require the same things every other human being requires. But I guess that because of the world we live in, I have to say "anarchist."

In response to Hedges, Suzahn wrote a note to her friends on Facebook, "An open letter from a human being":

You are coercing me into a box and then are surprised, hurt, and angered when the only thing I can think to do is to reject, resist, and break free from it (by destroying it or otherwise).

It ended, "p.s. fuck off, chris hedges."

But Hedges wouldn't apologize for his article. "It did what I wanted it to do, which is trigger the discussion," he told me. "I'm not trying to make friends." At a meeting a year later, I heard him say in passing, "It might surprise some people, but I consider myself almost an anarchist."

Said at the meeting of a feminist subgroup of Direct Action in January:

- A proposal for "a fem black bloc," "for being militant in the streets"
- "I want us to challenge what it means to be badass"—"find ways of doing direct action without it being so fucking macho."
- January 17 glitter-bombing action
- "This is a gendered class war."
- May Day women's strike
- Call to organize women workers at Walmart
- "We have to be really careful how we do actions involving rapists."
- In the media, "It's usually just men confronting the police."
- A repertoire of songs, rather than just chants
- "I have lots of self-defense hook-ups."

From its inception, OWS included people with many different long-tended visions of what resistance is supposed to look like—orderly or chaotic, peaceful or insurrectionary—and as the talk about violence continued, these latent tensions bubbled over into it.

During Occupy marches, one often heard participants muttering frustrations under their breath, seemingly with newsreels of Gandhi or King in mind: amid all the shouting and anger, they expressed a longing for more discipline, more grace. The conventional logic of nonviolent action is to heighten the contrast between the decorum of the protesters and the violence of the state, to force a dilemma upon those in power by winning public support and causing defections. Ruckus protests won't play well in Peoria. Fox News could get away with calling the events in Oakland on

January 28 a "riot," presumably inclining the couch potatoes at home to side with the cops.

Mixed in with calls for nonviolence, too, were concerns about safety, especially for children and people who couldn't afford a run-in with the police. These would have to be addressed for the movement to grow, but they're really a separate matter. Nonviolence doesn't equal safety, though ideally it does mean facing arrest, or worse, on one's own terms. Perhaps the movement's most Gandhian moment so far was the arrest of Pancho Ramos Stierle—as he sat in silent meditation, smiling—during the November 14 raid on Occupy Oakland. An undocumented Bay Area resident from Mexico (who had left his astrophysics PhD program at Berkeley because of the university's involvement in nuclear weapons), he knowingly faced deportation, at least until tens of thousands of people successfully petitioned for his release.

Those who'd been articulating the diversity-of-tactics framework tended to be less concerned with what would play well in Peoria than, say, in Harlem—in communities suffering most from the abuses of the system. They were tired of hearing the Egyptian revolution being talked about as "nonviolent" when protesters there burned police stations and cleared Mubarak's goons from the streets of Cairo by hurling rocks. They told stories of being assaulted by self-appointed peace police at past protests and argued that people in the movement should care more about being nonviolent toward one another than toward the police or a Starbucks window. They felt that focusing too much on whether a tactic is nonviolent would result in losing sight of whether it is strategic, while sanitizing the movement and keeping it from endangering the power of the 1 percent. In any case, most of them agreed that black blocs didn't make sense at Occupy Wall Street for the time being.

It was often defenders of diversity of tactics like Suzahn, actually, who had been training fellow Occupiers in nonviolent civil disobedience. For them, the whole opposition between violence and nonviolence seemed contrived to divide the movement—especially ever since Oakland mayor Jean Quan demanded that OWS denounce Occupy Oakland's behavior. "This is a really common tactic: bash the anarchists, or blame outside agitators," Suzahn said. "It just takes a very cursory look at the history of social justice movements that have been totally cleaved apart by the state to understand what's happening now."

What people on all sides seemed to fear most was not being able to trust one another—trust that a rock-throwing black bloc wouldn't come swooping in on a silent vigil or trust that nobody would be turned in for breaking the lock on a foreclosed home or slashing the tires of a police car. Trust among various factions takes planning and relying on one another's strengths. When there's even a little bit of coordination and synergy, you get scenes like what I experienced on November 19 in Oakland. That day, a black-clad group was at the head of a march from a rally for public education to a closed-off vacant park. Before the police could mobilize to stop them, those in black cut through the chain-link fence surrounding the park, and the rest of the marchers poured in. Minutes later, the entire fence had been neatly rolled up. As police watched from its edges, the empty park became a festival.

Really, there was no better display of what diversity of tactics meant for Occupy Wall Street than the variety of responses to the events in Oakland in late January. Every OWS meeting one went to became a discussion about violence and nonviolence and Chris Hedges. I sent out a flurry of e-mails to organizers to see what they thought might be done. Most of them were already up to something, each confronting the problem in a different way.

InterOccupy, the movement's new conference call network, hosted a series of national strategy conversations. Civil rights movement veterans were being invited to hold teach-ins. A group of unions and political organizations, from the Service Employees International Union to MoveOn.org, soon promised that "100,000 Americans will train for nonviolent direct action" in a "99% Spring."

Even while the Internet was still fanning Hedges's flame, members of Direct Action held a cathartic meeting about concepts like solidarity and diversity of tactics. "It was really important to get those conversations off an e-mail thread and into a room," said Sandy Nurse. Face-to-face, the Gandhians and the insurrectionists found they had more in common than they thought; they might not have the same aesthetics, but they could probably agree on strategies, and they could listen.

"The problem is not whether or not someone will throw a bottle—because somebody's gonna do that—but how you deal with it," one person said. "We have to learn how to talk to each other," another concluded. "It probably isn't the debate about violence or nonviolence that will break up the movement; it's how we talk to each other." At the end of the evening, hearts appeared around the room, made with index fingers curled and joined at the top and thumbs joined at the bottom.

The response to the crisis that really caught my attention, though, was the clown army.

At a semisecret meeting in the basement of Judson Memorial Church one Saturday night in February, a couple dozen of the busiest Occupy Wall Street organizers sit in a circle of folding chairs. Calling the group to order is Yates McKee, an art critic with aviator glasses and big sneakers. His hair, which he usually wears up, drapes down past his shoulders. This seems especially appropriate considering his choice to open the proceedings by reading from the Book of Matthew: turn the other cheek, love your enemies, pray for those who persecute you.

"A lot of people would agree that this movement is in crisis," he says. "We've had these discussions about so-called diversity of tactics, which I think makes a lot of people very uncomfortable." True. Just hearing those words puts the room on edge.

"I think right now is the moment to look to great men of history," Yates continues imperiously, listing the men he has in mind: Jesus Christ, Gandhi, and Martin Luther King. "They all show us that the way to build a popular revolutionary movement is through love, through harmony, and through the strength of nonviolence."

Natasha Singh, sitting on the other side of the circle, is furious. She interrupts: "I don't think this is the place to talk about diversity of tactics. Seriously."

His authority as facilitator challenged, Yates scolds her back: "The way you're talking right now is going to derail the movement." Sandy Nurse, who is sitting on the other side of me, gets up to storm out.

"Clown check!" cries a voice from the hall. "Clown check!" Out prances a figure in a full-body orange spandex suit, an orange cape, and a straw sombrero topped with two orange balloons and orange streamers. It is barely recognizable as Austin Guest, also part of Direct Action. Behind him comes a gang of clowns dancing and singing and shooting Silly String, with plus signs painted on their cheeks. Yates winds up with three cream pies in his face. Andy Bichlbaum—one of the Yes Men, a duo of activist pranksters, wearing a red pig-tailed wig—gets me with one too. (Yates and Natasha are in on it; Sandy and I aren't.) Then, with clown games and some Direct Action–themed rounds of Scattergories, the meeting begins in earnest.

The urge for a clown army first came from a frustration with the same old Occupy tactics that Natasha had been feeling for a while. "The marches were pointless," she said. Then, just after the January 28 incident in Oakland, her collaborator, Amin Husain, returned from a World Social Forum meeting in Brazil, where he'd learned about the Chilean student movement's creativity in the streets. He wanted to bring some of that home. The two of them recruited others and settled on a name: the Plus Brigades. They scoured photographs of movements past at the New York Public Library and scattered them through the next issue of *Tidal,* which they edited. The goal, said Amin, was "addition and supplement rather than negation, opposition and subtraction." Thus their answer to all the worry about black blocs: create other kinds of blocs of your own. "Plus it up," they'd say.

Amin, who with Natasha had been involved since the very earliest planning meetings, was part of the First Intifada as a teenager in the West Bank. After moving to the United States he became a corporate lawyer and then eventually quit. He had a strong build and a deep voice and usually wore an army-style cap. Whether speaking to a group around a dinner table or to an assembly of a thousand, his speeches reframed questions, or turned words upside down, or otherwise sought to put listeners in a more revolutionary plane of space and time. He enunciated every syllable and inflected them with pauses. Natasha, on the other hand, the daughter of an Indian general, was funny and fierce and spoke in her thick accent at a furious pace. Amin and Natasha were filmmakers—artists. The movement's problem, they thought, wasn't a matter of violence or nonviolence; it was a lack of imagination. There was too small a repertoire.

"Don't negate the things you don't like," explained Austin at that inaugural Plus Brigades meeting in the church basement. "Add the things you do, so we can get a *real* diversity of tactics." People started pitching ideas, like a Song & Dance Brigade, a Naked Bike Bloc, a Donut Brigade, a Gender-Bending Brigade, water balloon fights, TV smashing, a Male Prostitution on Wall Street Brigade ("We will do anything for money!"), and more. Each brigade was meant to be radical, sensational, and accessible, providing ways for new people to get involved in the movement and, as Natasha liked to say, "to do a ninja on the media."

The Plus Brigades debuted on Leap Day, February 29, during a rainy Midtown protest against several choice corporate skyscrapers. The Brigadiers gave reporters pictures of men in pantless business suits and a dancing clown in handcuffs. Within a few weeks of regular Plus Brigades rehearsals, each time drawing more people from Direct Action and the movement as a whole, nobody was arguing about violence anymore. Neither side had won; they'd both been plussed. And all this served another purpose, too.

One night, after running through the rain on Fourteenth Street, then seeking cover under the awning of Party City and ogling the aisles of clown supplies, I sat down for big bowls of pho with Amin, Natasha, Austin, and Yates. The conversation turned subdued, tinged with post-traumatic stress. Yates mumbled about "evildoers" on the fringes of the movement who were planning to do it in—ones worse than Chris Hedges had imagined. Austin talked about spending hours sitting in a jail cell and then having to organize a big demonstration the next day. Amin watched his father die in December and hadn't had time to mourn. They were out of money. None of them seemed to have come up for air since the movement began.

"We all need to do some healing," said Austin. If that meant wearing orange spandex and face paint while blockading a bank, so be it.

The political was getting more and more personal. At one of the discussions on violence and nonviolence hosted by the Think Tank, a working group devoted to fostering discussion, someone observed, "I feel like Occupy Wall Street is a lot like AA. For many reasons." It's true that one woman, who with her husband was homeless before and after living in Liberty Square, told me that she had actually kicked her hard-drug habit there. But people gave themselves to the movement to escape all sorts of things.

A guy I knew before any of this, a friend of an old roommate, was a video producer who didn't quite know why he was. The last time I saw him before Occupy, I think, was at a party supporting Obama's first presidential campaign. But then he appeared at the General Assembly or at this or that meeting, gradually assuming visible roles and being a voice and a presence. He talked the talk. He stopped producing videos. He made things happen. He got new tattoos.

I'd actually known Austin before, too, when some of our friends had been dating each other a few years earlier. Back then, he struck me as remarkably and inexplicably crazy, with energy and enthusiasm bigger than the ordinary pace of life. But not the pace of Occupy. There, in meetings and marches and wherever movement-time took him, his natural excess flourished—which was amazing, although like all excess it was also too much. Our old mutual friends, when I found several of them together in a bar, felt angry at him and abandoned.

And then there were stories of those who, sometime over the course of the winter, had fallen in love with a fellow Occupier and nearly left their spouses and kids as a result. E-mails arrived periodically, and frantically, making clear that this love was less about the other person as such than about the movement, which the other might have come to personify. It was always a little hard to tell who was really who, or what.

Jonah Bossewitch, the compiler of a pamphlet for the movement about radical mental health, described the situation to me this way:

> Our country has been in a social recession far longer than the financial one. It will take a long time to unlearn our self-defeating habits and embrace languages of compassion and liberation, instead of mistrust and fear. First, we need to believe in the future—vividly imagine it, talk about it, and manifest it. This movement, and activism in general, is notorious for its cycles of energetic bursts of creativity, followed by a crash. We have to be self-aware of these patterns and take better care of ourselves and each other. We need to be more honest with ourselves about what we can tackle, learn how to recognize our triggers, learn how to say no, and learn how and when to bottom-line, delegate, and collaborate. We especially need to avoid replicating habits of exploitation and oppression in our day-to-day interactions. We need to actively build our support networks when we are well and create wellness plans that our friends can use to help support us when we aren't. But, mostly, we need to relearn how to breathe, share, and love.

The public sympathy and the fawning reporters and the constant arrival of newcomers from the fall were gone. Most everyone in the movement had some reason to be frustrated or angry. Those who stuck around were determined to do their healing in the streets; even more than before, actions seemed designed for those taking part rather than for anyone else or any cause.

Weekly "Spring Training" marches started converging each Friday afternoon on Wall Street to replace the closing bell with a choreographed "people's gong" outside. The marches practiced new moves that had been coming out of the Plus Brigades' meetings, like "going civilian" by splitting up and regrouping elsewhere or momentarily "melting" together into the ground. The favorite chant was no longer "We! Are! The 99 percent!" but a crescendo of "A! Anti! Anticapitalista!" At the very least, if things got boring, marchers could break into a chorus of screaming "Fuck Monsanto!" as loud as they could, referring to the hated GMO-producing megacorporation. It was play, and anticipation, and practice for the spring that would inevitably come.

I had my first insurrectionary dream in early March. Aided by bizarre technology, I was part of a group working to disassemble the city, destroy the bridges, tear the thing apart—even firing missiles. There was a certain beauty to it. A few days later, I dreamed that Occupiers were trying to rent out occupied spaces for wedding parties.

Occupy Wall Street celebrated its six-month anniversary on March 17 in Zuccotti Park with ritual and repetition, a fast-forward replay of the previous fall: reoccupation, carnival, violent eviction, defiance. The big reunion began with a morning chalk-in for families and an early afternoon march around the Financial District. (Actually, there was a choice between two marches: one silent and one rowdy.) As re-renamed Liberty Square—or Plaza or Park—became full once again with hundreds of people, the hardy organizers who had spent the winter in meetings and arguments were drowned out again by joiners, curious visitors, drummers, and reporters. A twenty-four-hour reoccupation was called for, and the Plus Brigades crew led the rehearsal of new defensive formations en masse. People danced, chanted, and held an assembly. Their numbers swelled to close to a thousand when marches from the nearby Left Forum conference joined later in the evening. (I had to leave the reoccupation for a few hours to speak on a panel there about occupations.) The dull gray plaza came alive again. Liberty was back.

The police also seemed to be in a particularly nasty mood. There were arrests peppered throughout the afternoon, and they chased away a St. Patrick's Day procession that tried to stop by the plaza for a visit. As I stood in a line facing a line of cops, one of them snarled to me, "You haven't seen guys like us yet."

At around 10 P.M., tents and tarps appeared in the park. They were basically symbolic: glowing orange camping tents, marked with slogans and held on poles high in the air above the crowd. A giant yellow-and-black "OCCUPY WALL STREET" banner lined the north perimeter. Symbolic defenses went up too: the by-then-ubiquitous yellow caution tape marked "OCCUPY" and a similarly marked roll of orange netting—the same stuff that police had used before to surround and trap marches. Facing the police who were massing along Broadway, a line of Occupiers held up the orange net across Liberty's eastern end.

At last the order came, and at about 10:30 hundreds of police and Brookfield private security officers poured into the park—pushing, tearing, kicking. They seemed intent on clearing people out while minimizing arrest numbers, but dozens of Occupiers were beaten and arrested for staying put, then taken away in police wagons and a repurposed city bus. Not until twenty minutes later did ambulances arrive for the injured, including one woman who appeared to be suffering a seizure. A glass bottle flew over my head from behind and shattered near where some cops were standing, and the cops lunged into the crowd, pushing indiscriminately with their clubs.

Some Occupiers remained near Zuccotti, but others set out on a spontaneous march northward, throwing bags full of trash into the street as they were chased by police, with arrests and skirmishes all along the way. I followed the trail of broken trash bags and caught up with them just above Houston. There, what may have been Occupy Wall Street's first broken window came when a cop smashed a street medic's head against a glass door. As they proceeded up on Broadway, marchers belted out an old freedom song with an anarcho-twist:

> We shall smash the sta-a-ate!
> We shall smash the sta-a-ate!
> We shall smash the sta-a-ate! Someday-ay-ay!
> O-oh, deep in my heart,
> I do believe, we shall smash the state someday.

The march soon arrived at Union Square, holding up the "OCCUPY WALL STREET" banner on the square's main steps and facing several dozen police officers standing shoulder to shoulder. The crowd began to dissipate as the early morning wore on, but not entirely. The march's destination became an unplanned-for occupation.

Familiar feelings, all over again: courage, awe, exuberance, rage, sadness, pain, fatigue. The city succeeded once again if its purpose was to keep the protesters' attention on the police, rather than, for instance, on the financial institutions for which Mayor Bloomberg continually assured his support. The Occupiers succeeded if their purpose was to celebrate, reenact, and make a blip in the media. For all the joy of it, the nighttime police riot forced a recognition upon those in Direct Action who'd been holding out hope against hope: Liberty Square would not be coming back.

Unexpectedly to just about everyone, the occupation at Union Square held. Occupiers were sleeping there, mixed in with the usual nighttime population of loiterers and the homeless. During the day, info tables and food and meetings and teach-ins appeared. Each night, there would be a round of "eviction theater" as the cops tried to push Occupiers off Union Square's steps. The laboratory of the Plus Brigades meant there was a plentiful supply of activities for each little eviction. One night, when the cops had their riot gear on and barricades were arranged around the steps, Occupiers gathered in huddles and then, all of a sudden, charged the barricades at full speed, only to collapse right in front of them into a cuddle puddle. On another night the game was Hide and Seek, and on another it was a "people's rap battle" against the cops. Donuts were dangled in front officers' faces to chants like "Treat us like animals, we'll treat you like pigs!" and "Show me what a donut looks like! This is what a donut looks like!" and so on.

After one evening of eviction theater, in the subway station under Union Square, I waited for my train by a cop who was guarding the nearly empty platform. We talked about the reasons we were each there that night, playing our respective roles. She said that there have to be rules and order. If there weren't, society would fall apart. Chaos. When I asked why the cops weren't so violent down in DC, she chalked it up to a North-South divide. Anyway, she said, as if by rote, most of the trouble from both cops and protesters was caused by just a few bad apples. Right.

It was clear, anyway, that her uniform had kept her from the bliss—of Zuccotti, of Liberty, of society momentarily fallen apart, of the good stuff that chaos can bring.

For a lot of young white Occupiers in New York City particularly, getting habitually beaten up by police was a learning experience. With time they started realizing that this violence was a glimpse of what people in communities of color experience on a regular basis—when a hundred cameras aren't up, when the whole world isn't watching. Through Occupy Wall

Street, many thousands of people learned for the first time about the NYPD's stop-and-frisk policy, by which New Yorkers who look a certain way and live in certain places are systematically subjected to searches by police, as if they are guilty until proven innocent, as if they are less free than others to walk the streets. When you and your friends have experienced a taste of that criminalization while trying to protest banks and trying to march in the streets, the term *police state* starts to sound a whole lot less like an exaggeration.

A few nights after the six-month-anniversary extravaganza, on March 21, a "Million Hoodie March" expressed outrage at the fact that the killer of a black teenager in Florida, Trayvon Martin, had yet to be arrested or charged because of the state's corporate-sponsored "Stand Your Ground" law. (Martin died wearing a hoodie.) The march began with a rally at Union Square, which was still very much under occupation and became flooded with thousands of people from across the city, mostly people of color sick of not being treated equally under the law.

Soon, after dark, the rally poured into the streets, and in the process of evading containment by police the resulting march broke into two—one heading up to Times Square, the other heading down to Wall Street. Both made it off the sidewalks and into the streets, swerving around and overrunning the cops trying to herd them. The *Charging Bull* statue downtown, which had been barricaded and guarded twenty-four hours a day since the night before Occupy Wall Street began, was surrounded by marchers, who overwhelmed its defenses long enough to climb atop it in momentary conquest. Just like the Troy Davis march, which had come down from Union Square in the first days of the occupation at Liberty, this was a picture of what could happen if the movement learned how to mobilize the most aggrieved people of New York, those who had really and truly suffered enough, uniting the communities that always had been divided by culture and background and color and the scramble to get to the top of the capitalist dung heap. All of this and more.

In that spirit, then, Occupiers began planning a march for the following Saturday afternoon—M24—a march against police brutality throughout the city and the repression of OWS. It was advertised to be decidedly not a family-friendly march, but a "fuck the police" march, even if under the rather cheerful new slogan "Let Freedom Spring." Chris Longenecker, who was helping to organize it with Direct Action, predicted that this was "likely to be our biggest action since November."

It wasn't. The unions and community organizations and Trayvon Martin mourners who were expected to turn out their ranks didn't, so the result was a couple hundred mostly white Occupy regulars and a city councilman trying to take the lead. They carried a banner at the front that said "ACAB"—All Cops Are Bastards—and chanted, "From New York to Greece, fuck the police!" The marchers made their way from Zuccotti Park toward Union Square, getting caught up in the hidden, narrow streets of SoHo trying to evade the almost equal number of cops, only to be tackled and arrested in front of tourists having lunch at sidewalk cafés. Most of the time, though, as the march passed through some of the city's whitest and wealthiest quarters, those least harmed by the police department's racist practices, the marchers were the ones shouting as if crazed, while the cops—many of whom were black or brown themselves—walked alongside calmly in formation, taking the insults hurled against them. The marchers, remarkably, made the cops look good. The only thing that kept M24 from being utterly miserable, as far as I could tell, was the brigade that had dressed their bicycles up like police scooters, and dressed themselves up like officers, and put on skits about beating up protesters for fun.

What kind of revolution could have possibly come out of this, this tango with cops, this playful, puppeteer chaos, this asymmetric warfare? As time went on, the movement was getting smaller and smaller, tighter-knit, and more militant in its slogans while the violence used against it got uglier and uglier. There were overpowering, magnificent exceptions, which mattered infinitely, but nevertheless much of the time on marches when I heard "This is what democracy looks like!" or "Whose streets? Our streets!" I found myself hoping that what was being chanted wasn't literally true.

Another Occupy action took place on March 24, a few hours later, in front of the United Nations complex. It began with a small pack of typical OWS protesters, this time with messages mostly related to climate change etched on their signs. The police surrounded them as usual. But they were only a decoy. The real trouble was caused by a few people from the Disrupt Dirty Power affinity group who, while dressed in business attire, were busily setting up tents marked with corporate logos on the lawn at United Nations Plaza. "Bloomberg is in our pocket!" they cried as they were arrested. "We control everything!" Apparently taken in by their appearance, the police treated the "mock-upiers" gently. One officer said to the arrestees in the van, "I'm sorry we had to arrest you today. We support what you are doing."

The night of the Million Hoodie March, there was a meeting in the basement of a union office on Fourteenth Street—sparsely attended by maybe thirty people because of the action in the streets. The focus of it was immigrant solidarity, and, despite occasional interruptions from Occupiers rushing downstairs to report on what was happening outside, it went on as planned. Among those in the conversation were workers from Hot & Crusty, a bakery chain, whom Occupiers were supporting in what would be a successful effort to win a labor dispute by occupying a store. The festival up in the streets focused the minds of those in the basement on the dangers that many undocumented immigrants had come to associate with the Occupy movement. "I would like to see us really put the Occupy values to the test and be really inclusive," said one immigrant worker activist. He continued:

> If you do a DA, a direct action, and there are undocumented folks around you, they could get bagged. That's huge, right? The repercussions are just humongous. They don't just put you on a plane or wait for you to pack your bags. Today, they'll detain you for a year, or two. You're a prisoner.

"When they hold people like us," added a gray-bearded Jamaican man wearing a "Stop Stop and Frisk" button, "we get dealt with with exile."

An organizer briefed the Occupiers on why the movement needed to concern itself with immigrants like himself, on how the same corporate elite that runs Wall Street drives them from their home countries to find abusive, illegal work in the United States. "It doesn't matter where you're from anymore, because this has become a global imperialist power now that is taking over," he said. "Occupy Wall Street is no longer a United States movement; it is a global movement, and immigrants are global citizens." Through tears, a college student involved in the fight for the DREAM Act told her story of being brought north from Mexico as a child by her parents fleeing the poverty wrought by NAFTA and being unable to return for fear of never coming back to the United States. She once visited the border and saw the goods and money passing back and forth—inanimate, profit-making things—yet she couldn't cross it herself. Just by being in this country, she and the others had been doing direct action with their whole lives.

"We go through the struggle every single day," said another of the undocumented organizers. "We crossed the border without having someone to help us. I think it's about being cautious and realizing that there will be repercussions. We know the action that we have to take, because we're suffering."

Behold, the fecundity of movements. The students who rose up in the 1960s didn't manage to halt the Vietnam War, but out of the attempt to do so arose second-wave feminism, black power, and gay rights. Now, a movement premised on an imperative to occupy Wall Street had not yet even slept on that street itself and had lost its park, but it meanwhile informed whole swaths of oblivious New Yorkers about the humiliation that many of their neighbors in the city are experiencing daily. On Fathers' Day, when organizations based in the black community led a march against stop and frisk from Harlem to the mayor's mansion, they made it a solemn and silent one; Occupiers joined, helping draw the attention of many others. The *New York Times* published editorials against the policy, and the governor stepped in. The number of stops around the city started to plummet.

Everywhere Occupy went, it aimed for Wall Street but became mired in the many roads that lead there: debt, foreclosure, homelessness, food access, environmental crises, school closures, police brutality, mass incarceration. No single strategy could fight them all, and no one tactic could suit everyone willing to try. This movement was turning out to be a lot more complicated than anyone could have thought but also a lot more necessary and, actually, a lot truer to its original calling to occupy Wall Street than if it had restricted itself to doing only that.

SEVEN | CRAZY EYES

#Call2create #CorporateGreed #GeneralStrike
#Imagine #m1nyc #m1gs #MayDay #SleepfulProtest
#StrikeEverywhere #WeArtThe99

"I'm totally in love with the general strike," said Jerry Goralnick, a middle-aged artist and actor, at a Sunday afternoon visioning meeting about what the Direct Action Working Group's priorities would be in the coming year. It was January 8, and by then Occupy Wall Street's die-hard meeting goers could think of little else than the strike. He understood the impulse, but it made him nervous; his experience in the 1960s had taught him the allure of the unattainable as well as its fallout.

"To me," he said, "it's analogous to seeing the face of God."

The idea of a general strike had been circulating in the movement since who knows when. There was the woman who called for it back on September 17. Occupy Oakland tried to mount one on November 2, with some success and a few broken windows. Soon after, Occupy LA took the lead in announcing a target that seemed sufficiently far off to be feasible and sufficiently familiar to seem plausible: May Day.

That afternoon in January, a hundred or so people were crowded together, standing or sitting in an oval at the radical art space on the fourth floor of 16 Beaver Street, just a few blocks south of Wall Street. "We're somewhere between a movement and a revolution," estimated Austin Guest, who had recently shaved the sideburns off one side of what had been a full beard after many female-assigned Occupiers buzzed part of their heads over the holidays. There was talk about bringing down Bank of America, and resisting home evictions, and providing child care. But the discussion kept coming back to May Day, to the general strike.

Just a few days later, in the basement of the Communication Workers of America Local 1180's Tribeca office, the May Day planning process began in earnest. The meeting, which included people from unions and immigrant justice groups as well as Occupiers, had a carefully composed mandate only to "discuss, possibly explore, supporting" Occupy LA's call for a May Day general strike. The caution was a politic move to get potential allies involved early, to ensure they'd be as fully invested in the general strike as possible.

Facilitating that night was Direct Action's Chris Longenecker, a lanky twenty-four-year-old from Long Island. His dark brown hair was still shaggy from the months in Zuccotti, and he had stringy pink bracelets on his wrist. He led the meeting deftly, making sure all the curmudgeonly union members got their chance to speak, even while inserting delicate and occasional interventions about the need to "smash state and capital." The more than fifty people in the room went around introducing themselves with names, affiliations, and the gender pronouns they preferred to go by. The last aroused resistance among some union folks; the Spanish-speaking men who'd come with the organizer from the Laundry Workers Center skipped the gender pronouns entirely.

The topic of discussion was the big picture: What would a general strike even mean, and did it make any sense to call for one? The union members tended to think they knew exactly what a general strike means, that one was not likely to happen anytime soon, and that it would be a terrible idea to call for one. The Occupiers tended toward optimism and subtlety. They wanted to try out, as Yates McKee put it, "imagining and dreaming what the city would look like in a general strike."

The concept of a general strike raises tricky questions about what revolution could mean in a society where fewer workers are unionized than have been for generations, where employment is often precarious, inadequate, and undemocratic, training workers to forget that things could be otherwise. What new forms of organizing economic resistance might there be besides unions, whose hands are already tied in no-strike clauses and complacency? Could the Internet help? Could Occupy? The strike to come wouldn't look quite like a strike ever had before, and it might be all the more powerful as a result—"to the point," Chris added, "that we might actually overthrow state and capital." Or at least promulgate the idea of doing so.

For the Occupiers, it was clear, "strike" conjured little of the industrial imagery of workers walking off the job in lockstep; many had never seen the inside of a factory or had an opportunity to join a union. Rather, to them, a city on strike would look like a gigantic Liberty Square, only better—a nonstop festival of salvific creativity through ungovernable acts of defiance, an inescapable mass annoyance to the 1 percent with the side effect of bringing the financial system to its knees. OWS had done impossible things before, so why couldn't it again?

After the meeting, I stood outside the union building under a scaffold with Yates and Chris, together with Natasha Singh and Amin Husain. As we talked, trading half-serious nonsense about what May Day might amount to, Natasha scanned around the circle with an accusing glare. "Look at us!" she announced. "We all have *crazy eyes!*"

The morning of that visioning meeting at 16 Beaver, I killed some time beforehand by going to a large, depressing electronics store in the Financial District to satisfy a consumerist obsession I'd been harboring. I was caught red-handed there by Bill Dobbs, elder doyen of the Press Relations Working Group, a lawyer who cut his activist teeth in ACT UP and various antiwar mobilizations, a New Yorker of the variety one would expect in a cameo on *Seinfeld*. He was feeling triumphant that morning because he'd dropped his keys down a subway grate and, after some misadventures, managed to recover them with a string and a magnet. But as always, Bill was also on the job. He made sure to serve me the latest metanarrative he was trying to feed into the news cycle.

"We're like a novelist whose first book was a best seller," he said. "Now we have to write another one that's even better." It's this kind of moment, this kind of pressure, that makes talented and successful people turn into drug addicts. At the time there were far more smart, connected, and experienced organizers working in OWS than during the planning of the original September 17 occupation. Yet somehow everybody knew this was no guarantee that the movement would get anywhere near making a blip on the national radar again.

The more I thought about it over the subsequent months—at the twice-weekly-or-more planning meetings for May Day, and in countless walks and meals whose sole and constant subject of conversation was revolution—what he'd said seemed right. He was right, in particular, to imagine the movement as analogous to a work of art. Maybe more than analogous, actually.

The realization was creeping upon me, or in some cases creeping me out, that this political movement I'd been mixed up in for months was really, truly, and above all best understood as a gigantic art project, which unwittingly I had been helping to carry out. It was like the "ancient astronaut" trope in a science fiction story—in which, at the end, it's revealed that the whole human race is the outcome of a science experiment rigged by aliens. This turns the meaning of everything upside down.

Think about it. Where did all of this begin but with a poster in the cen-terfold of an art magazine and a corresponding e-mail blast? The initial plan-ning and occupation emerged from the combination of political types from the Bloombergville occupation with artist types who'd been meeting at 16 Beaver; what made OWS work where Bloombergville didn't seems largely reducible to audaciousness of imagination. Georgia Sagri, who played such a usefully disruptive role in the early Tompkins Square Park meetings, was a performance artist, part of the latest Whitney Museum Biennial. Could it be that she was just doing her art? Was I just participating in her art by writ-ing about her? What about Amin and Natasha and Yates, who had known each other before through a program at the Whitney? From the beginning of the occupation onward, artists like them spread out among the working groups and facilitated the General Assembly meetings. They managed the finances. For major days of action, art studios around the city were used for staging and storage, and works of art—like the ladder that took people over Trinity's fence on December 17 and the levitating tents of March 17's reoccupation—were key props for the movement's most consequential direct actions. Insurrectionist and anarchist books circulating in art schools had prepared a critical mass in the movement to demand only the impossible and became the basis of its theoretical leading edge. Famous artists became some of the movement's major funders and public advocates. And nothing was more artsy than the prospect of a May Day that would turn the whole city into a canvas.

The usual expectation in a protest movement is that political people set the agenda and artists come in and decorate it. But with OWS, the more empirically accurate story was the reverse. The paradigm vocation of the civil rights movement was the pastor; for the Occupy movement, it was the artist.

Obviously this has been tried before. One thinks, for instance, of the Situationists, who inspired the students of May 1968 in Paris; the slogans of artists and critics nearly brought down the government. Kalle Lasn of *Adbusters* told me that he fancied himself their successor. Politicians make movements through organizations and memberships and coalitions, but art-ists spread their political works by inspiration, promulgation, and replica-tion—which is to say, by making them go viral.

There's decent strategic logic to having a movement conceived of and run by artists and to thinking of it as a work of art. Lots of people join movements not principally because of an ideology or by political calculation but because the movement is cool, or beautiful, or fun. They join a march for a lot of the same reasons that they pay exorbitant prices to stuff themselves into packed stadium concerts or camp out for the chance to catch a glimpse of a celebrity. If the artist or the movement can create that magnetism, that experience, that effervescence, then people will come and sacrifice in order to take part. Thus it was a rock band, the Plastic People of the Universe, that helped launch Czechoslovakia's resistance against Soviet rule and a playwright, Václav Havel, who followed through. Artists specialize in making us imagine and realize a different kind of world.

The artists' strategy, though, also faces a recurring danger. The Situationists might have inspired French students to rise up and scrawl absurdist slogans on the walls of their occupied university buildings, but it was the unions that finally stepped in, and mounted a general strike, and negotiated with the government. The outcome ended up bolstering the unions and leaving the students choking on tear gas. It happens in every upheaval that comes from reckless enthusiasm and fragile unity; the French Revolution went to Napoleon, and the Iranian one went to Kohmeini, just as the uprising at Tahrir Square devolved into another skirmish between the military and the Islamists. If Occupiers had created a Tahrir-sized rupture, who would really have benefited? Corporations and megachurches would be my guess. Again and again, the idealists create an opening, but those who are actually organized move in to fill it.

The older and more experienced folks in OWS, by and large, didn't want a viral meme; they wanted a "mass movement," full of middle-class Americans taking peaceably to the streets and knocking on doors for a new batch of candidates. They wanted the 99 percent, not so much the Occupy. They wanted to see winnable political goals concerning banks and taxes, and they wanted to meet those goals, with success leading to success. They wanted mailing lists and buttons and matching T-shirts. These are sensible things. This is what democracy looks like. This is what organizing has typically looked like. But it wasn't Occupy.

The meetings went on. A wrenching standoff between anarchists and unionists had produced a short and cautious yet spirited text, which was presented to Occupy Wall Street's moribund General Assembly on Valentine's Day and approved, to cheers and heart-themed balloons:

Occupy Wall Street stands in solidarity with the calls for a day without the 99%, a general strike and more!! On May Day, wherever you are, we are calling for:

- No Work
- No School
- No Housework
- No Shopping
- No Banking

TAKE THE STREETS!!!!!

Notice that slippery word, *solidarity,* and the just as open-ended "a general strike and more!!"—plausible deniability. No, OWS didn't call for a general strike. Yes, it sort of did. Unions could say no; anarchists could say yes. Both of them could "TAKE THE STREETS!!!!!"

What had been accomplished politically, meanwhile, was actually quite significant. OWS had brought into one fold unions and immigrants' rights groups, which have often-diverging agendas and typically hold separate May Day rallies. There would be a "solidarity" march from Union Square, where the immigrants usually gather, which would move downtown past Foley Square, where the unions normally do. The details were being worked out in "4 × 4" meetings, with members of Occupy, unions, immigrants, and community organizations. But Occupiers insisted on treating these as spokes councils, making their decisions by consensus rather than empowering representatives. They boasted to each other that their horizontality was rubbing off on the coalition partners, at least a little. Overseeing it all was a matronly Jackie DiSalvo, an English professor and labor organizer whose involvement in OWS went back to the Tompkins Square Park planning meetings, where she sat above the fray in a portable folding chair.

There were moments, glimpses, when something truly radical and huge seemed to be happening. The immigrants from the Laundry Workers Center, when they told their stories in bits and pieces of English but mostly in tears— those struggles were for real. "Any campaign you have is our campaign," one of them told the coalition. In turn, Occupiers showed up to the immigrant workers' actions against abusive bosses. Occupiers and transit workers tied open the gates at subway stations around the city one day in March, alongside posters for May Day, causing celebration and rage on the organizing e-mail threads. But these scenes of escalation toward May 1 weren't always distinguishable from the mirages.

Occupiers made a point of investigating the history of general strikes, pouring through old radical texts and archival films and making zines of their own. Labor historian Jeremy Brecher spoke on the subject in the CWA Local 1180's basement. Gayatri Spivak wrote a pair of articles on general strikes for the Occupy journal *Tidal*. But the historical indications were as foreboding as they were encouraging. A century earlier, the great agitator Rosa Luxemburg chided, "The mass strike is not artificially 'made,' not 'decided' at random, not 'propagated,' but ... results from social conditions with historical inevitability." All the planning and coalition building in the world might therefore seem futile. Frances Fox Piven, speaking in February at NYU, noted a contradiction in what was being called for: "A general strike doesn't last for a day—that's a demonstration."

Regardless, there were more meetings. The process continued. The various committees went on with their work, reporting to one another from behind placards like "Action" and "Mutual Aid," with circles around the *A*'s. In the coalition, Occupy Wall Street brought the energy and the youth, and it changed the game. It made possible a unity that wasn't possible before. It made big, crazy-eyed promises. May Day meetings became OWS's most vibrant and populous gatherings, especially after the General Assembly and the Spokes Council went from moribund to deceased. But without access to funds of their own through those bodies, Occupiers had to rely on the coalition to foot a lot of the necessary bills, and it took work to keep their partners happy. Such politics had a consumptive effect.

Yates McKee, who'd entered the May Day process as a prophet of weird, became one of the most patient and persistent negotiators, balancing week after week the nonnegotiables of various stakeholders in order to ensure their backing for the all-important cultural extravaganza that would precede the big solidarity march. His time was consumed not only in booking acts for the stage at Union Square but also in the painstaking building of consensus with the coalition about the most basic content of fliers and websites. ("Legalize, Unionize, Organize" was the final slogan. "Occupy," though originally part of it, was blocked for being potentially offensive.) He continued wearing neon green every day I saw him—a neon green knit cap and shoelaces, especially—because aliens from the future are green, he'd whisper, and because green represented his ambition of making the environment a uniting issue for Occupy. This ambition was semiarticulated at the end of a pseudonymous essay that appeared in the March *Brooklyn Rail*:

we don't pour fuel onto the fire.
we are the fuel, we are the fire.
green fuel, green fire
green is the new red
green is the new black
#occupygreen
electric green revolution
a sustainable power-grid for the energies of the 99%
(lol)

Later in March, Yates e-mailed me: "just had a deep convo with Michael Azzerad about why Sun Ra is the secret avatar of OWS." And the like. The wilder the ambitions the better. But as the weeks went on, more and more of the Occupiers' energy went toward the business of haggling with unions.

In the mix of all this, the idea of the general strike was spoken of less and less in the May Day meetings. First, the Strike Cluster became folded into Action, which in turn became bogged down in planning the big permitted solidarity march, which, by very virtue of its permit, didn't interest many Occupiers anyway. The strike was at worst taboo or at best forgotten. This outcome could've seemed, and in fact did seem to some, like a dastardly plan on the part of liberals to quash the prospects (such as they were) of the radicals' general strike. The historic coalition came at a cost.

At a sparsely attended press conference with the coalition at Union Square, OWS spokesperson Diego Ibañez couldn't even say the words that were supposed to be the whole point. But at the end of his speech he pulled away his plaid overshirt to reveal, under the green bandana around his neck, a white T-shirt on which were scrawled in red the unspeakable call: "GEN-ERAL STRIKE."

Georgia Sagri occasionally came to the May Day meetings, mostly with the apparent intent of defying the coalition-building process. I remember one time in particular, in mid-March. The long, light hair she'd worn at the Tompkins Square Park meetings was now close-cropped and dark. She was not frantic or dominating as usual, but mostly quiet, sitting on a table in the back. During announcements at the end, she said, innocently enough, "I'm part of this new group called the Occupy Central Park Exploratory Committee." They were having strolling meetings on Tuesdays, starting on the steps of the Metropolitan Museum of Art. She said, "We're gonna farm, we're gonna build houses." A quarter-page flier was meanwhile being passed around the room, with a picture of a shantytown in a snow-covered Central Park, with Upper West Side high-rise apartment buildings in the background. "NEW YORK IS ON INFINITE STRIKE," it said. "MAY 1st we occupy central park forever."

One of several anthropologists participant-observing the meeting confessed to me at the end, as we were heading up the stairs and out to Fourteenth Street, "I literally had a *dream* about Central Park, about us occupying Central Park."

As momentum for the general strike faltered in the main May Day meetings, others came forward to take it up. There was no shortage of general strike posters appearing on Occuprint.org and spreading like wild on Facebook and Pinterest and Twitter. In person in New York, the preeminent forum for such agitating was Strike Everywhere, a group of "anarchists, anti-capitalists, and autonomists," some of whom had been in and out of OWS circles since the first planning meetings in the summer. Once again, this group included more than a fair share of artists and critics, who seemed in league with Natasha Lennard, the reporter who'd been arrested on the Brooklyn Bridge and then dropped by the *New York Times* as a stringer for uttering anti-authoritarian sympathies in public, only to rise again through her Occupy columns in *Salon*.

"A lot of Strike Everywhere propaganda is . . . black," Chris Longenecker once astutely observed. A lot of it also said "fuck." One member of the group made it his special mission to hand out fliers at high schools calling for "no skule"—along with a terrifically funny Tumblr website. He told me that bad words helped get the kids' attention. My favorite picture on the site was of a tyrannosaurus rex with dynamite and an Uzi riding on the back of a great white shark.

I didn't last for more than twenty minutes at my first and only Strike Everywhere meeting. It was in late March, at an activist space often used by Occupiers on Atlantic Avenue in Brooklyn. There were twenty-five or so people sitting in a circle in chairs. "This is an open meeting," someone said. "Don't say anything crazy."

Proceedings began with report-backs. Georgia mentioned the Central Park Exploratory Committee. Another person summarized the recent doings of "some of the more politician types of Occupy Wall Street." Yet another mentioned the organizing for a general strike happening in Korea and Japan. They spoke of the Precarious & Service Workers Assembly that the group was organizing. They were working toward the Wildcat March on May Day, a march more militant than anything OWS or its precious coalition were planning.

Meanwhile, a woman I recognized by sight but not by name moved across the circle to sit next to me, saying nothing but poised so she could see my notebook. She interrupted the meeting and asked if they'd discussed reporters yet. Someone intoned the mantra, "No cops or reporters," which back in August had launched that harrowing debate about whether I could stay at my first Tompkins Square Park planning meeting. Some of the people in the room at Strike Everywhere had been there. They could have blocked my staying back then but didn't. This time, though, they did, and I had to walk out in silence.

No hard feelings, though. The Strike Everywhere–aligned account @strikeisaverb tweeted to me a few weeks later at @wagingnv, "We disagree more than you know, but we'd def de-arrest your pacifist ass." A high compliment.

Somewhere on the May Day spectrum between the coalition meetings and Strike Everywhere, the "Strike Cluster" reemerged among leading OWS people who'd been at the center of the coalition process and then become frustrated by it. They'd had enough with that but didn't want to throw in entirely with Strike Everywhere. Chris Longenecker was part of it, and Marisa Holmes, and Mike Andrews, and Shawn Carrié—a communications-system guru with an anarchist *A* on his lighter, a bandage on his left hand from having his thumb broken by police on March 17, and an "OWS non-violent" button on his jacket with the *non-* markered out.

They set themselves to the task of making up for lost time, to agitate, agitate, agitate. They planned street teams to spread the word about the general strike, and Marisa and I launched a pair of strike-related Tumblr accounts. If the strike came off as it should, it was imagined, other things would fall into place. "I wouldn't discount the possibility that we will have a park or a building after May 1st," Chris said at the first meeting, squatting in his chair, eating an orange.

Mike agreed; the world beyond the May Day event horizon was unknown and unknowable. "We shouldn't make a lot of plans," he said, "because if May Day fulfills our wildest dreams, what follows will come naturally."

During the early morning of April 10, people from the occupation that had been stationed at Union Square shuttled back downtown, beginning what would be the first time that the movement actually, literally occupied Wall Street. Forty people slept on the sidewalk that night. Night after night this continued, and each time the cops woke them up and shifted them across the street. Eventually the occupation settled, catty-corner to the Stock Exchange, on the steps of the Federal Hall memorial—a National Park Service site outside the NYPD's jurisdiction. The steps, full of protesters, became like risers for a chorus chanting down the business all around them. A few days later, though, one side of the steps had been surrounded by a box of barricades with a single entry-and-exit point at the bottom. The occupation turned from a chorus to a zoo.

This was quite unexpected to many of the movement's "organizers," as opposed to the grungier "occupiers" actually carrying it out. Approvingly, Amin Husain said of the occupiers, "Fucking vanguards!" But another organizer suggested to me that the occupiers were behaving like a bunch of toddlers. The occupiers, in turn, grumbled about the organizers: "Stop trying to *organize* us!" Conditions in the "freedom cage" deteriorated. But at least they were on Wall Street.

All the frustrations and shortsightedness and limitations could feel overcome, at least then and there in the midst of it, by this movement's fecundity. One could have in it something like the same kind of faith one tends to have in automobiles—that every year, a new model will come out better than its predecessor, in unexpected and habit-forming ways. Except here it seemed to arise out of nowhere. Someone would always come up with the next salvific poster, the next Plus Brigade, the next feat of mutual aid, the next viral video, the next website, the next committee to serve the next need. Of course so many necessary things went undone, and one had reservations about the general direction of the whole movement and every detail therein. But at least there was something always new and creative and unexpected, always somehow better than the last.

So it was with May Day. One couldn't keep track of everything if one tried: May Day radio (thanks to pirate transmitters and specially rigged iPhones), the maypole (decorated with words from the Declaration of the Occupation of New York City), the Occupy Guitarmy: ("Enlisting 1000 Musicians for a May Day Music March"), the Free University (the "collective educational experiment" of striking students and professors), the Wildcat March (of Strike Everywhere and company), mutual aid (in forms ranging from free food to a "really really free market"), and the 99 Pickets (a litany in itself, with dozens of unions and community groups planning actions in Midtown related to their various ongoing struggles). "And more," as the call to action promised. That night, we were to expect mysterious, militant, affinity-group-led actions in the Financial District, the kind of thing it was better not to know about in advance.

At a May Day meeting in early April in Washington Square Park, organizers went around the circle trying to remember all these things to help orient the newcomers. It took a long time, and they knew there was a lot they were still missing.

"I can't sit through meetings," one participant eventually whispered to me as she stood up. She took out a piece of chalk and began writing on the steps and on one of the park's main walkways. The police were making a special point of ticketing people for smoking in the park that day—one of Mayor Bloomberg's recent policy innovations—but a pair of cops paused to scrutinize her as she did, not sure whether they should do anything about it.

A little boy walked up to the chalked steps and started reading aloud, loudly and robotically, while pointing: "MAY-DAY. NO WORK. NO SCHOOL. ANOTHER WORLD IS . . . POSS-I-BLE."

"Whatever," said his father, pulling him away.

The park was getting full, meanwhile, mostly of college students who perhaps should've been organizing against their loan sharks. But instead they were carrying pillows. It was International Pillow Fight Day. Occupy hadn't mobilized that many people in months.

Mid-April brought with it the anxiety that May Day might not be everything it would need to be to rescue the world—much less, the movement, which for months had been glaringly absent from headlines. The city evidently wasn't bracing for an impending general strike. People in the streets and on the subway looked innocent of any such thing. The list of unions and organizations endorsing the solidarity march was growing, perhaps, but workplaces weren't gearing up for a work stoppage. On the InterOccupy conference calls, the national situation seemed even more bleak; Oakland and LA had interesting plans, perhaps, but Honolulu, for instance, wasn't up to anything more than "art and labor-related fun." Among the true believers, drastic measures seemed more and more necessary.

On April 14, for instance, OWS-affiliated participants in the anarchist book fair at Judson Church earned the unfortunate *Gawker* headline, "Feeble Anarchists Fail to Smash New York City Starbucks Window," as well as some serious criminal charges. A few days earlier, at an after-party at the Odessa diner near Tompkins Square Park, someone had scrawled on a chair, in permanent marker, "MAY DAY @ GENERAL STRIKE." Other Occupiers put down their beers and started collecting money to replace it. Outside, some of the drunker ones were sitting in the way of a police car.

Where before I had been thinking about art, now I was thinking about apocalypse. This theological frame of mind might have been simply because in the midst of it all I was also scrambling to finish my book manuscript about proofs for the existence of God. Yet it was also plainly true that those of us in the midst of this process were staring constantly in the face of the end of the world. The intention, of course, was to end the world of systemic oppression, the world of the 1 percent, the world made of debt. Whether or not they deep-down believed it, Occupiers talked as if such an end might be near. The likeliest explanation for such terrific credulity, however, was the recognition that the real end we were in danger of experiencing was that of the movement itself.

"Everybody knows that May Day is kind of Occupy Wall Street's last hurrah," said Diego Ibañez at one of the last May Day meetings, in a moment of desperation while trying to push through the passage of a controversial proposal. But then Diego corrected himself: "Sorry, I didn't mean to say it that way." Too close for comfort.

There was a mood of collective insomnia—or of a lucid dream, in which you know you are asleep, and dreaming, and that knowledge makes you feel in control. Perhaps this is what it feels like to be in the middle of a work of art, as neither the model nor the artist but as the brush and the paint. Or the self-awareness of helpless human beings in the midst of a world that will be considerably warmer by the time our kids grow up—if we can ever get enough out of debt to afford to have kids. This is life in a flourishing democracy, as we were relentlessly told, with a government that protects the profits of the largest corporations at all costs while leaving the rest of us to scrounge for the trickle-down. End-times politics starts to seem far more reasonable than giving oneself over to the ritual delusion of an election year, through which we're offered a choice between two slightly different approaches to achieving world domination as a means of securing, for those who are lucky enough, the very middle-class existence that is making us fat and destroying our planet.

One of the kinder, gentler Occupiers—an original one, from the planning meetings before the occupation began—had a banner atop his Facebook time line from the History Channel series *Life after People:* an artist's rendition of a cityscape after which all the humans in it somehow disappear. Trees are growing out from the sides of crumbling buildings. The scene is quiet, and still, with life, but not our kind of life.

To say that this image had anything to do with the movement's plans for May 1, which the person who posted it was involved in making, might have caused both paranoid-style right-wing radio hosts and the most anarcho- of primitivists to froth at the mouth. And so they should have. Ever since the idea of working toward May Day started catching on in Occupy Wall Street, its overriding impulse was not merely to discipline the banks or get money out of politics but to stop this world in its tracks and unveil the image of a very different one.

With exactly a week left before May Day, Occupy organizers were coming and going from an East Village townhouse. In the basement, enormous banners were being painted for mutual aid stations. Upstairs, Ingrid Burrington and Chris Longenecker sat on meditation cushions on the hardwood floor of a room where Chris and three other Occupiers were living. The walls were covered with general strike posters, and a record player was spinning an Allman Brothers album. On the floor in front of Ingrid and Chris were intricate maps of New York, which Ingrid had obtained from the Department of City Planning and laminated. As her computer attempted to process a data trove related to the NYPD's stop-and-frisk policy, she explained to Chris how to transfer information from a spreadsheet to the JavaScript code that was controlling a Google map.

"Does that make sense?" she asked.

"It doesn't completely *not* make sense," he replied.

Chris had already begun marking the targets of the 99 Pickets on the laminated maps with colored markers: police precincts in blue, pickets that might involve arrests in red, and safer ones in green. Each picket was numbered. The map would be used by the people in the clandestine control center tasked with coordinating the day's actions. "This has way more moving parts than anything we've ever done before," Chris said.

It was fortunate, then, that Ingrid was around. "I'm only good at two things," she'd explained a few weeks earlier, as she showed me a map in Adobe

Illustrator of police patrol routes for Union Square. "Organizing large amounts of data in useful ways and making pies."

Ingrid started creating maps as an art student in Baltimore. Charting that city's patchwork of neighborhoods, with its stark divisions between black and white, rich and poor, she'd come to appreciate the political nature of cartography—how maps shape people's experience of space and how they thereby wield power. She later edited a diagrammatic periodical, the *Schematic Quarterly,* and produced a geographical analysis of "missed connections" postings on New York's Craigslist.

When Ingrid first became involved with Occupy Wall Street, she was surprised at how little the movement was using maps, and she began charting sites of interest: corporate headquarters, privately owned public spaces, accessible bathrooms. "This is entirely a social movement about geography," she said. That line of thinking places her within a tradition of resistance that includes the Situationists' experiments in psychogeography, the Czechs who removed street signs to disorient Soviet troops during the Prague Spring, and the Syrians who changed the names of streets and bridges on Google Maps from ones associated with the ruling Assad family to others honoring heroes of the resistance.

Occupiers in Los Angeles were also using cartography in their May Day plans. To reach across the city's vast sprawl, they set up caravans of bicycles, cars, and subway trains that would converge on the downtown along four arteries—the "Four Winds"—starting in the north, south, east, and west ends of LA County. Their hope was that the Winds would become the basis of future organizing after May Day, linking disparate communities in the shape of a bull's eye around the city's financial district.

I asked Ingrid and some of the other May Day organizers in New York what a postrevolutionary map of the city might have on it. "Mutual-aid stuff," one of them said. "Where you can go for resources," Ingrid added. Then she thought of something else: "I think we would probably create monuments and weird new memorials." The November 15 police raid that ended the occupation of Zuccotti Park, she said, had seared certain scenes and places into her memory.

A few days before the mapmaking session with Ingrid and Chris, I had sat with a group of Occupiers on the steps of the Federal Hall memorial, surrounded by barricades. One of them was Amin, who pointed to a fist-sized gash in the side of a building on the other side of Wall Street. Looking at his phone, he read aloud from a Wikipedia page that explained its cause: a 1920 bombing by Italian anarchists that killed thirty-eight people. It was a quiet reminder that Wall Street had had enemies before. But the gash was unmarked and unmapped; I'd passed by it many times and had never even noticed.

I came late to the last of the big May Day meetings. It was wrapping up already, and people were busily moving from cluster to cluster, making last-minute plans. One person told me the meeting had been powerful and moving and deep; another said it was boring.

I was in time, at least, to get a copy of a new zine that Yates said I should definitely look at—one among tables full of posters and fliers and booklets and stickers on display. It stated nothing about its authorship, though it apparently came from the direction of Strike Everywhere. On the cover, sandwiching a photo of riot police beating people and a man in a suit looking on, it said, *Mayday 1971 or, How to Lose Street Battles and Alienate People.*

Inside the ninety-two-page, photocopied zine was a series of period documents directly or indirectly related to the massive 1971 May Day action in Washington DC. Affinity groups from around the country converged in an attempt to shut the city down and, in the government's stead, declare the war in Vietnam over. I'd never heard of this before. The zine included the complete "May Day Tactical Manual" used for the action, as well as an article from the time about how impressed Pentagon officials were by it. There were news reports about the "comic trek" as affinity groups briefly clogged the federal workers' commute and suffered thousands of arrests for their trouble. Activists' reports told much the same depressing story in a different voice. The last quarter or so of the zine consisted of a 1979 article by a pair of sociologists recounting the demise of the 1960s counterculture over the course of the subsequent decade as disappointment with "the freak vision of an anarchist communard post-scarcity society" carried people into such "post-movement groups" as the Hari Krishnas, the Weather Underground, the Symbionese Liberation Army, the World Christian Liberation Army, and Jim Jones's People's Temple, which came to its suicidal end in 1978 in Guyana.

Thus Andrew Kopkind began a 1973 essay, "Mystic Politics: Refugees from the New Left," which I would later come across while staying with a group of Occupiers at the commune he fled to in Vermont:

The topography of American political culture in this strangely suspended season is strewn with the skeletons of abandoned movements, lowered visions, dying dreams—No truces but tacit cease-fires have stilled the war on poverty, the war of the classes, the war of the worlds. In the white and middle-class field of action, at least, explicitly political energy and imagination are in short supply. Ideologies based on mechanistic analyses of power and history may not be wrong, but they are seen to be external to the lives of many whom they once moved, and irrelevant, too, to long-untended needs for peace of body, soul or mind.

I read the whole zine that night, from beginning to end, in a trance of déjà vu. And while people I knew who had been there in '71 contested the implication that whatever happened on May Day had destroyed their movement once and for all with its ambition-cum-cataclysm, they couldn't take away my feeling of having gone to a palm reader and been told that we were causing our own undoing, Oedipally enough, precisely by trying to escape it.

When May Day finally came, I'd been attending the planning meetings for four months, and I still went into the day feeling that I had no idea what would come out of it. All along, May 1 had been talked about among organizers in addictive, beatific terms. In the process of getting my fix, I became witness to the politics of assembling the coalition of Occupiers, labor unions, immigrants' groups, and community organizations—not always pretty, though occasionally it actually was. Much the same could be said of the day itself: come for the dream, trudge through the reality.

I woke to the news on Twitter that letters containing white powder had been sent to bank offices and City Hall; no one claimed responsibility. Strike Everywhere people had received preemptive visits from the NYPD. Soon, the FBI would announce that five men had been arrested in Cleveland for attempting to blow up a bridge—all goaded by an undercover agent. Somebody was evidently out to ensure that May Day would look like terrorism.

In New York, the day's first arrest was of OWS regular Bill Steyert, a white-bearded Veteran for Peace who momentarily blocked the intersection at Forty-Second Street and Sixth Avenue, waving a yellow flag. Just then, the 99 Pickets were beginning, and a pack of black-clad youngsters went off to shout down "fucking Disney." A few hundred people slogging their way through pickets on a rainy Midtown morning swelled to closer to a thousand filling Bryant Park at midday. Hard-boiled eggs, first-aid, and the movement's latest publications were on offer, while across the park Rage against the Machine's Tom Morello led a rehearsal for the Occupy Guitarmy, the hundred-strong orchestra of stickered-up guitars playing old protest songs, a Morello original, and a particularly hypnotic arrangement of Willie Nile's "One Guitar." By early afternoon, the Guitarmy steered the crowd at Bryant Park in a march downtown. Picking up students from the Free University being held at Madison Square Park, the first wave of marchers defied police attempts to keep them on the sidewalk and took over Broadway before arriving at Union Square, where they were greeted by the maypole, with dancers weaving together ribbons marked with the movements' grievances.

News from elsewhere around the city and the country came in over Twitter, bit by bit. There were arrests downtown, both before and during the Wildcat March. In Oakland, the cops had already started shooting flash grenades.

The May Day coalition had secured permits for actions in Union Square and the subsequent march down Broadway to the Financial District, ensuring that the whole area was surrounded by metal barricades. Bystanders couldn't enter, and marchers couldn't exit, except at designated points. Police protected this gigantic pen with zeal, suffocating scooter exhaust, and occasional arrests. They also managed to split the OWS contingent, trapping thousands of marchers in Union Square and refusing to let them enter Broadway.

Still, it was during the permitted march that the day's numbers reached their peak—around thirty thousand. The unions themselves didn't seem to turn out great masses of their own, nor did they even try to mount any kind of strike. But by arranging for a permit, as Occupiers would never do themselves, the more institutional allies did provide space for a considerable show of support for the Occupy movement's concerns, which Occupy itself hadn't been able to even approach since the fall. The vast majority of people came for the permitted portion of the day and left after it was over.

Down Broadway, I walked alongside two elderly marchers—a nun and a priest—together holding a pillowcase on which was written, "BREAD NOT BOMBS." Beside us was a gigantic blue tarp covering a hundred or so of OWS's rowdier troops, threatening, in thus far only theoretical chants, to burn banks and smash the state. Undocumented immigrants, often reluctant to take part in Occupy's usual unpermitted actions, led the way ahead of us.

The nun, no stranger to the front lines of protests, couldn't believe the level of police presence. "When did it become like this?" she kept asking. Four NYPD helicopters hovered overhead. The department's taste for pageantry was on display most of all downtown, where multiple rows of officers and a line of horses blocked the entrance to Wall Street. Those under the tarp shouted, "Fuck the police!" while the priest thanked individual cops for their service—a diversity of tactics.

As dark came, plans to hold an after-party in Battery Park were foiled by police blockades. Text-message alerts guided those who remained to Vietnam Veterans Memorial Plaza, tucked along the East River waterfront between buildings that house Morgan Stanley and Standard & Poor's. The memorial includes a space that served as a perfect amphitheater for a thousand-strong "people's assembly," and it turned into one of those moments of collective effervescence and speaking-in-one-voice that won so many discursively inclined hearts to the movement in the fall. After a tiring and tedious day, I reveled in it. People of other inclinations danced to the familiar sound of the drum circle on the far side of the park.

The topic of the assembly soon became whether to stay, to try to occupy. At first it seemed that maybe people would. (What better place to spend the summer than by the water?) Led by Tarak Kauff and Ellen Davidson, the pair I'd met during the planning for the Freedom Plaza occupation, members of Veterans for Peace formed a uniformed bloc of military veterans and allies ready to stand at the front lines. With them were two clergymen from Occupy Faith—including Bishop George Packard, the first to have gone over Trinity Wall Street's fence on December 17. Their commitment won cheers, but as the discussion wore on, the assembly seemed less and less inclined to stay after the park closed at 10 P.M. and repeat another sequence of beatings and arrests. Even after being told that the Occupiers would retreat to the streets, the Veterans for Peace members and the clergymen stood their ground at the memorial and were apprehended by police.

For the next two hours, the improvised after-party dissipated as police chased black-masked marchers through the neighborhood's narrow streets and clubbed some of them bloody. Mini-assemblies formed on sidewalks to plan what to do next and were broken up, too, when discovered. All roads eventually led to Zuccotti Park, where the two hundred or so people remaining assembled, and rested, and then left.

There, I found a huddle of Direct Action folks who'd been trying to orchestrate the night's events. They were cursing the unions. Amin urged

Sandy Nurse to get up and do a mic check, and she did, announcing that there would be "Summer Disobedience School" every Saturday until the next big action, on September 17, the movement's birthday—"Black Monday." Just the thought of it, by then, to me, was exhausting. But others seemed primed for more.

"I'd say this was the best day of the year," I heard one person say in a small circle of Occupiers near Zuccotti Park, debriefing over kebabs from a street vendor. "Just this year, though." On the corner beside them, I heard a cop tell another, "They say they want free education. Sure, we all do—but that's not how society works." An unchanged heart, a still-chained imagination.

At around two in the morning, I got on the subway to head home—befriending, on the walk there, a Methodist minister from Korea who'd also been around for the actions. The subway car that finally arrived to take me from the platform smelled terrible. Inside was a man, half-clothed in rags and hunched over himself, neither alive nor dead. In a city where we all depend on one another, as cells of the same organism, his condition was our shared failure. A revolution would have been nice right about then and there, but, for my part, the best I could think to do was move to a different car at the next station.

When the Second Coming of Jesus failed to occur on October 22, 1844, as thousands of Americans expected it to—the "Great Disappointment"—their reactions varied. Some picked another date. Others reinterpreted failure as success. Others returned to less excitable congregations, while still others became Shakers.

If May Day was disappointing, the disappointment was disappointing too. A lot of those who'd planned it were simply tired. Some skipped town for a while to rest. Others started turning to other movement projects, like the actions against austerity in the middle of May. For many of us who had been living in an alternate universe since September, it was a time to pay mind to our jobs and families and regular lives a bit more again; I finally turned in my overdue book manuscript. Still others redoubled their revolutionary efforts but with less attachment to the "Occupy" label.

Calls for a general strike and mass economic noncompliance went mostly unheeded. The financial markets followed a trapezoidal journey over the course of the day—apparently unperturbed by the movement's threat to shut down the flow of capital with the 99 Pickets—spiking in the morning and crashing back down to where they had started by late afternoon. The main-stream press wasn't much impressed either, which may or may not have had anything to do with the morning pickets at News Corp. and the New York Times Building.

The disappointment was there but not exactly "great." Maybe it was less a matter of having failed to see the promised face of God than of having produced a work of art that was good but not quite a masterpiece. Maybe nobody else really believed the transcendental expectations in the first place. But I know that from time to time I did—in glimpses, like passing a seductive canvas in a gallery.

A few days after May Day, I got a call from Marisa Holmes. She wanted, it seemed, to set the record straight about certain details of the events of that night, especially the fact that she had always opposed the idea of an occupation or a mass arrest at the memorial. She was upset that others in her affinity group had tried to push for those things.

"I'm not completely satisfied by anything that's going on right now," she confessed. "I'm not happy, overall."

Marisa continued, "We have to go beyond the symbolic. What does it *really* mean to Occupy Wall Street?" Hearing her, I felt ashamed for all my reveries about art and about the end of worlds. She didn't want to talk about imagination this time, and she didn't even want to talk about process.

"People want to see, like, actual results."

PART FOUR

SUMMER TO FALL

EIGHT | ETERNAL RETURN

#Anarchives #ClimateSOS #ClimateStrike #FreeMarkAdams
#OccupySandy #OccupyYearTwo #RollingJubilee #S17 #StrikeDebt

At the corner of Spring and Varick Streets, in the ethereal white halls of a Manhattan Mini Storage, two members of the Occupy Wall Street Archives Working Group assembled competing visions of how the movement should be remembered. Their collections looked deceptively similar: cramped, high-ceilinged closets packed with cardboard signs, boxes, banners, and stray objects such as a mannequin, a pig mask, a miniature tent, an orange mesh police net, and hundreds of unopened letters. Neither self-appointed archivist had access to the other's stash. They rarely even spoke to each other, having undergone a philosophical falling-out—one that, as the first birthday of OWS approached, seemed to hinge on the question of whether the movement should be spoken of in the past or the present tense.

Amy Roberts was in her midthirties and worked for a public library in New York while studying for her certification as an archivist. She had an acute, quiet awareness of the people and things around her, a quality I appreciated when we were watching out for each other in the streets during the eviction in November. She hoped to deliver the contents of her storage unit to New York University's Tamiment Library, which specializes in "labor and the left," and which for months had been courting the Archives Working Group. The materials would be professionally cataloged and preserved there, allowing easy access for whatever future historians might want to see them.

As we went through the objects in her storage unit, we played memory games, trying to pin each to a particular time and place. "It's nice to go through this again," Amy said, holding a letter that accompanied a donation of clothes from a trendy retailer in Los Angeles.

On another floor of the same building, Jeremy Bold kept his branch of the OWS archives. He was in his late twenties and had a wispy beard that was most profuse in the region between his jawline and neck. Jez, as he was called, had been working as a philosophy librarian at NYU but now was entering a more transient period. "There is no such thing as permanence in my life," he observed—speaking, as he often would, about ordinary things in metaphysical terms.

Like Amy, Jez collected signs, documents, and other ephemera throughout the occupation and its aftermath. Since he was part of the earliest planning meetings in New York, some of his objects had particular historical significance. But by late summer, unable to keep paying for the storage unit, he wanted to give them away. "I guess my part is over," he said. "If people still feel strongly about this stuff, I think they'll want to take care of it."

To this end, he had been theorizing what he called the "Anarchives"—a system for preserving the movement's material history outside pernicious institutions like NYU. Rather than all of the objects being kept in one place, they'd be divided among those who helped create them, who would then catalog and interpret their holdings in an online database.

"The history is left to be preserved by the people still living it," Jez explained. Rather than the ossified existence offered by Tamiment, the Anarchives would play an ongoing role in an ongoing movement and in a manner consistent with the movement's do-it-yourself ideals. Bold's proposal, however, assumed that there was still a movement in the first place.

During the fall of 2011, op-ed pages and cable news shows constantly referred to "the Occupy Wall Street protests" and tried their darnedest to explain what exactly had caused this sudden and unhygienic uprising. The encampments indisputably "changed the conversation," specifically by making it permissible to talk about wealth and inequality again, and by identifying some of the basic pathogens and symptoms of corporate domination over politics and everyday life; even President Obama would be able to win reelection by railing against Mitt Romney as a 1 percenter in their debates. But after the destruction of the Zuccotti Park encampment, the media's gaze turned away from the movement as such, contributing to a widely held impression that it no longer existed.

Both Jez and Amy were part of that rarefied clique of Occupiers still pressing on, however, and they had reasons to think that there was reason to do so. "Sleepful protest" encampments continued on the sidewalk in front of Trinity Church and at sites around the country. (Although small, Occupy Trinity was New York's longest encampment yet.) There were still more meetings going on than one could count, many of which were laying plans for the one-year-anniversary actions on September 17. Some were even being held under the Hare Krishna Tree in Tompkins Square Park, where planning meetings had taken place for the original occupation with about the same number of people. A year later, the déjà vu was palpable, complete with much the same precariousness, naïveté, and uncertainty.

As a summer of record-setting heat sweltered on, Occupy faced more and more of the persecution that always batters and hones apocalyptic uprisings. Meetings over the winter and spring had seemed especially rife with infiltrators, and such suspicions were confirmed in May, when undercover officers lured isolated activists in Cleveland and Chicago into terrorism charges that could put them in prison for decades. That further harmed the whole movement on the news. Mark Adams, a much-admired member of Direct Action, served about a month in prison on Rikers Island for his role in the attempted reoccupation on December 17. Whenever Occupiers gathered in public spaces in New York, police seemed especially willing to use force to ensure that no new occupation could establish itself. "Across the United States, abusive and unlawful protest regulation and policing practices have been and continue to be alarmingly evident," concluded a report produced by the Protest and Assembly Rights Project, a coalition of several law school clinics. Occupiers tended to respond to repression with reaction rather than thoughtful counteroffensive, which made the repression that much more effective.

In July, NYPD officials claimed to have found DNA evidence that resulted in a slanderous *New York Post* front-page headline: "OWS MURDER LINK." The alleged "link" to an eight-year-old crime was entirely circumstantial, and even that turned out to be just the result of sloppy lab work—but the damage was done. At a peaceful action in Zuccotti Park the day the story ran, passersby clutching the paper confronted Occupiers and demanded, "Where's the murderer?"

The backlash thus came not only from the law and its enforcers but from the media as well. The late reactionary pundit Andrew Breitbart, with the help of FBI informant Brandon Darby, would soon strike from the grave with a documentary hit piece, *Occupy Unmasked*. Such counterattacks would have been less troubling were the crude stereotypes they perpetuated about populist resistance not finding their way among some of the most hallowed icons of pop culture. A new Batman movie came out in July whose villain takes all of Gotham hostage, resulting in an anarchic spree as the city is handed over to "the people." "The people" then avenge themselves by tearing the rich out of their mansions to be sentenced to death by a hipster judge. A climactic sequence, partly filmed on Wall Street while OWS was still in Zuccotti Park a few blocks away, depicts a battle in which a column of gallant police officers—backed by the crime-fighting vigilante superhero, the alter ego of a billionaire arms dealer—charges down what appears to be Wall Street against a mob of 99 percenters armed with AK-47s. By the end, Catwoman is rescued from her anarchic and lesbian tendencies by Batman's kiss. The only concern for the poor that the movie condones is picking up capitalism's mess by exercising charity toward orphans. It is difficult to imagine a more telling self-portrayal of American corporate fascism or a more callous attempt to discredit its enemies through the caricature of superherodom. The movie's release occasioned a young man in full body armor going on a shooting spree in a Colorado theater.

Such physical and psychological attacks took their toll. Younger Occupiers, with mounting rap sheets and untended fatigue, were struggling to learn the art of "self-care"—taking breaks, traveling, finding a balance. There was a long-overdue backlash against the movement's glamorizing of arrests, coming especially from those tired of playing supporting roles to their serial-arrestee friends. Meanwhile, more casual supporters who didn't want to risk arrest were successfully spooked away by the same grisly police violence that had helped draw their sympathy to the occupations in the first place months earlier.

Many of the movement's internal features, which once lent an aura of inclusivity—the subversion of demands, the improvisational structure, the shunning of paid organizers—were becoming less and less fruitful. In a society still ruled by capital and hierarchy, anarchist utopia wasn't easy to keep up for long. Working groups splintered into project groups and affinity groups, and some proceeded to go on strike against the others. Even if these groups could agree about anything, there were no adequate venues for making collective decisions. Occupy as a whole was in danger of becoming a catastrophic disappointment, of convincing another generation of the futility of resistance and the need to retreat into ironic distance. Then again, some would argue, maybe having "changed the conversation" was victory enough.

It wasn't enough for Ravi Ahmad. While holding her day job as an administrator at Columbia University, Ravi's specialty in OWS was keeping track of the disparate project groups and helping them connect through social media, a weekly e-mail blast, and the Project List, an occasional print publication enumerating all the groups one could plug into. "We've moved out of the spectacular phase," she said. "The main focus of what we do now is day-in, day-out organizing." For her, that part was even more important. And so was a sense of perspective.

"The failure of Occupy is that it didn't *smash capitalism*," she reminded me at a planning meeting one night in August. "That's the standard we measure ourselves by."

"Changing the conversation," by the way, was only the movement's most superficial effect. Because news reporters don't make a habit of paying attention to activist networks the way they follow presidential exercise habits or wobbly stock tickers, they weren't attuned to the sea change brought about by Occupy: people organizing for economic justice—especially young people—now knew one another. Together, they had practiced direct democracy in general assemblies and risked their bodies in direct action. They were talking with one another over networks that they had created themselves. They were traveling, connecting, and building their capacity for future action.

"Occupy unleashed this heightened sense of resistance," said Chris Longenecker—who, after being such a driving force for May Day, took a break to drive a pedicab in Boston. "We've formed really close bonds," he continued. "The people I worked with most in Occupy I'm going to trust the rest of my life." Occupiers I talked with around the country kept telling me the same thing.

Distance and time lessened many people's attachment to the Occupy label. "I've been working with all the same people I worked with in Occupy," said Kate Savage, who specialized in facilitating assemblies at Occupy Nashville, "only it's not called 'Occupy' for a variety of reasons." As onetime Occupiers joined struggles in communities where the movement had not taken hold or was not widely embraced, they were finding that the Occupy brand, with its associations of police violence and ragged protesters, could hurt more than it helped.

The summer witnessed, for instance, a wave of direct actions against the worst culprits of the environmental crisis across the United States. For the first time, a fracking well was blockaded and shut down in Pennsylvania, and a mountaintop-removal coal mine in West Virginia received similar treatment. The Keystone XL oil pipeline, which had inspired ritualized protests at the White House a year earlier, now had locals and out-of-towners putting their bodies in the way of construction machines in Texas. In New York, the fight was against the Spectra Energy pipeline, posed to funnel explosive fracked natural gas into Manhattan. To each of these campaigns Occupy veterans brought their bravado, their experience, and their new friends.

"Lots of folks are going from eco-action to eco-action," said Chris. "They're building their skill sets."

The environmental campaigns were only one such beneficiary of the movement. Occupiers were serving as hired guns for big unions, helping to agitate in unusually militant campaigns against corporations and austerity budgets. Soon, in part because of them, the Chicago teachers would be on strike, and Walmart workers, for the first time in the company's history, would follow. Others were working to draw attention to the massive influx of corporate cash into the electoral system, while still others were challenging the National Defense Authorization Act's most troubling provisions in federal court. Home liberation efforts were taking place around the country—from Occupiers' support of a rent strike led by Latino women in Brooklyn to under-the-radar house reclamations in the poorest neighborhoods of Chicago's South Side. A grad-student-heavy contingent at OWS launched the Strike Debt campaign through online memes, assemblies, and public debt-burnings with the hope of mobilizing victims of crippling debt into an "Invisible Army of Defaulters" and setting off a "Rolling Jubilee," named after the biblical tradition of debt erasure. The group collectively authored and published the handsome 132-page *Debt Resistors' Operations Manual,* which offered both rousing propaganda and form letters to send to collection agencies. The fecundity of this movement was ever more on display, under ever more names.

People who before Occupy had focused on only one of these issues were working closely with those involved in others, stitching their grievances together through action. They created venues to keep nursing their anticapitalist tendencies. Through Occupy Nashville, Kate Savage became part of the Anarchist Cotillion, a group meant, she said, "to support each other in terms of being political radicals." In New York, a regular reading group on direct action was gathering at spaces previously used for OWS meetings.

"There's something every day of every week to follow. So much is going on," said Joan Donovan, an organizer with Occupy LA and InterOccupy, which had grown from a series of conference calls to a full-service online platform for organizing. "Occupy has always felt to me like a social experiment, a beta test for a much larger-scale global movement." To this end, InterOccupy had plans to swell into "InterMovement," making its tools available beyond the subculture of self-identified Occupiers.

"The idea of occupation as a tactic—it had an expiration date," Joan added. "But what doesn't are all the networks we can build."

Text message on August 1 from David DeGraw:

Any use for free tents? Have a thousand of them!!

The uprising in Tahrir Square at the start of 2011 inspired American malcontents to believe in their own capacity for civil resistance, but it also left them with a misconception. News reports furnished the impression that, with the help of Silicon Valley's latest gizmos, a revolution can begin and end inside of a month. The outcome after a year and a half in Egypt, however, was a painful reminder that this isn't so. Rather than the tech-savvy upstarts, those who'd been preparing for revolution the longest—the Muslim Brotherhood—were most prepared to lead it. Here in the United States, at least, the absence of total upheaval by the end of the fall convinced those Occupiers who hadn't simply given up to start thinking in terms of not months but years, not sudden outbursts but patient, untelevised organizing.

Throughout the summer, fresh inspiration came from other movements abroad. The students in Quebec filled the streets night after night, and Occupiers banged on pots and pans in concert with them, pinning the Quebecois red-felt squares to their clothes. In Mexico, another movement named after a hashtag, #YoSoy132, shook up the presidential election with open assemblies. Members of the Russian punk band Pussy Riot went to prison for blaspheming Vladimir Putin in a cathedral. Occupiers saw their own reflection in each of these and saw their movement as only one part of a larger nexus of movements all over the world.

Before Occupy Wall Street, few people my age in the United States knew what a general assembly or an affinity group was; after a year, many more had participated in one. Thousands occupied public spaces and were arrested for their convictions who might otherwise have thought the police were there to protect them. People who were once merely interested in social change became committed to it.

"A year ago, the movement was something I could schedule into my life," said Marisa Holmes. "Now the movement *is* my life."

She and others who were planning for the anniversary celebrations around September 17 were consciously trying to avoid overpromising, as they had for May Day. S17 was being thought of less as a turning point than as a necessary milestone, a reminder of the duty to keep resisting. Rather than a May Day–style apocalypse, it was more like a holy day of obligation.

They called for people from around the country to converge on New York for a weekend of music, art, and organizing. On Monday—S17 itself—they would show that "all roads lead to Wall Street" with civil disobedience in the Financial District. In anticipation, Occupiers were doing "99 Percent Pub Crawls" through the city's bar scene to spread the word and practice causing trouble. "It's largely symbolic; we're not really shutting down Wall Street," Marisa assured me. "That's more long-term, not something you can do in one day."

There was a press conference at Zuccotti Park on the Wednesday before the anniversary to announce the release of a new statement by the Council of Elders, a group of sage veterans of past movements. A couple dozen people showed up for some songs and speeches there on the steps as these various heroes attempted to pass the baton of resistance on to their beleaguered counterparts in Occupy. But precious few of the latter came to receive it.

As the event was winding down, I met a woman from LA, Wawa. Her presence was unrelated to the Council of Elders, though she could have been an honorary member. She had been holding her signs at Zuccotti day after day for weeks. That day her sign said, "NO BIG DEBT," and she wore a green T-shirt, with a pair of reading glasses and a pair of sunglasses up on her head. As we talked, she swayed to the beat of a guy near us beating a drum.

Wawa wanted to give the Occupiers an earful. "You have to plan ahead!" she said, with a Caribbean accent. "Five months in advance it should be all ready! You can't do everything at the last minute." She told me about her attempts to get people to organize themselves, though I couldn't recall having seen her at the meetings I'd been going to.

Wawa talked like she was carrying the whole movement on her shoulders—which might have seemed reasonable to the casual observer, since she was often the only protester holding her ground in the park. But when one passed by Zuccotti Park and saw only one or two people holding signs, as was typical then, it was hard to see anything reasonable at all about what they were doing.

There was perhaps some sign of life in the fact that Occupy Wall Street's most painful, divisive, and distracting controversy was still capable of being revived. As the anniversary drew near, in the basement of the City University of New York's Grad Center in Midtown, Chris Hedges appeared onstage alongside B. Traven, of the anarchist collective CrimethInc., to rehash the nonviolence-versus-diversity-of-tactics debate. Since March or so this debate had mostly faded from the movement itself, but what a few months earlier had been a genuine crisis was now being reenacted in the form of a spectacle. The mastermind was Andy Stepanian, a PR man for the activist set who had served prison time when convicted of terrorism for his animal-rights work.

In their introductory remarks, the moderators kept referring to Occupy Wall Street in the past tense, as a movement no longer in the streets. Some of those who were still sleeping in front of Trinity Church defiantly held up their sleeping bags in disbelief. No one ended up charging the stage to tar and feather Hedges, as Andy had feared, but there was a lot of heckling and boo-ing and hissing intermixed with the cheering. None of it deterred Hedges from pressing on with his humorless sermons about the "collective suicide" nearly upon us, peppered with stories from his years dodging bullets as a war reporter, quotations from nineteenth-century literature, and gender analysis of a similar vintage. "The forces arrayed against us are working over-time to crush us," he muttered, his gaze unshaken by the insults being hurled at him.

The irony of the whole crisis Hedges's article had provoked that winter was thus laid bare once again: the person by far more intimately familiar with violence was the one contending that it wasn't a good idea, given the circum-stances. Hedges squarely won over those middle-aged and older, while the younger Traven satisfied the idiomatic needs of the anarchist-y Occupiers, not least by continually reminding us of his discomfort with the hierarchical format of the debate in the first place.

When asked near the end about their respective theories of social change, Hedges turned once again to fatalism: "Whatever we do, change is coming," he said, grimly. All that matters, then, is "how we cope with this change"—

ideally, by mounting a mass nonviolent resistance movement against the masters of the universe who are destroying us.

Traven summarized his own theory with concision: "Just keep at it, basically." Throughout the evening he had articulated his primary strategic objective as getting more people "feeling more entitled to act"—against authority, the state, or its various proxies. Despite the collectedness of his own demeanor, though, Traven's words did little to dispel the notion that anarchism is just an excuse for angry young people to do whatever they wish without much thought for anyone else. That he won so many cheers seemed fitting, as his vision most accurately described what a lot of Occupy Wall Street seemed to have become: a self-referential subculture acting out by and for itself.

Facebook update by Sparrow Ingersoll, whom I hadn't seen in months, on September 12, 2012:

> seriously, i'm not going to go to your occupy event. stop inviting me.

Group e-mail on September 15 from Harrison Schultz, the movement's web traffic analytics guru, in reference to OccupyWallSt.org:

> The graph is startling because the numbers for our Occuversary are LOW. I realize it's early in the weekend but the numbers are low, low, low, low. The number of visits are exactly where they were at a year ago. This isn't necessarily a bad thing provided … provided we critically reflect and realize that we've been running in circles.

By the light of the setting sun on September 16, three or four or five hundred Occupiers from occupations everywhere are sitting close together in the plaza under the NYPD's headquarters, just across the street from Foley Square. This public conspiracy, technically, is the affinity group spokes council. The facilitator is Lisa Fithian, who has been around on and off since day one, a rare elder whom OWS's main direct actioneers trust in their midst. You can see why: having organized more movements and mobilizations and campaigns than most of them have ever heard of, she handles the crowd masterfully, waving her hands as if doing hypnosis or parting a sea. She has on a black T-shirt that says in white letters, "STAY HUMAN," a slogan often used in reference to the Palestinian cause. Crouched over a bit by back pain, her gestures move the conversation like pieces on a board.

"Even if you're not an anarchist, please use consensus decision making to make sure everybody gets what they need," she instructs.

And so they do, surprisingly smoothly. People are arranged according to their various affinity groups, and those groups, in turn, are in clusters. That fact in itself is impressive—people actually formed affinity groups. Among the groups are such names as

- The Myles Horton Pyramid Scheme
- Debtasaurus
- Education Is a Human Right
- Youth Liberation Front
- Occupy Las Vegas
- Occupy Faith
- Strike Debt
- The Big Jaded Elephant
- Debt Boulder

The group behind Lisa, apparently orchestrating things, is ICU—according to their handmade buttons, Insurrectionary Care Unit. It includes such familiar faces as those of Marisa Holmes and Mark Adams and Austin Guest and Ingrid Burrington. At each juncture in the meeting, Lisa consults with them in a huddle.

"This is so great!" I can't help but whisper to Ingrid.

"I know, right?"

"Why did it take so long for this to happen?" I ask.

She thinks for a second. "Because revolution takes a long time!"

All this came at the end of a weekend of events and trainings, reunions and preparations, first at Washington Square Park on Saturday and then during the concert at Foley on Sunday. Strike Debt released the *Debt Resistors' Operations Manual* on Saturday night with an event at Judson Memorial Church, and out-of-towners practiced their new Plus Brigades tactics on the grass. Now, in the soft orange light, people were ready and focused as together they worked out the basic plan of the mayhem they'd create in the Financial District the following morning, and then a contingency plan if the police—

surely listening to every word—foiled that. There was also a further backup plan for heading to Midtown, just in case. Handouts went around with a map of the area and various convergence points, which had been made by Ingrid, of course, still the sole member of the OWS Cartography Department.

The Mutant Legal affinity group gave their spiel about what to expect from the law, wearing their cool new upturned hats. Like them, lots of groups seemed more organized than ever. Smaller than before, maybe, but tighter, more serious, and acting like there was really business to be done.

Finally, Lisa Fithian ended the proceedings: "I think we have a fucking plan."

As dusk fell, Sister Susan and Bishop Packard held a mic check and led the group down on a solemn march to Zuccotti. There, a Rosh Hashanah service filled the eastern part of the park, inciting murmurs among Jews about whether they were comfortable singing prayers to the tune of Bob Marley songs or referring to God as "Cha-Cha." Behind them, a middle-aged man held a handmade sign denouncing theocracy. The whole park was packed full of people, full of expectation. On the other side of it, I saw a Muslim man do his *salat* prayers on a rug.

Rosh Hashanah is the Jewish new year. This wasn't just Occupy Wall Street's birthday, the officiant pointed out: "It is also the birthday of humanity." All weekend people were wishing one another a happy birthday, as if it really were each of ours, individually and together.

Less than an hour into the hours-long liturgy, a young woman sitting near me closed her prayer book and got up to leave in tears. "I can't be in this space," she said to the friend beside her. "Apparently I have a lot of PTSD that I didn't know about."

The first arrest of the morning, at seven o'clock sharp, was on the northeast corner of Zuccotti. Once again, it was Bill Steyert—standing in the middle of Broadway and waving the flag of Veterans for Peace, just as he had first thing in the morning on May Day at Forty-Second and Sixth. It was him and his flag, too, that I remembered seeing at Broadway and Wall Street as I arrived exactly a year earlier, when all this was first getting started.

Through the people's mic, one of the planners rallied those beginning to gather nearby: "Today I want to show Wall Street what I learned this year. I learned about organizing. I learned about *love*."

And so the day began. Dozens of affinity groups were assembling in four zones, each on a different side of the Stock Exchange, several blocks away.

Police, dressed in various amounts of armor and fearsomeness, were everywhere. The only vantage point from which one could come close to seeing the big picture of what was taking place was that of the airspace overhead, apparently closed to all but the two hovering NYPD helicopters. Organizers stationed at a secret location—high up in an office building on Wall Street—did their best to monitor the action with smartphones and social media.

The opening act was the "People's Wall," billed as a "civil rights–style" sit-in along the barricades blocking the entrances to the Stock Exchange area. But the mayhem of protesters, cops, and businesspeople ensured that little could be formal or disciplined about it. Father Paul and Bishop Packard and Tarak Kauff and others were arrested for kneeling in prayer at Wall and Broadway, across the street from Trinity Church and in front of a barricaded press pen full of television cameras. There was so much commotion all around that few people saw them do it. By then, the traffic on Broadway was at a standstill up well past City Hall, and commuter buses were letting passengers out to walk the rest of the way to work.

Overheard at the entrance to Wall Street:

Cop: "You should've stayed home today."

Wall Streeter: "I need the money."

Cop: "You and me both."

By midmorning, the People's Wall more or less gave way to the next phase of the plan, the "99 Revolutions." Throughout the area, packs of marchers moved along sidewalks and then held up intersections by swirling around in circles, stormlike, holding and blocking them for minutes at a time before enough police arrived. Repeat.

We learned more specifics of what was taking place only later, during report-backs at the midday spokes council in Battery Park. Each affinity group had an adventure of its own. Members of the Disability Caucus were arrested in their wheelchairs. A couple got engaged. One group handed out money to people in suits, and another made videos of the suits saying what they thought of it all. Almost the entire Occupy Faith and veteran contingents were arrested at the entrance to Wall Street. Code Pink and friends shut down bank offices; they did a die-in at a Citibank and liberated a couch. Yates McKee and others in Strike Debt tossed red-square confetti in a Chase lobby and mic-checked the bank's embattled CEO, only to be tackled by police in riot gear and detained until late the next day. There were over a hundred arrests in the morning alone.

"Moving in a large group only got us cops," reported one of the remaining members of Strike Debt at the spokes council. Other groups had the same experience. Instead of uniting, they dispersed, swarmed, made trouble, and reassembled.

Observed Mike Andrews, a tactician of the initial occupation, "We finally learned how to turn our disorganization in our favor."

That was the point. The affinity groups and the clusters and the 99 Revolutions were born of Occupy's long year of anarcho-curiosity. Rather than having an elaborate plan made in advance, this was a protest that everybody was expected to help plan for themselves, in their groups and on the fly, and it was up to them to make their plans go viral. The periodic pauses for meetings and spokes councils that so baffled the police and the reporters were not really pauses at all; they were the heart of the action. The day was practice in becoming ungoverned and ungovernable, a movement full of organizers pressing on until global revolution. As one banner that day suggested, "DON'T STOP UNTIL WE GET THERE."

The 99 Revolutions concluded with an eco-themed convergence at Bowling Green, under the Museum of the American Indian, right where the first big gathering had been that day a year earlier. It was about the same number of people, too—about two thousand. I milled around and reminisced with others who'd been there last time. One of them was the Real Radio Rahim, Bed-Stuy educator and hip-hop pioneer. He was more excited than anyone.

"I know this is going to work, because I was there for the start of hip hop," he said, towering over me in too many ways to count. "It was just like this. We're going to win."

The afternoon brought more, which didn't necessarily seem like so much at any given place or time, but which taken together was quite a lot—including but definitely not limited to

- a disruption of the Wall Streeter lunch crowds
- several simultaneous marches to the World Financial Center, forcing its buildings to be locked.
- a sit-in at a Goldman Sachs lobby ("Everybody pays their tax, everyone but Goldman Sachs")
- a blockade of the West Side Highway for a few minutes

- a celebration at Zuccotti involving thousands
- a group of college students who got up close to the Stock Exchange and made a speech through their people's mic about how white privilege enabled them to get through the barricades just by tucking in their shirts

I spent the latter part of the afternoon doing jail support for Father Paul and Bernice, our Occupy Catholics taken prisoner. This support consisted of waiting outside a pizza place near Central Booking, until some cops pushed us off the sidewalk and across the street. There, we waited and shared stories and danced to the Rude Mechanical Orchestra marching band before greeting our comrades with cheers, snacks, and legal forms when they came out. We learned that in jail there had been assemblies, sermons, and breakout groups.

"I do believe jail support is the best thing to come out of Occupy Wall Street," said Steph McGuinness, sitting there on the sidewalk. She would know; her partner was Jason Ahmadi, one of the movement's most prolific arrestees, so jail support had become a way of life. While living in Zuccotti Park, she would take the subway up to the Upper West Side to walk the dogs of 1 percenters. She'd stayed up until two the night before S17 making a piñata of the *Charging Bull,* which was smashed to bits during the midday spokes council. For all the attention I'd been paying to Jason's arrests, it was far too long before I noticed all that she'd been doing.

The folks from Mutant Legal had said earlier, "A culture of care *is* a culture of resistance."

Night fell over a big assembly in Zuccotti Park, where hundreds traded stories of the day and whatever else they needed to say. But even more people were just milling around, or drowning out the assembly with drums, or running into old friends. Hours passed, and the crowd thinned. As midnight got closer, messages went out on the text-message loop gently reminding people that there were rules against structures and sleeping in the park and that the police presence was still really strong. "Make a choice that's right for you," one message said. "Keep your center and help the person next to you keep theirs." That was the end, pretty much.

S17 a year before could've been like this, really: a day of messing around downtown with more ambition than unity, then ending in some mayhem, maybe, or in quiet, all without blowing up into the public consciousness. Or Occupy Wall Street could have just as easily lasted only a few days, lightly affecting only a few thousand people, cops included. What happened, then?

Was it grace, or luck, or necessity that bestowed even this momentary rupture? Or was it really our doing? Will anyone remember?

Andrew Ross Sorkin in the *New York Times,* September 17, 2012, where "it" refers to Occupy Wall Street:

> It will be an asterisk in the history books, if it gets a mention at all.

After getting out of jail from his arrest on S17 with other members of Veterans for Peace, Tarak Kauff complained in an e-mail to his comrades:

> Of course most of us don't even believe in the concept of a reality based on actually winning, do we? I mean seriously, would you even give odds on it?

A few days earlier I'd had a conversation over lunch along similar lines with Yotam Marom. A member of the Organization for a Free Society, in his midtwenties and living with his parents in New Jersey, Yotam was part of Bloombergville and the planning meetings for Occupy Wall Street. In the movement he often played the role of a spokesperson and an orchestrator of big actions, including the intricate sequence of events on November 17. His prominence was part of what eventually swelled into a backlash against him, driving him to the periphery of the movement, and then as it shrank he found he was no longer in it much at all. (Months later, I heard an Occupier say, only half joking, "I kind of miss when it was just Yotam telling us what to do.")

When September rolled around again, Yotam was a revolutionary without a revolution. He was looking for new projects and was starting some of his own. He was also seeing Occupy Wall Street from the outside, as he couldn't have before, and it started seeming less and less like the seeds of a revolution anyway.

"Look at the people who think the world is about to end, who really believe it," Yotam said. "See how they act. None of us is acting like that."

It was true; nobody was making serious preparations for a revolutionary endgame, about how and when a shift in power might take place and what it would take to arrive at the breaking point. That would have seemed far too remote. I knew a Chinese cyber-dissident, for instance, who had a plan sketched out for how to bring down Communist rule inside of a decade, including which members of the politburo need to be turned against which other members, when the moment will be right to return to Tiananmen Square, and how to organize the roundtable negotiations about the details of the transition. Why did one never hear talk like that at Liberty Square, despite all the talk of revolution? Is it because we couldn't really believe revolution would happen in our lifetime?

Persevering in this movement—a movement so multifarious and unpredictable and ever still discovering itself—was always an act of faith of some sort. People believed less in what it was than in what it should be or what its hidden meanings were beneath the clumsy surface. They gave hours and hours and months of their lives; they quit jobs and moved to a different city. But I found myself wondering if even that was faith enough.

Recall the scene at the end of the 1999 movie *Fight Club,* as the great (evacuated) towers of a financial capital fall upon themselves in a cascade of explosives against the night, eerily predictive of the calamity in New York that was only two years away. The towers' destruction, we are to understand, spells the erasure of some considerable portion of the world's credit as computer servers, records, and files melt in the inferno or flitter away in free fall. Atop the lone tower that has been spared, the silhouettes of Edward Norton and Helena Bonham Carter stand watching, like Adam and Eve at the Fall, holding hands. The Pixies' "Where Is My Mind?" plays, with the drone of its opening guitar riff grating against the fireballs.

"Trust me," says Norton's character to Bonham Carter's, as the first demolition charges glow against his face, "everything is going to be fine."

Norton's character, unknowingly and unconsciously, was the architect of this. After surviving a self-inflicted bullet wound to his face, he finally accepts what he has done. He realizes that he did it for a reason, and, though it nearly killed him to endure it, the reason was good. The two look lovingly at each other, and the movie is over.

I have a theory that *Fight Club,* with its vision of postyuppie liberation, played a role in training the relevant subset of the generation that birthed Occupy Wall Street. As a teenager I thought it was the greatest thing I'd ever seen—a fantasy of exit from corporatized boredom. But it's also masochistic and viciously sexist and dangerously incomplete. *Fight Club*'s ending teaches us that revolution requires just a single great rupture, after which "everything is going to be fine." This is a lie—one bewitching enough to compel us to start the revolution without equipping us with what we'll need to finish it.

One faces two options after experiencing an apocalyptic moment. Neither is comfortable. First, one can return to the world outside, in defiance of the knowledge still creeping within oneself that the world is not in fact the same and should not be. But one can keep that thought suppressed well enough, most of the time, and manage to carry out a decent enough life. Or, second, one can try to keep the spirit of that moment alive within and in one's way of being, aiming one's defiance at the world outside, which carries on in ignorance. In doing so, one is true to self but a stranger among the principalities and powers that still pretend to rule the world—an exile and a prisoner. It becomes tempting, when the demand to conform mounts more and more, to relocate to a commune in Vermont or to an asylum. But there are other coping strategies as well. One might even win the world over.

This is more or less the choice for so many of us who underwent the Occupy apocalypse in the fall of 2011. I've seen quite a lot of people opt for the first option and go back to their lives mostly as they were before, to try to make a living and make do. Despite the various irritations and disappointments of Occupy Wall Street and its consequences, however, I find myself in need, clinging to what it got right against a social order gone gruesomely awry: occupying parks against occupying countries, mutual aid against ruthless competition, horizontalism against mounting inequality, direct democracy against the rule of profit, no demands before a system that wouldn't listen to them anyway. But these general features are only the most surface-level reasons for the hold this movement has on me. Far firmer has been the grip of so many thousands of people, particularly those in my young and unsettled generation, discovering better parts of themselves than they'd known before, claiming a politics more of their own making and driven by their formidable creativity. I'm compelled by the rooms and assemblies I've been in, surrounded by people each made brilliant and effulgent by the others and by what they were trying to accomplish together. They are why I cannot let go of this apocalypse or allow it to let go of me.

Protest movements can and do change the world, though it takes time and never happens quite the way anyone expects. The initial occupation made this point in microcosm: it had to *stay*, for days and weeks, before the world would even notice. If Occupy Wall Street had only been a protest on September 17 or even a weekend sleep-out, it would have been a forgettable failure. Instead, it pressed on through intimidation, awkwardness, fear, and frustration. It made its demand a process, its goal a means of getting there—which is the only way we ever will.

"Destruction has never been enough to make things irreversible," concludes *The Coming Insurrection,* an apocalyptic French manifesto that could be found by the cash register at trendy bookstores in the years between *Fight Club* and Occupy Wall Street (and that literate Occupiers either loved or hated). "What matters is how it's done."

Movements don't work without human sacrifice, without consecrating our lives to something beyond. They demand that we turn society into a school to study power, organize, clarify visions, and sustain one another. Movements survive when they keep on moving and keep on re-creating themselves. There are no plans for this, there are no maps. There are strategies, but they're always provisional. An apocalypse is when we enlist our reason to faith, the already to the not-yet.

The spirit that made so much sense to so many people in the Occupy movement is finished only if we let it be—or if we wait for someone else to carry it for us. Organizing to build power and resist corruption is something we can all do, wherever we find ourselves. What would happen if families were sitting around their dinner tables discussing how corporate hegemony is vulnerable and how to exploit its vulnerabilities? What if some of the ingenuity that we normally put into weighing consumer choices, or artfully complaining, went into sucking out the marrow of capitalist culture and the modes of thinking and acting that uphold it? What if there were as many people going to neighborhood assemblies as playing the lotto? If a people-power campaign had as many Facebook followers as your average breakfast cereal, it would be a force to reckon with online. If there were as many people marching in the streets of a given city as regularly fill its football stadium, the whole city would have to listen. Revolution really isn't as far off as it might seem. Nor is apocalypse. "THE BEGINNING IS NEAR," said a popular slogan on Occupy's cardboard signs.

The New York Stock Exchange was finally shut down the week before Halloween in the fall of 2012, after being flooded by the freak "Frankenstorm" Hurricane Sandy—a creature of the system's own making. With an election just days away, the presidential candidates still said nothing about climate change, but the climate itself did. Sandbags lined the front of the Goldman Sachs Tower, which stayed lit as the rest of Lower Manhattan went dark. The remnants of a battered construction crane dangled alongside the shell of a new Midtown luxury apartment building, and explosions shook a ConEdison substation in the East Village.

The next day, remnants of Occupy Wall Street became Occupy Sandy. InterOccupy built the go-to website for New Yorkers who wanted to help out. Thousands of volunteers-turned-organizers brought the skills of self-reliance honed at Liberty Square to devastated neighborhoods—many heavily populated by city police officers—where official agencies were scarce. They set up distribution hubs in churches that they helped to dig out of the wreckage, and they helped the congregations organize themselves against the onslaught of developers and disaster capitalists who were sure to come. The National Guard made a photogenic amphibious landing on Rockaway Beach, then asked Occupiers what they should do next.

"Occupy Sandy has been miraculous for us, really," the parish manager at St. Margaret Mary, a church in Staten Island, told me. "They are doing exactly as Christ preached."

Meanwhile, the Rolling Jubilee went massively viral online. It raised enough money in donations from everywhere to buy millions of dollars of defaulted medical debt at a discount and abolish it in a "People's Bailout." Business magazines competed to heap praises on the idea, and debt resisters' groups formed across the country to follow suit. Occupy was on a roll with crisis relief.

When I would stop by the Occupy Sandy hub near my apartment—a gorgeous, asymmetrical Episcopal church—and join the mayhem of volunteers carrying boxes this way and that, and poke my head into the upper room full of laptops and organizers around a long table, and see Occupiers in line for communion at Sunday services, I kept thinking about how the Alcoholics Anonymous twelve-step program ends. That was kind of what had happened. The twelfth step is where you cap off all the self-involved inner work you've been doing, and get over yourself for a bit, and heal yourself, and find yourself by reaching out to someone else.

Sparks like this won't be long in coming. They're flashing all the time. They can't be planned for, but it's for us to lay the kindling, it's for us to be ready to catch fire—or others will be ready in our place. What makes an apocalypse an apocalypse is the veil-lifting revelation that the world has definitely and decisively changed, that the new order has been set into motion already. There's no going back now, which is a start. The end is a beginning.

ACKNOWLEDGMENTS

Portions of this book have been adapted from articles that previously appeared in the *Boston Review,* the *Catholic Worker, Harper's Magazine,* the *Indypendent, Killing the Buddha, n+1's Occupy!* gazette, the *Nation,* the *New York Times,* the *Occupied Wall Street Journal, Religion Dispatches, Tidal, Truthout, Waging Nonviolence,* and *YES! Magazine.* Two of these also appeared as chapters in *This Changes Everything: Occupy Wall Street and the 99% Movement,* published in 2011 by Berrett-Koehler, and *We Are Many: Reflections on Movement Strategy from Occupation to Liberation,* published in 2012 by AK Press.

WORKS NOT CITED

Texts that I was reading, rereading, or meaning to read at the time.

1. SOME GREAT CAUSE

DeGraw, David. *The Economic Elite vs. the People of the United States of America.* Amped Status.com, 2010. http://is.gd/NoSl3v.

Graeber, David. *Debt: The First 500 Years.* Brooklyn: Melville House, 2011.

Khalil, Ashraf. *Liberation Square: Inside the Egyptian Revolution and the Rebirth of a Nation.* New York: St. Martin's Press, 2011.

King, Mary E. "Getting Out the News." In *Hands on the Freedom Plow: Personal Accounts by Women in SNCC,* edited by Faith S. Holsaert, Martha Prescod Norman Noonan, Judy Richardson, Betty Garman Robinson, Jean Smith Young, and Dorothy M. Zellner, 332–43. Champaign: University of Illinois Press, 2010.

Landes, Richard. *Heaven on Earth: The Varieties of Millennial Experience.* Oxford: Oxford University Press, 2011.

Mailer, Norman. *Armies of the Night: History as a Novel, the Novel as History.* New York: New American Library, 1968.

Mason, Paul. *Why It's Kicking Off Everywhere: The New Global Revolutions.* London: Verso, 2012.

Penny, Laurie. *Penny Red: Notes from the New Age of Dissent.* London: Pluto Press, 2011.

Schiffrin, Anya, and Eamon Kircher-Allen, eds. *From Cairo to Wall Street: Voices from the Global Spring.* New York: New Press, 2012.

Schneider, Nathan. *God in Proof: The Story of a Search from the Ancients to the Internet.* Berkeley, CA: University of California Press, 2013.

Sharp, Gene. *From Dictatorship to Democracy: A Conceptual Framework for Liberation.* East Boston: Albert Einstein Institution, 2010. http://is.gd/40BIlN.

2. NEW MESSIAH

Butler, Anthea, et al. "God Dissolves into the Occupy Movement." *Religion Dispatches,* October 16, 2011. http://is.gd/9UMVIh.

Cox, Harvey. *The Secular City: Secularization and Urbanization in Theological Perspective.* New York: Macmillan, 1966.

Graeber, David. *Direct Action: An Ethnography.* Oakland: AK Press, 2009.

King, Mary Elizabeth. "How We Made the Media Pay Attention." *Waging Nonviolence,* September 16, 2011. http://is.gd/ugosGg.

Trillin, Calvin. "Back on the Bus." *New Yorker,* July 25, 2011.

Writers for the 99%. *Occupying Wall Street: The Inside Story of an Action That Changed America.* New York: OR Books, 2011.

3. PLANET OCCUPY

Amster, Randall. *Anarchism Today.* Santa Barbara, CA: Praeger, 2012.

Arquilla, John, and David Ronfeldt. *Swarming and the Future of Conflict.* Santa Monica, CA: RAND Corporation, 2001.

Bey, Hakim. *T.A.Z.: The Temporary Autonomous Zone, Ontological Anarchy, Poetic Terrorism.* Brooklyn: Autonomedia, 1991. http://is.gd/fhBBIk.

Deleuze, Gilles, and Félix Guattari. *A Thousand Plateaus* (in French: *Mille Plateaux*). Minneapolis: University of Minnesota Press, 1993.

Harcourt, Bernard E. "Occupy Wall Street's 'Political Disobedience.'" *New York Times,* October 13, 2011. http://is.gd/FwiuT4.

Hardt, Michael, and Antonio Negri. *Declaration.* New York: Argo Navis Author Services, 2012.

Holloway, John. *Change the World without Taking Power.* London: Pluto Press, 2002. http://is.gd/odwBYm.

La carta de los comunes. Madrilonia.org, 2011. http://is.gd/tily5M.

Le Guin, Ursula K. *The Dispossessed.* New York: Avon, 1974.

Marshall, Peter. *Demanding the Impossible: A History of Anarchism.* Oakland, CA: PM Press, 2010.

Raasch-Gilman, Betsy. "Chaos Theory and Nonviolence." Training for Change, June 2000. http://is.gd/kwemi8.

Signer, Rachel. "Mic Checked." *Killing the Buddha,* November 14, 2011. http://is.gd/BkHCqR.

Sitrin, Marina. *Horizontalism: Voices of Popular Power in Argentina.* Oakland, CA: AK Press, 2006.

Sitrin, Marina, and Dario Azzellini. *Occupying Language: The Secret Rendezvous with History and the Present.* Brooklyn: Zuccotti Park Press, 2012.

Alexander, Michelle. *The New Jim Crow: Mass Incarceration in the Age of Color-blindness.* New York: New Press, 2010.

Carr, David. "A Protest's Ink-Stained Fingers." *New York Times,* October 9, 2011. http://is.gd/vBG5Wq.

Coleman, Gabriella. *Coding Freedom: The Ethics and Aesthetics of Hacking.* Princeton, NJ: Princeton University Press, 2013.

———. "Our Weirdness Is Free." *Triple Canopy* 15 (January 13, 2012). http://is.gd/mYNYgG.

Frank, Thomas. "To the Precinct Station: How Theory Met Practice and Drove It Absolutely Crazy." *Baffler* 21 (November 2012). http://is.gd/2ZSI51.

Grant, Melissa Gira. *Take This Book: The People's Library at Occupy Wall Street.* New York: Glass Houses, 2012. http://is.gd/FsUqGx.

Greenberg, Michael. "In Zuccotti Park." *New York Review of Books,* October 13, 2011. http://is.gd/JjcN6N.

Hess, Karl. *Dear America.* New York: HarperCollins, 1975.

Hughes, C. *Occupied Zuccotti, Social Struggle, and Planned Shrinkage.* Pamphlet published by WarMachines.info, 2012.

Khatib, Kate, Margaret Killjoy, and Mike McGuire, eds. *We Are Many: Reflections on Movement Strategy from Occupation to Liberation.* Oakland, CA: AK Press, 2012.

King, Mary Elizabeth. "Leaderless Movements Trump Patrilinial Tyrants." *Waging Nonviolence,* October 25, 2011. http://is.gd/KPLPUG.

Olson, Parmy. *We Are Anonymous: Inside the Hacker World of LulzSec, Anonymous, and the Global Cyber Insurgency.* New York: Little, Brown, 2012.

Sharlet, Jeff. "By the Mob's Early Light." *Bookforum,* December–January 2012. http://is.gd/zkomEL.

Vradis, Antonis, and Dimitris Dalakoglou, eds. *Revolt and Crisis in Greece: Between a Present Yet to Pass and a Future Still to Come.* Oakland, CA: AK Press, 2011.

5. SANCTUARY

Baker, Ray Stannard. *The Spiritual Unrest.* New York: Fredrick A. Stokes Company, 1910.

D, Savitri, and Bill Talen. *The Reverend Billy Project: From Rehearsal Hall to Super Mall with the Church of Life after Shopping.* Edited by Alisa Solomon. Ann Arbor: University of Michigan Press, 2011.

Ellul, Jacques. *Anarchy and Christianity.* Translated by Geoffrey W. Bromiley. Eugene, OR: Wipf and Stock, 1991.

Guzder, Deena. *Divine Rebels: American Christian Activists for Social Justice.* Chicago: Lawrence Hill Books, 2011.

Hoffman, Michael. *Usury in Christendom: The Mortal Sin That Was and Now Is Not.* Coeur d'Alene, ID: Independent History and Research, 2012.

Manson, Jamie. "Occupy Catholics Seeks to Make Tradition Relevant to a New Movement." *National Catholic Reporter,* July 9, 2012. http://is.gd /CeaEzL.

Pinto, Nick. "Lead Us Not Astray, Reverend James Cooper." *Village Voice,* December 12, 2012. http://is.gd/FYpU2P.

Rieger, Joerg, and Kwok Pui-lan. *Occupy Religion: Theology of the Multitude.* Lanham, MD: Rowman & Littlefield, 2012.

Stout, Jeffrey. *Blessed Are the Organized: Grassroots Democracy in America.* Princeton, NJ: Princeton University Press, 2010.

Stringfellow, William, and Anthony Towne. *Suspect Tenderness: The Ethics of the Berrigan Witness.* New York: Holt, Reinhart and Winston, 1971.

Taylor, Astra. "Occupy and Space." *Occupy! An OWS-Inspired Gazette* 3 (December 15, 2011). http://is.gd/pRae1X.

6. DIVERSITY OF TACTICS

Boyd, Andrew, ed. *Beautiful Trouble: A Toolbox for Revolution.* New York: OR Books, 2012. http://is.gd/axgocV.

Cox, Harvey. *The Feast of Fools: A Theological Essay on Festivity and Fantasy.* Cambridge, MA: Harvard University Press, 1969.

Farrell, Bryan. "Finally, OWS Gets Police to Arrest the People in Suits." *Waging Nonviolence,* March 26, 2012. http://is.gd/efRBBy.

Fuegoverde, Talib Agape. "Occupy Criticism, Occupy Spring." *Brooklyn Rail,* March 2012. http://is.gd/VwGXhc.

Gelderloos, Peter. *How Nonviolence Protects the State.* Cambridge, MA: South End Press, 2007. http://is.gd/i2jMB3.

Gottesdiener, Laura. "A New Face of the New Labor Movement" *Waging Nonviolence,* December 1, 2012. http://is.gd/DBXw0E.

Graeber, David. "Concerning the Violent Peace Police." *n+1,* February 9, 2012. http://is.gd/UQzoZy.

Hedges, Chris. "The Cancer in Occupy." *Truthdig,* February 6, 2012. http://is.gd /HMic4Z.

Klein, Naomi. "Occupy Wall Street: The Most Important Thing in the World." *Nation,* October 6, 2011. http://is.gd/X9Fmli.

Lakey, George. *The Sword That Heals.* Philadelphia: Training for Change, 2001. http://is.gd/nobzDw.

Marom, Yotam. "Making Our Arrests Count." *Waging Nonviolence,* April 18, 2012. http://is.gd/8icu87.

Occupy Mental Health Project, eds. *Mindful Occupation: Rising Up without Burning Out.* Oakland, CA: AK Press, 2012. http://is.gd/O4Q2Yl.

Solnit, Rebecca. "Throwing Out the Master's Tools and Building a Better House." *Occupy! An OWS-Inspired Gazette* 2 (November 14, 2011). http://is.gd/Dq6eL3.

Williams, Kristian. *Our Enemies in Blue: Police and Power in America.* Cambridge, MA: South End Press, 2007.

7. CRAZY EYES

Brecher, Jeremy. *Strike!* Cambridge, MA: South End Press, 1997.

Kopkind, Andrew. *The Thirty Years' Wars: Dispatches and Diversions of a Radical Journalist, 1965–1994.* Edited by JoAnn Wypijewski. London: Verso, 1995.

Lakey, George. "Activism for the End Times: Mass Actions or Focused Campaigns?" *Waging Nonviolence,* February 28, 2012. http://is.gd/G6inHu.

Luxemburg, Rosa. *The Mass Strike, the Political Party and the Trade Unions.* Translated by Patrick Lavin. Detroit: Marxist Educational Society of Detroit, 1925. http://is.gd/JH4MnZ.

Malina, Judith. *The Enormous Despair.* New York: Random House, 1972.

Melville, Herman. *Bartleby the Scrivener.* Brooklyn: Melville House, 2004.

Quattrochi, Angelo, and Tom Nairn. *Beginning of the End: France, May 1968.* London: Verso, 1998.

Rosenberg, Tina. *Join the Club: How Peer Pressure Can Transform the World.* New York: W. W. Norton, 2011.

8. ETERNAL RETURN

Dean, Michelle. "The Struggle for the Occupy Wall Street Archives." *Awl,* December 21, 2011. http://is.gd/5Rp043.

Eliade, Mircea. *The Myth of the Eternal Return: Or, Cosmos and History.* New York: Pantheon, 1971.

The Invisible Committee. *The Coming Insurrection.* Los Angeles: Semiotext(e), 2009.

Keller, Catherine. *Apocalypse Now and Then: A Feminist Guide to the End of the World.* Boston: Beacon Press, 1996.

Knuckey, Sarah, et al. *Suppressing Protest: Human Rights Violations in the U.S. Response to Occupy Wall Street.* Protest and Assembly Rights Project, August 25, 2012. http://is.gd/5bbkdl.

Sitchin, Zecharia. *The End of Days: Armageddon and Prophecies of the Return.* New York: Harper, 2007.

Solnit, Rebecca. *A Paradise Built in Hell: The Extraordinary Communities That Arise in Disaster.* New York: Penguin, 2010.

Strike Debt and Occupy Wall Street. *The Debt Resistors' Operations Manual.* September 2012. http://is.gd/afamsy.

Taylor, Astra. "Occupy 2.0: Strike Debt." *Nation,* September 24, 2012. http://is.gd/qpZU4m.

Wilcox, Susan. "Forgive Us Our Debts, As We Forgive Our Lenders." *America,* November 14, 2012. http://is.gd/5vbRjo.

TEXT
11/14 Garamond Premier Pro

DISPLAY
Knockout, Univers

COMPOSITOR
IDS Infotech Ltd.

PRINTER AND BINDER
Maple Press